VISIONS OF PRACTIC

Sonia Nieto, *Series Editor*

Embracing Diversity:
Teachers' Everyday Practices in Secondary English Language Arts Classrooms
SARAH BICKENS, FRANCES BITTMAN, & DAVID J. CONNOR

Families With Power:
Centering Students by Engaging With Families and Community
MARY COWHEY

Embracing Diversity

Teachers' Everyday Practices in Secondary English Language Arts Classrooms

Sarah Bickens, Frances Bittman, and David J. Connor

Foreword by Sonia Nieto

TEACHERS COLLEGE PRESS
TEACHERS COLLEGE | COLUMBIA UNIVERSITY
NEW YORK AND LONDON

Published by Teachers College Press,® 1234 Amsterdam Avenue, New York, NY 10027

Front cover design by Holly Grundon / BHG Graphics. Artwork by David J. Connor.

Library of Congress Cataloging-in-Publication Data

Names: Bickens, Sarah, author. | Bittman, Frances, author. | Connor, David J., 1961– author.
Title: Embracing diversity : teachers' everyday practices in secondary english language arts classrooms / Sarah Bickens, Frances Bittman, and David J. Connor ; Foreword by Sonia Nieto.
Description: New York, NY : Teachers College Press, [2023] | Series: Visions of practice | Includes bibliographical references and index.
Identifiers: LCCN 2023016816 (print) | LCCN 2023016817 (ebook) | ISBN 9780807768440 (paperback) | ISBN 9780807768457 (hardcover) | ISBN 9780807781777 (ebook)
Subjects: LCSH: English language—Study and teaching (Secondary) | Language arts (Secondary) | Multicultural education. | Critical thinking—Study and teaching (Secondary)
Classification: LCC LB1631 .B46 2023 (print) | LCC LB1631 (ebook) | DDC 428.0071/2—dc23/eng/20230517
LC record available at https://lccn.loc.gov/2023016816
LC ebook record available at https://lccn.loc.gov/2023016817

ISBN 978-0-8077-6844-0 (paper)
ISBN 978-0-8077-6845-7 (hardcover)
ISBN 978-0-8077-8177-7 (ebook)

Printed on acid-free paper
Manufactured in the United States of America

To

My mother, Patricia Bickens,
a public school educator for over 30 years,
and my first and best teacher

—Sarah

My first class of students at Manhattan Village Academy,
the 9th-graders who attended from 2003–2004. Without them
putting up with me as I worked out the inevitable kinks as a
first-year teacher, I would not be the teacher I am today

—Fran

My nieces and nephews,
Ethan, Lilly, Jake, Eve, Abbey, Lucy, Joe, & Emily

—David

Contents

Foreword

The word "diversity," not to mention the topic itself, was not yet in the pedagogical lexicon when I became a teacher of language arts, Spanish, and English as a Second Language in the mid-1960s. Those were also the days when only White children were on the covers of teacher education texts, as if the multicultural and multiracial reality of our nation had not existed since the founding of what would become the United States. Fast-forward 2 decades to the 1980s, and "diversity" was everywhere: on textbook titles and photos, university syllabi, state requirements, and more. It was as if the nation had awoken to the previously invisible and unacknowledged students in our schools, as if they just recently had appeared.

The pervasive nature of diversity caught some educators by surprise, as research articles, white papers, and entire textbooks on the topic were becoming ubiquitous. Yet, despite some earnest attempts at defining and clarifying the concept, many early attempts left teachers and other educators confused and unsure of what it meant to understand and adapt to the more multicultural reality that our nation, and indeed our world, had become. Reasons for this are not hard to find. For one, teacher professional development had not caught up with the reality of our nation's population. Also, the high school literature textbooks of the 1950s and 1960s, many of which were still found in U.S. literature classrooms, no longer reflected our reality. Consequently, a sizable discrepancy exists between the student population and teachers' knowledge as related to the dramatic demographic changes that schools have undergone in the past several decades. For instance, the K–12 student population in the United States has changed tremendously. By 2020 the percentage of White students had dipped to 46%, while BIPOC students now account for 56% of all school-age children (National Center for Education Statistics [NCES], 2022). On the other hand, the U.S. teacher workforce is still predominantly White, although it dropped from 84% in 2000 to 79% in 2018 (NCES, 2018).

Currently, the notion that diversity must be an essential part of school curricula and pedagogy has become largely, although certainly not universally, accepted in our nation and in teacher certification requirements. But it did not take long after diversity entered the lexicon for a backlash to emerge. Recently, the backlash has become even more fierce and meanspirited: from book banning to state laws forbidding the use of conversations about race, gender, and identity; from gaslighting to curriculum suppression; and even to the firing of teachers for supposedly "brainwashing" their students when all they wanted was to teach a more complete and authentic understanding of, in the case of English Language Arts, U.S. literature. All these attitudes and behaviors have taken a toll on teachers and other educators: Many have left the profession entirely; others have become silenced and reluctant to speak up. The result sometimes has been a whitewashing of our nation's history and literary canon.

Enter David Connor, Fran Bittman, and Sarah Bickens, three educators with a passion for literature and social justice, and a love of teaching. When David first approached me with the idea of this book for the Visions of Practice series, I was immediately captivated. Having worked on another project with him in the recent past, I knew he was a serious scholar with a primary interest in disability studies, another increasingly central aspect of diversity in education. I was convinced the result would be an excellent textbook for preparing preservice and practicing teachers of all backgrounds for their actual multicultural classrooms. When he and his colleagues Fran Bittman and Sarah Bickens sent me their prospectus, I was even more impressed. The three educators had worked closely for years, David in teacher education and Fran and Sarah as high school classroom literature teachers. Originally Fran's and Sarah's mentor, David eventually became a trusted colleague in a years-long relationship in which they became mutual mentors.

Until recently, much of what had been included in high school literature classes was outdated. As White educators, David, Fran, and Sarah knew they had a special responsibility to reach students of all backgrounds through the literature they selected. They also recognized that the stories, experiences, and voices of students of numerous backgrounds had been poorly represented and, in some cases, completely invisible in U.S. high school literature classes and curricula. David, Fran, and Sarah also understood that not being a member of the diverse groups they were teaching posed another challenge. Thus, they immersed themselves in learning about the backgrounds, lives, and experiences of the students who currently grace our classrooms. In addition, their willingness to confront the gaps in their knowledge and address them openly and with humility, as well as a willingness to learn, shines through these pages. Through their long collaboration, they have worked to critically examine and select literature that is inclusive, and strategies that will motivate the interests of students. While not throwing the proverbial "baby out with the bathwater," they insisted on framing a more accurate literature to engage students.

This book is the result of their work. A thoroughly documented and creatively designed text that educators will turn to again and again, *Embracing Diversity: Teachers' Everyday Practices in Secondary English Language Arts Classrooms* provides an extraordinarily rich and comprehensive treatment of how to connect theory with practice in secondary literature classrooms. It is a book for teachers and other educators who, although wishing to create more inclusive classrooms, may need guidance in doing so. But this book is not about lesson plans or units; instead, it provides important questions for teachers to consider in crafting their curricula and strategies to engage students in learning a more robust understanding of U.S. literature.

Embracing Diversity is a treasure trove of resources, ideas, and pedagogical practices that will be a lifeline for teachers wanting to make their classrooms havens for creativity and critical thinking. I wish this book had been around when I began teaching and, later, when I was a teacher educator who was always on the lookout for excellent multicultural resources to share with my graduate students. This book would certainly have filled that gap.

—*Sonia Nieto*

REFERENCES

National Center for Education Statistics. (2018). Race and ethnicity of public school teachers and their students.. Retrieved from https://nces.ed.gov/programs/coe/indicator/clr/public-school-teachers

National Center for Education Statistics. (2022). Racial ethnic enrollments in public schools. Retrieved from https://nces.ed.gov/programs/coe/indicator/cge/racial-ethnic-enrollment

Acknowledgments

We'd like to thank the following people for their invaluable help in developing this book.

Dr. Sonia Nieto, for her encouragement, guidance, and feedback that was always thoughtful, supportive, and very helpful. We couldn't have wished for a better editor and are honored to be included in this book series dedicated to the practice of teaching.

Brian Ellerbeck, editorial director, Teachers College Press, for his helpful feedback, guidance, and belief in our ideas.

Caritza Berlioz, assistant acquisitions editor, Teachers College Press, for helping us navigate the process of submitting our manuscript.

Amanda Gorman, National Youth Poet Laureate, for giving us permission to include lines from "The Hill We Climb."

The two anonymous peer reviewers of sample chapters from the manuscript who were invaluable in helping us push our thinking and ultimately refine and expand our ideas.

Dr. Gholdy Muhammad for permitting us to share her words of wisdom from a Twitter post.

Dr. Jody Polleck and Dr. Melissa Schieble, both authors with TCP and professors of literacy in the School of Education at Hunter College, City University of New York. Your informal peer feedback, generously provided during your busy schedules, truly strengthened our work.

Sara Barber-Just, head of the English Department, Amherst Regional High School, for the policy on approaching the "n-word" in texts and documents in the English classroom.

Neal Shopick, humanities educator (and Fran's coteacher) at Greenwich High School, for generously sharing materials.

Christopher Harter at the Amistad Research Center for providing information about Countee Cullen's "Incident."

Harvard University Press for acknowledging that we may use "Hope Is a Thing With Feathers. (Source: *The Poems of Emily Dickinson*, edited by T. H. Johnson, 1960, Belknap Press of Harvard University Press. Copyright 1951, 1955, 1979, 1983 by the President and Fellows of Harvard College.)

Acknowledgments

Embracing Diversity

Introduction

Welcome. This book is about embracing diversity within secondary English Language Arts (ELA) classrooms. We are three career-educators who believe that centering diversity in ELA classrooms is imperative within a pluralistic society—and should be close to, if not *the* heart of, every teacher's thinking. It is our sincere hope that all kinds of educators will read this book; find the contents useful in terms of engaging with ideas, big and small; and try some of the varied practical approaches to teaching.

The Pledge of Allegiance of the United States of America holds itself to an ideal in which all the nation's people are "indivisible, with liberty and justice for all." As citizens, we value an ideal that inspires working toward unity and mutual respect. We also know that this ideal—symbolized in the concept of equality—has been out of reach for many Americans throughout our history. The disparate realities of American people have been drawn along lines of race, gender, ethnicity, social class, ability, sexual orientation, language, immigration status, and other markers of identity (Cuauhtin et al., 2019; Zinn, 2005). These realities also have been complicated by intersectional experiences, each person's life and views shaped by how they were/are simultaneously raced, gendered, ethnicized, classed, or otherwise labeled within the cultural norms of a specific time and context in society. Complex experiences of what it means to be human in a particular time and place usually are represented within literature. There are novels, plays, poems, short stories, memoirs, and screenplays that capture both past and present societies—allowing us to vicariously enter a multitude of worlds like time travelers. Writers always have been driven to create stories reflecting the values, concerns, and interests of their times. As English teachers, we believe that by engaging with writers' stories, readers expand their own world.

In this Introduction we seek to inform the reader why we wrote this book and how we envision the book's audience. Given the disparate realities of the American experience and education system specifically, we frame our positionality as White educators teaching a diverse student body through a theoretical grounding in social justice and critical self-reflection. Finally, we briefly describe each chapter to share the various angles where teachers can embrace diversity throughout their careers.

WHO IS THIS BOOK FOR?

This book is for teachers by teachers. Over our combined 75 years in the classroom, we have observed that a growing number of educators in secondary ELA seek to engage students about diversity, asking themselves: In what ways do issues of race, ethnicity, gender, social class, ability, sexual orientation, and other markers of identity resonate with students, and how might I incorporate these issues into my lessons? How can I leverage students' interests to take a deeper dive into the texts we're studying? How can students' life experiences be accessed to explore these issues? In brief, many teachers value these topics as a means of opening up the conversation and enriching lessons through reaching all students. In contrast, we recognize that for other teachers, diversity may have the opposite effect—namely, closing them down. For such teachers, their uncertainties may influence their avoidance of specific issues, curtail discussions, and limit questions, through fear of losing control in managing classroom conversations, floundering in public, and putting a proverbial foot in their own mouths. To some degree, this type of response is understandable. Teaching is a multilayered, demanding profession, and for teaching to be effective, classrooms have to be brave, community-minded spaces for students and teachers alike.

That said, the premise of this book is to uphold the value of teaching diversity. While we examine issues of race and racism, we also strive to encompass other aspects of identity such as gender, religion, social class, disability, immigration status, and other categories of "difference." We, therefore, seek to encourage and support *all* teachers in embracing diversity as a core value within secondary ELA classrooms. Teachers who already share this disposition will find many ways to approach their craft by engaging with students about what it means to be human through classic, contemporary, and alternative literature. For teachers seeking to grow in confidence, and even for those who may be reticent, we also provide a strong rationale to justify why this work is imperative within a pluralistic society. In addition, we realize some readers may view us with a critical eye—three White teachers who claim to value and promote diversity as a core element in our teaching. On our part, we don't seek to cultivate a "White savior narrative," often depicted in popular films such as *Dangerous Minds* (Smith, 1995) and *Freedom Writers* (Lagravanese, 2007), where the prototype White, middle-class, usually female teachers "save" inner-city students (Aronson, 2017). Rather, we invite *all teachers* to think about what it means to teach a diverse student body—because, in the course of our careers, it is an inevitability.

WHY DID WE WRITE THIS BOOK?

The book speaks to the everyday reality of classroom teachers, offering ways to proactively and practically teach about diversity, an order we see as a moral imperative in light of our nation's history and current inequities. Our hope is that fellow educators will benefit from learning about our successes, risks, struggles, and—importantly—failures. In reflecting upon what motivated us to write the book, we identify essentially two reasons: (1) We have always loved literature, enough that it determined our career choices to teach it in secondary schools, and (2) we value diversity within our society in a country that historically has struggled to meet its own ideal of asserting equality for all. As teachers of ELA, it has been our desire to share our love of literature, introducing students to writers and their ideas, opening doors to different worlds and ways of thinking. At the same time, being teachers in urban settings, we became cognizant of standing at cultural crossroads within our classrooms every day. On one hand, we wondered, should students all be taught the classical canon of U.S. and English literature? We knew it would provide them with a form of cultural capital for when they went to college or be part of their general knowledge if they did not. On the other hand, it was clear that the traditional canon of the ELA curriculum was highly Anglo-American, decidedly Eurocentric in world matters, and written mainly by White, middle-class, male authors, often mirrored in the characters of their protagonists. We believe that if classic texts are taught uncritically, they serve to reinforce outdated colonial values and further disenfranchise people of color and other marginalized groups within the general population. Worse, knowledge we have been conditioned to assume was good for students to know actually can play a role in oppressing them by omitting, negating, or minimizing their existences. As White teachers interested in teaching about diversity, these thoughts weigh heavily on us. Consequently, this book materialized from our realization that texts, the themes they raise, and the pedagogical methods we use, have to be as diverse as the students in our classrooms. More important, we also believe it's not enough to simply teach diverse books and be done with it. There is so much to think about in terms of *how* teachers teach, interact with students and build relationships, and reflect on their own identities. Over our long careers in diverse classrooms, we have developed and refined these aspects of our craft to make for a more inclusive and empowering classroom. As we continue our work in schools, we recognize that this is an ongoing, lifelong journey, one of personal and professional growth; we are not (nor ever will be) "done," but wish to share some of the things that we've learned along the way.

Teaching in a Pluralistic Society

It is a well-known fact that U.S. demographics have shifted toward a more multiracial society (see Table I.1). While students of color continue to grow in number, the teaching force has remained largely the same—approximately 80% are White, of middle-class origins, monolingual English-speaking, and mostly female. In many ways we—the authors of this book—reflect this demographic. Our experiences have impacted us profoundly as, through the practice of teaching, our existing knowledge about human diversity has expanded greatly. We also came to discover that teachers, as well as students, can be continually enriched through explicitly engaging with diversity. As teachers, this engagement helps us to hone our craft while constantly enlarging our knowledge, always in the service of educating students.

Embracing Diversity in Troubled Times

In recent times, important issues directly related to a pluralistic society have been raised, including the expansion of the Black Lives Matter movement; the terms "White privilege" and "White supremacy" becoming commonplace; demonstrations of anti-Semitism; violence against Asian Americans; mistrust of Muslim Americans; the virtual absence of Native Americans in society; the severe diminishment of women's reproductive rights; increased numbers of people living in poverty and without access to health care; discrimination against transgender people; the need for public information to be accessible in multiple formats (including American Sign Language and languages other than English); the tenacious grip of the standardization movement and the marketization of education; using fear of critical race theory and the 1619 project to prohibit almost any discussions of race; the banning of both classic and modern literature; the barring of books deemed to feature components of social and emotional learning; and immigrants and students in poverty being among the least well-served children in public schools. All of these topics are foregrounded to varying degrees in mainstream media and amplified by social media, reflecting a national landscape filled with concerns about longstanding and recurring racial, ethnic, gender, and economic disparities in our society. Our students have access to this

Table I.1: Percentage Distribution of Students in Public Schools by Race and Ethnicity 2000, 2017, and Projected 2029

Demographic Group	2000	2017	2029
White	61	48	44
Black	17	15	15
Hispanic	16	27	28
Asian	N/A	5	7
American Indian	1	1	1
Pacific Islander	N/A	<1	<1
Two or more races	N/A	4	6

Note. From NCES, 2019.

information and are keenly aware of the world in which we live. We therefore feel it is our responsibility to help students develop the educational tools to be critical actors in response to these issues.

In many ways, this book strives to locate itself somewhere in the middle ground of "the curriculum wars" (Nicol, 2008), replete with battles over what knowledge gets included or excluded for students. Above all, we value the diversity of human experience that literature provides access to. After all, literature allows us to enter the thoughts of any character in any location during any period of time—past, present, and imagined future—transcending the limitations of our own bodies. For this reason alone, we advocate for a wide variety of texts to be used in ELA classes, knowing that many teachers are required, to different degrees, to continue teaching canonical texts. Here, we realize we run the risk of appearing "middle of the road," but we feel our decisions recognize the reality of many teachers in a vast variety of school environments across the United States. Put differently, we don't want to "throw the baby out with the bathwater," as we seek to recognize established texts, while being mindful of teaching acclaimed works with a critical eye adept at using multiple lenses. Simultaneously, we support grassroots teacher initiatives such as #Disrupt Texts (https://disrupttexts.org) that strive to create an antiracist, antibiased, more inclusive curriculum, agreeing that varied literature provides access to a rich diversity of experiences. After all, a diversity-centered approach to teaching ELA goes far beyond simply varying texts and includes pedagogical philosophies and practices.

THEORETICAL GROUNDING IN SOCIAL JUSTICE

The theoretical grounding guiding this text is the value of multiculturalism, creating a more socially just society that strives for greater equality among all people. We respectfully acknowledge the work of pioneering scholars of multiculturalism, such as Banks (1993), Gay (1994), Nieto (1992), and Sleeter and Grant (1987, 1988), whose ideas have been influential throughout our teaching, centering multiculturalism's core concepts, which include valuing a diverse student body, challenging cultural misperceptions and stereotypes, decentering White norms, and developing curricula and pedagogies to effectively engage all students. We also recognize that multiculturalism has played an important role in influencing the rise of culturally responsive pedagogy (Ladson-Billings, 1994), culturally sustaining pedagogy (Paris & Alim, 2017), culturally responsive literacy (Muhammad, 2020), and anti-oppressive education (Kumashiro, 2000)—all of which seek, among other things, to actively redress power differentials in our society by affirming the cultural identities of all students.

The implications of the overwhelming demographic disparity between teachers and their students—in terms of race, gender, and social class—has been of concern for some time (Cannella & Reiff, 1994), along with the best way to prepare teachers, given the multiple and often conflicting demands placed upon them (Sharma & Lazar, 2019). A recent report by the NCES (2020) revealed that public school teachers shared the following about their preparation programs: 65% took courses in students from diverse economic backgrounds, 70% in educating students with disabilities, and 41% in emergent bilingual students. While clearly 100% of all teacher programs should include all of these groups of students, it is important to note that some progress has been made over time (for example, the same report reveals that only 14% of teachers in 1980 had courses in teaching emergent bilingual students). We share these statistics to illustrate some points that support our larger argument, namely, that while promising, these statistics don't necessarily reveal the *content* and *quality* of what is being taught and by whom. In addition, they don't indicate how teachers themselves view their readiness to teach a diverse body of students. For example, in regard to different socioeconomic status groups, Ladson-Billings (2008) points out, "The preparation of novice teachers is dominated by psychological notions almost to the exclusion of other social science paradigms" (p.104), thereby shaping already limited perceptions of what constitutes "culture" without really grappling with the implications of economic differences (and their entanglement with other markers of identity) between students and teachers. In considering students with disabilities, a recent report revealed, "Only 17% of teachers surveyed feel very well prepared to teach students with mild to moderate learning disabilities (National Center for Learning Disabilities, 2019, p. 11). Regarding teacher preparation of English language learners (ELLs), Lopez et al. (2013) found that no state required their teachers, including ELL specialists, to be exposed to or be proficient in all 10 skills deemed key to the instruction of ELLs (Gándara & Santibañez, 2016). In sum, substantial evidence points to teacher preparation in our country being significantly uneven, resulting in vast variations among teachers' confidence to work with, and learn from, a diverse body of students.

And yet, as we've indicated, it is a fact that demographic shifts in our society will continue, placing the onus on teachers to personally reach and effectively teach all of their students. This is why having a grounding in a social justice approach to teaching is important, because it consciously blends the personal, professional, and political. As Nieto (2013) notes, having a social justice approach "is more a stance than a set of strategies or lesson plans. It requires being open and flexible, willing to learn, and humble. One also needs to become a *multicultural person* rather than just being a *multicultural teacher*" (p. 20, emphasis in original). Below, we take the four components of Nieto's description of social justice within education, highlighted in italics, and apply them to teaching ELA in the secondary classroom.

1. *It challenges, confronts, and disrupts misconceptions, untruths, and stereotypes that lead to or exacerbate structural inequality and discrimination.*
    - Texts can be analyzed to illustrate representations of characters in terms of authenticities of representation (according to race, ethnicity, nationality, gender, sexual orientation, social class, and so on).
    - Emphasis can be placed on a variety of representations that work against stereotypes and show a variety of experience, including those that expose oppression and, importantly, move beyond a singular focus on suffering to celebrate resilience, creativity, and the human experience in general.
    - Societies in which stories take place can be analyzed in terms of representation and correlations to power, including disempowering assumptions and systemic policies that may perpetuate social inequities.
    - Instances of discrimination can be identified and discussed in the context wherein they occur and can be linked to student experiences and perceptions.
    - Critical readings of current events can be applied to literary contexts so students may make connections between current and past injustice, interrogating ways unjust cultural practices are (re)produced and what can be done to counter them.
2. *It provides all students with the resources they need to learn to their full potential. This includes both material resources (books, curriculum, adequate funding, etc.) and emotional resources (believing in their ability and worth, caring for them as individuals and learners, honoring both their individuality and their group membership, having high expectations for them, and giving them the cultural and social capital to succeed, among others).*
    - Curricula rich in diversity can be developed.
    - Books representing diversity can form the core of the curriculum, including texts with a variety of positive, complex representations of diverse people that move beyond tropes of suffering.
    - Students can have choice in selecting literature that interests them, in seeing characters, settings, and culture that reflect their own.
    - Students may engage with literature as individuals and groups.
    - Varied literacy skills can be built upon and developed to ensure cultural and social capital, for example, the confidence to grow as learners and continue their educational trajectory in college.

   - » Classrooms are developed as communities where students' voices are valued and incorporated; while these spaces may not always be safe, they support students' social–emotional needs and encourage students to take academic risks essential to reach their intellectual potential.
3. *It draws on students' talents and strengths. This requires having a critical perspective while also rejecting deficit theories about children of particular backgrounds and understanding that all children have strengths that can enhance their education.*
   - » Students are seen through a strength-based perspective (countering pervasive deficit-based perspectives of difference).
   - » Students' interests can be acknowledged and nurtured.
   - » Students can play different roles in engaging educational activities.
   - » Teaching is understood as multimodal, drawing on a variety of cultural traditions and breaking from the stereotype of "chalk and talk" to include call and response, oral tradition, and "collectivist" activities.
4. *Finally, social justice education is about creating a learning environment that promotes critical thinking and supports agency of social change, in effect providing students with an apprenticeship in their role in a democratic society* (p. 21).
   - » Students grow as critical thinkers, with the ability to analyze and evaluate socially pertinent issues in texts.
   - » Students develop confidence in exploring complex issues using skills such as intrapersonal reflection and interpersonal dialogues to exchange ideas and perspectives.
   - » Students develop not only as critical thinkers but as creative thinkers.
   - » Students have opportunities to connect classroom work with real-world issues and activism, seeing education as a means for social change.

These examples are far from exhaustive, and we encourage readers to contemplate other ways in which students can flourish in ELA classrooms through engaging in diverse texts that keep expanding their knowledge and interests.

WHY IS IT IMPORTANT FOR TEACHERS TO CRITICALLY REFLECT?

We came to write this book because we enjoy our career choice and wanted to share some of our learnings, observations, experiences, and hopes—with a view to supporting both new and practicing teachers who teach in secondary ELA classrooms. In many ways, we have come to see our work as dissolving the lines between the personal, professional, and political realms of experience. The degree to which these three realms are separate, somewhat overlapping, or intertwined varies enormously among educators. From our own perspective, we consider these realms as inextricably intertwined and will illustrate how.

The *personal realm,* to perhaps state the obvious, is synonymous with who we believe we are—our personal identity. Identities are based upon all kinds of influences such as when and where we're born, the family structure we were born into, and our gender, race, religion, nationality, social class, sexual orientation, dis/ability, and so on. Some of these markers are permanent, some fluid, while others are acquired during the course of our lives. In other words, our identities have multiple components—all of which are embedded within history, society, and culture—and are subject to change. Each of our experiences to date has influenced us, providing us with various degrees of privilege, power, and oppression that have shaped our belief systems about everything—including how we view ourselves and other people.

The *professional realm* relates to our place within the ever-evolving profession of teaching and how we see our roles within the continually changing assumptions and responsibilities that come with owning the title of "teacher." Teaching comes with expectations of how we perform our job as employees, including adhering to federal, state, local, and school requirements. Working within a profession with many regulations, we nonetheless strive to create unique, welcoming spaces for students in which to feel a sense of belonging and where learning occurs—by using creativity, originality, and flexibility to promote engagement. All of these characteristics that make teaching effective come from our personal realm.

The *political realm* refers to how we view and understand the dynamics of power. It's important to be clear that we're not using the term "politics" in a way that reduces associations to political parties. Rather, we use the term to describe how power works among humans, namely, recognizing *who is empowered and who is disempowered* in every interactional context. In schools, such interactions can range from personal exchanges between people (e.g., teacher and student, or parent, or administrator), in meetings (e.g., school curriculum committees), via rule enforcement (e.g., school disciplinary proceedings), in operational systems (e.g., school placement options), and in standard practices (e.g., tracking, gifted classes, special education services). These examples also are echoed by society at large, such as in media (e.g., who is featured in news items, representation of different groups), cultural depictions of people (e.g., accepted norms of ideal citizens vs. aberrations of undesirable citizens), as well as historical examples (hierarchies of racial and gendered worth, such as that all U.S. presidents have been males and, except for one, White).

We invite readers to see ways in which these three realms are intricately bound, playing a part in all of the decisions we make as teachers. For example, personal beliefs that form who we are influence all of our choices and actions as professionals who work in a society that historically has empowered some groups and disempowered others. As educators in ELA we must be cognizant of (1) which authors are represented in the curriculum; (2) who characters represent and how they're portrayed in the texts that we teach; and (3) respectfully engaging students about the issues authors raise. Additionally, at the school level, we must be conscious of—among other things—Who has the right to make decisions about curricula? Whose voice matters, and whose doesn't, at faculty meetings, departmental and schoolwide committees, and parent/teacher associations? Who speaks, or is silent, on school policy? Where and when are student voices heard, or ignored? Moreover, we ask teachers to contemplate—by embracing diversity—what can be done in classrooms and schools to create practices that seek to counter historical imbalances of power among people?

To be blunt, educators should always be aware of their own personal beliefs in relation to historical and contemporary inequalities based upon race, ethnicity, gender, dis/ability, nationality, and other markers of identity. As simple as it sounds, a person who acknowledges inequalities, and desires to do something to counter them, is a starting point for contemplating change. In other words, our accrued experiences and personal knowledge can inform professional choices that seek political change. What assists us in this process is the ability to develop, and nurture, a critical consciousness that includes the crucial element of self-reflection.

CRITICAL SELF-REFLECTION AND WHITENESS

The value of critical self-reflection as praxis was recognized by Freire (1976, 1985) as integral to creating the possibilities of social change through education. Critical self-reflection means we become aware of our presuppositions in order to engage with our own beliefs and ways of thinking (Fernández-Balboa, 1998). This approach to teaching, rooted in our own experiences and practices, is an ongoing process The importance of critical self-reflection has been recognized in other caring professions as well as teaching, such as nursing (Grech, 2021) and social work (Theobald et al., 2017). Widespread recognition of critical self-reflection affirms the idea that professionals can not only link theory and research to practice but also incorporate their experiences, acknowledge their intuition, and develop a greater professional self-knowledge within the context of their own workplace.

We are all a work-in-progress and, by the very nature of our profession, should be open to expanding and refining our knowledge about any topic.

Furthermore, we recognize that practicing cultural humility is integral to an ongoing critical examination of our own positionality. As Nomikoudis and Starr (2016) assert, cultivating a professional stance of *listening to* the people whom professionals serve helps to better understand them. We recognize that listening can be done in a variety of ways within school communities, such as facilitating engaging classroom activities (Salend, 2015), integrating elements of social and emotional learning (Philibert, 2017), using culturally sustaining methodologies (Paris & Alim, 2017), talking with students (Griffith, 2016) and their parents (Harry & Ocasio-Stoutenburg, 2020), and attending events organized by community members (Cowhey, 2022). Additionally, teachers can listen indirectly by subscribing to periodicals committed to centering diversity, such as *Rethinking Schools* and the *Journal of Multicultural Education*; reading scholars who have specialized in affirming human differences (Nieto & Bode, 2017); and engaging with writings by authors of different identities (Anderson & Hill Collins, 2022) and multiply marginalized intersectional experiences (Kumashiro, 2003). Admittedly, this is a tall order, as we know no educator without time constraints, or one who always "gets things right," including ourselves. It is, however, vital that teachers hold themselves responsible for being knowledgeable about both themselves and their students.

These necessities bring us to an important aspect of this book—our own positionality as White teachers who strive to be critically reflective practitioners in a multicultural society. Before addressing the concept of Whiteness in general, and then as individual authors, we wish to stress again that this book is designed for *all* teachers; each one of us should be self-knowledgeable about the ways in which our identities potentially can impact our teaching. In foregrounding the issue of Whiteness here, we know it will resonate with many White readers, who still make up the majority of the teaching profession. At the same time, the phenomenon of Whiteness as currently understood in our society—including within educational theory, research, and practice—has informed much about the values and goals of our educational system and should be of interest to everyone.

The concept of Whiteness is a fairly recent development within public discourse and as an academic discipline, although its roots stretch back to the ideas of W. E. B. Du Bois (1903/1989), and it has been directly engaged by Toni Morrison in *Playing in the Dark: Whiteness and the Literary Imagination* (1992) (Matias, 2022). Whiteness has been manifested implicitly as representing what constitutes "the norm" in our society. Other racial groups have not had the same opportunities in all aspects of life, including, but not limited to, access to quality education, employment, freedom of movement, and accrual of wealth. The historical oppression of people of color created many barriers—including physical, social, emotional, attitudinal, and financial—that made being White easier in our society. The pervasiveness of structural racism has remained with us, even if it is not always acknowledged by White people. That nonrecognition in itself is a form of what has been termed "White privilege" (McIntosh, 1990), denoting ways in which accrued social, cultural, and economic benefits of Whiteness have been inherited. Whiteness has always been central to how the history of the United States has been uncritically represented (Yacoveone, 2022). Paradoxically, the omnipresence of Whiteness has been matched, at least until recently, by its intangibility. There is, for many Whites, what can be characterized as a tangle of feelings, including a sense of unease, guilt, awkwardness, and defensiveness, about defining a White racial identity even though identities of all other racial groups commonly are articulated in our society (Rothenberg, 2015).

In Kincheloe's *The Struggle to Define and Reinvent Whiteness* (1999), he noted how the concept was "slippery and elusive. . . . Even though no one at this point really knows what whiteness is, most observers agree that it is intimately involved with issues of power and power differences between white and non-white people" (p. 162). Over the last couple of decades, the subject of Whiteness has gained greater interest and has been taken up by other scholars within education—exploring its implications such as recognizing "deep-seated contradictions that are produced in the unequal racial experiences that define modern education and society" (Mccarthy, 2003, p. 127); illustrating how Whiteness works in all aspects of society, including schools and teacher education programs (Leonardo, 2009); analyzing the relationship of Whiteness and teachers' perceptions of students of color (Matias, 2016a); calling upon White educators to teach one another about Whiteness (Tanner, 2019); and using critical pedagogy to understand Whiteness (Allen, 2004), confront anti-Blackness (Matias & Mackey, 2016), and promote social change (Trainor, 2002). As can be seen, studying Whiteness in teacher education can be challenging, but it is also necessary (Sleeter, 2016, 2017), as failure to do so risks White teachers—and we'd also argue some teachers of color—maintaining and enacting historically dominant racial ideologies (Picower, 2009).

In the following section, as White educators who have embraced diversity in teaching, we each share aspects from this element of our journey, illustrating ways in which the personal and professional merge with the political, shaping us as educators.

Sarah

I grew up in a very segregated racial setting that is unfortunately very common in America. My small hometown on the Jersey shore was less than 60 miles from New York City, but there was one African American student and one Filipino student in my *entire* otherwise-White high school. Thus, for much of my youth I had the privilege of assuming White as the norm and really ignoring race altogether. I was raised by Left-leaning parents, so if you had asked 12-year-old me about race, I would have acknowledged that racism existed, that it had "improved" from the past, but that inequality was still a problem in the world.

College expanded the diversity of my friend group and my thoughts on race as I read bell hooks (2014) and Lisa Delpit (1996) and began to work as a college volunteer in schools with a majority of students of color. Here, as I will describe below, I began to see systemic inequities that my White privilege had shielded me from thus far. I had assumed my adequate public school education as the baseline norm, not recognizing the systems in place to drastically increase the likelihood that schools serving students of color would be underfunded, with crumbling buildings, few supplies, and teachers who often didn't last the full year. This experience drove me to want to teach in urban schools serving BIPOC students, helping in a small way to improve a system that did not seem to believe Black and Brown students deserved qualified teachers. If you had asked 19-year-old me if I thought I was swooping in to "save" these students, I would have rejected this White savior stereotype. *Dangerous Minds* (Smith, 1995) had come out 4 years prior and had been mocked sufficiently by then to make me see the error of this trope. Plus, after working with Black and Latinx high school students for a few years, I knew the creativity and engagement of these students enough to know that "saving" was *not* what they needed; they needed a good English teacher so they could learn to write papers, pass those state tests, and have the skills to succeed in college. That said, I had yet to grapple with my position as a White teacher in a room full of students of color.

When I graduated and became a full-time teacher in a school with a majority of students of color, I felt my Whiteness in a powerful way. It made me self-conscious and, if I'm totally honest, on tough days sometimes made me feel alienated from my students, like I could never fully relate to them. On more positive days I would try to avoid wrestling with race by adopting not exactly a "colorblind lens" but a "they're all just kids and we're all just people" platitude to avoid the sticky topic of race. As my teaching years progressed, I realized that, while true on one level, this concept of shared humanity was in many ways a "cop out" from considering my positionality as a White authority figure—creator of curricula, selector of books, enforcer of rules, arbiter of grades—in a classroom with mostly Black and Brown students. Looking to more authentically engage my students, I began to select more books by authors of color, plan creative activities that were linked to pop culture and student interests, and work harder to learn about my students' backgrounds and families. These changes made my classroom a place that was less "White focused" and more connected to students of color as I attempted to make it what is now called more culturally responsive (although in the mid-2000s I was not aware of the term).

The final piece of my Whiteness "journey" came with the more recent focus on this concept in the past few years. After reading *White Fragility* (DiAngelo, 2018) and *Raising White Kids* (Harvey, 2019), not to mention working with Glenn Singleton's *Courageous Conversations About Race* (2005) with my colleagues, I truly began to engage with the "self-work" around my own Whiteness.[1] Rather than glossing over my own identity or ignoring the influence of Whiteness on the literature that had most likely shaped my students' prior English education, I started to reflect on what it had meant to my own formation as a person and a teacher. This work included much reading, writing, and conversations with other White people about Whiteness. Naming Whiteness and dissecting the advantages it had afforded me, sometimes without my awareness, opened the door to thinking about privilege and structural inequities in ways I had not done before. This is the self-reflection we encourage all teachers, but particularly White teachers, to engage in throughout this book as they read about, discuss, and think about Whiteness, power structures, and identity. Personally, this work has led me to more deeply interrogate my own privilege and biases I bring to the classroom and to my beliefs in general. I continue to "edit out" books from the White, male, Western canon as I see the systems that led to the ascension of these books in the first place. In checking my assumptions and biases, I have been able to deepen relationships with more students. I've been able to see more of the brilliance students, especially students of color, bring to my classroom that I previously may have been unaware of, especially if this brilliance fell outside of the strict parameters of stereotypical "good student" behavior. And then, I've tried to change. I've tried to find ways to make space for these aforementioned students to shine in ways schools don't always value. I've changed the way I teach these texts to respond to my students, rather than meeting some internal idea of teaching that is an antiquated relic from my own White childhood. Perhaps most important, I've realized that as a White teacher who has chosen (and loves) working in diverse New York City schools, this work in regard to race, but also my own Whiteness, is ongoing. This is not a journey that will end or resolve with a neat bow. It is continual and challenging but also essential.

Fran

I grew up in a wealthy, homogeneous suburb outside of Washington, DC. I experienced almost no diversity in students or teachers until I attended an all-female Catholic high school in Washington, DC, where many of the students were from the capital and clear initiatives were in place to make sure the school had some diversity. For all 4 years in high school I was a volunteer tutor at a Catholic elementary school in the city, working with Hispanic students. It was then I began to realize the inequities in education and started to enjoy my role as a teacher. By college I planned on becoming a teacher and volunteered at a local in-house drug rehabilitation center to help patients get their GEDs. I loved working with this diverse group of women, who shared amazing stories, and had their children staying in the facility with them. It was here that I started to question more fully the access to and role that education plays in people's lives.

While I knew I wanted to be a teacher since high school, I never thought about who my students would be. Having gone to mostly private schools, I actually abhorred the unlevel playing field that "elite" schools often provide. I knew I was committed to public education, but beyond that, I had no preferences. When moving to New York City for graduate school, I planned on staying for a little over a year before moving out of the city. I did not think I was a "city person," so I was going to get my master's and run. However, I did my student teaching, first at a middle school in the Bronx with an amazing seasoned 8th-grade teacher and then at a small high school in the Lower East Side with an equally amazing seasoned 10th-grade teacher. Both placements were Title I schools, receiving federal support for students from low-income families. It was the first time in my life that I was the racial minority. In fact, other than my cooperating teachers, I was the only White person in the room. It was a humbling experience. I began to understand what it felt like to be an outsider and was thankful for my two mentor teachers who showed me how to navigate these new waters. I loved my two student teaching placements so much that I decided to apply to teach only in New York City and, before I knew it, I was working at another Title I school in Manhattan for the next 11 years.

I don't think I really ever thought about what it means to be White until my race made me the "other." All of a sudden, the burden was on me to convince my students that I was respectful, fair, and committed to a world where all students could succeed. Over a decade later, when I moved to a suburb of New York City, I was astonished by the lack of diversity found there. I couldn't believe how different the suburban schools were from most of those in the New York City public school system, not only in terms of who attended, but in the sizes, teachers, and resources of these schools. It's impossible to ignore the racial and economic segregation that occurs in different communities. It's also impossible to overlook the drastic inequities in education that exist from one school to the next. While all children are guaranteed an education in the United States, those educations are often not comparable at all.

Furthermore, when I worked in the city with a very diverse group of students, I didn't worry about which books I was teaching. The selections we had at that school were wide-ranging, and the principal would order any book I requested. Now, with everything becoming increasingly highly politicized in our society, I consciously try to navigate this landscape. The big questions that constantly absorb me are, "What are we *not* reading?" and "What are we *not* studying?" The high school I now teach in is much less diverse than those where I taught in the city—but my job is still the same. How can I ensure that every voice is heard, even if it is not in the classroom? One program that I have become part of is Advancement Via Individual Determination (AVID). It's a national organization that helps mostly students from low socioeconomic backgrounds and racially underrepresented students get the skills and assistance they need to get to college. I recently finished working with the same group of students for their entire 4 years of high school. I gave a speech for their graduation and couldn't help, despite not being a crier, getting choked up when I saw the level of success the students achieved. All of them are going to college, several with full scholarships, and many others with substantial scholarships.

In February, 4 months before this graduation, a student in my AVID class told me, "It's my month." I said, "Oh, when is your birthday?" He said, "No. It's my month." And I smiled and said, "Oh, Black history month. Yes. The shortest month on the calendar." He turned to a friend in the class, another Black student, and said, "See, Mrs. Bittman isn't White. She gets us."[2] This simple, spontaneous exchange made me reflect upon several things, including how all teachers and students navigate historically racist systems, often from different perspectives; how the work of teaching can encompass building alliances with students; and how the creation of spaces in which everyone continues to learn from one another is essential to learning.

I know there are no quick and easy solutions for ameliorating racial disparities in the United States. Our racist roots are so ingrained in every aspect of our society that it is a formidable challenge to rectify where these roots have led us. As a White American, I feel like I am enmeshed in the problem. While my ancestors didn't arrive here as immigrants until the early 1900s, they certainly benefitted from the continued racial stratification that ensued post-slavery. Recognizing racial and economic disparities is an issue I grapple with every day, forcing me to continually ask myself: How can I, as a teacher, help students understand the complexities of our society and the world at large, and the problems that exist within it, and, most important, how can we find ways to address these problems?

David

I come from what was then a largely monocultural environment in northeast England and grew up in the 1960s and 1970s without thinking about being White at all. In retrospect, this was because being White was the norm, and to identify someone according to their color was viewed as "rude" (a far cry from the civil rights movement in the United States). Attending university in a different region of the country allowed me to meet a greater diversity of people. Additionally, studying English and American literature and film brought greater awareness of issues of race, social class, gender, and other identity markers. However, it wasn't until I immigrated to the United States that I began to grapple with what being White means.

New York City's population is made up of people whose ancestors come from the entire world, and I found people casually used racial markers such as White, Black, Asian, Hispanic, Middle Eastern, Native American, and so on, in everyday language. It may sound strange to some readers, but I felt I became White—at least in the sense of growing a consciousness about it—in the United States. Given the racially divisive history within the country, I was being assigned a label by which others defined me and according to which I was expected to define myself, which felt odd. However, I understood that Whites should not be exempt from categorization if everyone should be viewed as equal. I felt the need to keep asking myself: What does being White mean *to me* and what does that mean *for me* in our society?

If I'm honest, I simply wanted to ignore it. It made me feel uncomfortable because I'd been grouped with a race that had invaded, seized, and colonized lands of Native Americans, then built the country's wealth on enslaved Africans and forcibly tried to maintain racial segregation post–Civil War through Jim Crow laws (I also became more cognizant of alternative perspectives of colonialism in general, including European colonialism). These were all aspects of history that I found greatly disturbing, because *this was not me*. But I also realized I arrived in the United States during the early 1980s with a very naïve attitude, thinking that civil rights movements had changed the country, eliminating structural—if not personal—racism. It was a quick and rude awakening to find otherwise. My friends of color would call attention to all kinds of things I'd not been sufficiently aware of, such as how White people made assumptions about them, glass ceilings in the context of work, restrictive choices of where to live and educate their children, being regularly stopped by police, being followed in stores, people crossing to the other side of the street in certain neighborhoods, having taxi drivers refuse to stop, not seeing themselves accurately portrayed in media, and so on. I didn't like to look at these harsh realities, because I did not want the world to be this way. However, I had to accept that there was a difference in our daily experiences, and it was because of race.

When I was a rookie teacher, the topic of race often would surface in class, a new situation for me—a White person now being reminded of that by classes of Black and Brown students I taught. It made for an odd situation, as I'd never been in the racial minority before, nor had I been made to feel uncomfortable, sometimes purposefully. To counter this, I often made humorous responses (*"Oh my God, I'm White, nobody told me"*—looking at my hands in mock horror), which made them laugh. I'd heard how high school students would test their teachers in different ways and, in pushing through my own original discomfort, saw their comments as similar to those of my friends of color in letting me know very real differences existed in life because of how race is experienced.

I wondered whether students thought I was prejudiced against them and, simultaneously, wondered whether they mistrusted me—thinking I represented White people as a whole. After all, I wanted them to like and trust me. I came to understand that the liking part was easier, and the trust part harder, for I knew I could never force it. Ultimately, it was the student's decision as to the degree of trust. I found trust could be earned, in part, by being a teacher respectful of students, interested in their backgrounds and cultures, having high expectations, and proving I'd support them in their learning process. I also found that the professional knowledge I sought, the skills and practices of how to be an effective teacher, were always in conversation with who I was as a person. And in the students' eyes, I was a White person. Sometimes, after a student got to know me well, they'd say, "You're not really White." I took this to mean I differed in what they thought White people were like (see Note 2). Comments such as this caused me to further reflect on what it means to be White, analyzing the segregation in people's lives across the city and deepening my interest in race and schooling. Because of this, I began to read multicultural literature in education, just starting to proliferate in the late 1980s.

It became clear to me that much of the curriculum did not adequately reflect the diversity of students in my classes. When I was required to teach *Our Town* (Wilder, 2003), they felt comfortable enough to say, "These are White people's stories." At first, I winced at hearing this but, on reflection, thought my students had a good point, triggering me to question the curriculum. Of course, I recognize that Wilder's play is a classic, has merit, and was enjoyable when I saw it performed on Broadway. But in class, it felt dated, with the concerns of the rural, White community missing the mark in terms of resonating with learners in a multicultural urban setting (despite my best efforts to engage them in activities that included performing the wedding scene, which they hammed up spectacularly). So, I began using more texts by authors such as Toni Morrison (2007), Piri Thomas (1967), Alice Walker (2003), and Ntozake Shange (1997), which increased their engagement, giving rise to richer conversations. At the same time, classics such as *Macbeth* (Shakespeare, 2003 edition) and *A Streetcar Named Desire* (Williams, 2004 edition) were kept in the curriculum, as I'd found it easier to make connections with their universal themes of power and ambition, and subterfuge within family tensions, respectively. In brief, I sought to connect with students through more culturally diverse readings

After 7 years in the classroom, I became interested in teacher education and changed positions to that of district office staff developer, specializing in inclusive education. My motivation was an increased awareness of pervasive structural and systemic inequalities within education based on race and dis/ability. While *Brown v. Board of Education* (1954) had made it illegal to exclude based on race, it was still socially acceptable to do so based on disability, creating the phenomenon of many minoritized children and youth being placed in segregated classes and receiving an inferior education to that of their nondisabled peers, particularly White peers (Losen & Orfield, 2002). I saw a connection between teachers' deficit-based perceptions of students of color and the rates of referrals for an evaluation of a disability, noting the Whiteness of the teaching profession—and how removed many teachers' lived experiences and norms were from those of their students. One of the most powerful books I read during this time was Lisa Delpit's *Other People's Children: Cultural Conflict in the Classroom* (1996). This book opened doors to conversations about differences in the educational experiences of teachers and students according to race and social class—illustrating the complexities of being a teacher in an educational system located in a history, if we are to be honest, of White superiority (or what commonly is now referred to as White supremacy) and anti-Blackness.

It wasn't until I entered a doctoral program in 1999 that I listened to, and participated in, conversations about Whiteness in education. What had been a group of disparate observations, emerging ideas, and somatic feelings, now had a name. I was impressed by scholars who wrote about what it meant to be White in America (Stalvey, 1970) and the unrecognized privileges that being White brought (McIntosh, 1990). In a presentation I attended at the American Educational Research Association's conference one year, a researcher (regrettably, I don't recall his name) shared interviewing random White people on a busy street and asking, "What does it mean to be White?" He revealed that most were confused, thinking it was a trick question, some sort of setup. In sum, the majority were uncomfortable and could not answer. This social experiment did give me pause to think, again, about how elusive Whiteness can be, if White people are unwilling to even contemplate its existence (Lipsitz, 2018).

I wish to close my thoughts here with several simple, but important, points—including the difference between being biologically White and the notion of Whiteness as an ideology. The ideology of Whiteness is an invention that has accrued social capital over centuries (Baird, 2021). It is a constellation of interlocking ideas that forms the basis of a theory of superiority—a system that we all have inherited. To recognize that we all exist within, and the ways we've been differently impacted by, this system, is necessary in order to challenge it with a goal to dismantle it. Working against centuries of the ideology of Whiteness feels formidable, and yet it is what people of color do every day. To move toward the ideal of greater equality in our society, it must be done. That work starts with critical reflectivity. Speaking personally, challenging the ideology of Whiteness as a White person is not about feeling bad, guilty, or simply equating it with evil (although I respectfully recognize that these may be initial responses to be worked through). It is, rather, about the work of naming it and actively working toward undoing its power, manifested in all aspects of society, including our classrooms in schools (see, for example, Brookfield & Hess, 2021). Finally, all of us recognize that the topic of Whiteness can be a very sensitive area, for it is a highly complex phenomenon, requiring all people to (re)think about ourselves and the world in which we live. And while this book is not about Whiteness per se, our racial identities have been one of our fundamental influences to write it. For readers who are further interested in exploring Whiteness as a way of gaining self-knowledge to inform their professional practice, we have included some resources in Appendix A (see www.tcpress.com). In addition, some further thoughts on Whiteness are featured throughout the book, including in our final chapter.

What this book *is* about are our earnest attempts to diversify curriculum and pedagogy in the ELA classroom, with a view to cultivating and maintaining respect for, and representation of, students. This work is done, in part, by striving to be critically reflective practitioners who seek to constantly examine the complex issues raised within literature that can serve to help students not only understand our world, but strive to make it a better one.

STRUCTURE AND CONTENT OF CHAPTERS

We have utilized an active verb in the titles of Chapters 1 through 8 to reflect the practical aspect of the book's main topics. Each of these chapters features the following components:

(a) An opening narrative of one or more occurrences that we call "critical incidents" that actually happened in our classrooms—and are related to the main topic of the chapter.
(b) A discussion about the importance of the topic based on personal and professional experiences, explaining why we believe the topic is valuable to explore in terms of embracing diversity, including an overview of associated issues.
(c) Descriptions of a selection of pertinent classroom practices that are related to classic, contemporary, and alternative texts, including aspects of planning, implementing, and assessing lessons. Descriptions are in the form of narratives, featuring examples of ways to engage students with literature that develops critical thinking skills through reading, writing, listening, and speaking. Our narratives integrate reflections upon relevant aspects of teaching—including successes, partial successes, struggles, and failures—to illustrate knowledge gained from teaching that can be of potential use to readers. We also feature examples of methods and/or student responses highlighted in figures.
(d) A short summary to recap the essence of the chapter.

(e) Questions for the reader to reflect upon in their future or current practice in relation to the chapter topic. These questions allow readers to reflect and self-evaluate where they currently stand in relation to the issue we raise and the pedagogies we suggest.

In Chapter 1, Assessing How Students' Identities and Communities Influence Their Learning and Our Teaching, we discuss the need to know who is in your classroom, the importance of cultivating a disposition mindful of differences among students, and using what you know about your students to engage, teach, and support them. Selected practices include (1) ways of getting to know students, (2) giving students varied opportunities to explain themselves, (3) building criticality by requiring students to hear the other side of an issue, and (4) "keeping it fresh," that is, providing choices for students to creatively produce ways of sharing their knowledge. We also examine why various markers of identity are important in regard to understanding and teaching our students, and encourage teachers to self-analyze their own (un)conscious biases when they teach about these aspects of identity.

In Chapter 2, Building Relationships With Students, we explore how a crucial part of teaching is to connect with students. Our experience has taught us that building and cultivating relationships is the heart of effective teaching. The more students feel safe, the more they're willing to share. The notion of "safe spaces" are where students feel comfortable enough to share their views and perspectives of the literature we're engaging in. In addition, we describe the value of taking safe spaces a step further, to "brave spaces," where students decide to share information with the teacher (such as journals, specific assignments) or with the whole class (in discussions, presentations). We also address when things can "go wrong," as lessons don't always go according to plan, leaving students unresponsive and disengaged. Additionally, we recognize how teachers may struggle in finding their "management style," veering between the polarities of being tough or nurturing. Finally, we explore the concepts of "classroom management" and "discipline," offering multiple ways to reconsider these, and constructive, nonpunitive approaches to working with disengaged students.

In Chapter 3, Creating a Balanced Curriculum, we discuss teacher influence in creating curricula that center diversity, including different scenarios to contemplate teacher leverage. For example, in one school, Fran describes how her principal, an advocate of centering diversity in a robust curriculum, trusted her judgment and allowed her to order whatever texts she chose. This same trust existed in a second school where she taught. In contrast, in a third school, she encountered procedures that inhibited procuring more contemporary and diverse texts, resulting in the preservation of what have been called "dead white males" (Nicol, 2008) remaining as the central texts of ELA classes. Culling from these, and other personal experiences, we explore ways in which teachers can maximize their locus of control in diversifying curriculum and, even in the most restrictive circumstances, strategize about ways to supplement existing limited syllabi, including interdisciplinary approaches to developing curriculum and integrating the arts.

In Chapter 4, Developing Cultural Responsivity and Culturally Sustaining Practices, we advocate for the use of culturally responsive and sustaining pedagogies. Drawing from the work of H. Samy Alim, Geneva Gay, Zaretta Hammond, Gloria Ladson-Billings, Gholdy Muhammad, Sonia Nieto, Django Paris, and others, we make a case for valuing these approaches to teaching literature with an eye toward recognizing and exploring inequities within various contexts, times, and places—including our current society. In addition, we demonstrate the practical use of culturally responsive and sustaining pedagogies through learning and reflection, by first doing the work on oneself; using cultural archetypes in everyday teaching techniques; considering the use of criticality inside classrooms and outside in the world; and the core value of creating and maintaining relationships to build community. We also offer approaches for teachers to integrate reflective practices in time-efficient ways to help them better plan lessons, including activities, and options for students to demonstrate their knowledge.

In Chapter 5, Confronting (Dis)Comfort Zones, we look at teachers becoming comfortable with the idea of taking risks. Good teachers push themselves in many realms—from piloting new activities to selecting new texts, from developing new assessments to trying new teaching methods. The common denominator in all these examples is the willingness to try new things as an integral part of self-nurturing. We feature a variety of examples about risks we have taken, including teaching new texts, creating simple to complex activities, and deciding how far to engage with sensitive issues such as women's reproductive rights, sexual orientation, socioeconomic inequalities, and all forms of discrimination. In doing so, we champion the centrality of classroom discussions, ways they can be structured, the art of facilitation, and the value of "messy" conversations.

In Chapter 6, Adapting to Different Educational Contexts, we consider teachers' career spans and how they almost certainly will work in different schools that may vary in regional location, demographics, and core values. We share instances of transitioning to different institutions and ways in which we continued our commitment to embracing diversity in multiple ways. We also discuss how the process of adaptation requires being flexible in our practices, requiring us to be open to reflect, reorient, and rethink, as needed, by exploring topics such as how we engage with new colleagues who may have different viewpoints about diversity, what texts should be in the curriculum, and the most effective ways to teach. These observations encourage teachers to be reflective about (1) issues of diversity (in particular, race) in teacher education programs, (2) their student teaching experiences,

(3) their first full-time school position, and (4) how they can work independently to deepen their knowledge.

In Chapter 7, Considering What the Pandemic Has Taught Us About Teaching, we consider, from our current perspective, that in a post-pandemic world, teaching likely will never be quite the same as it was. We share what we have experienced, observed, and learned, offering thoughts and suggestions about effective ways to engage students within diversity-centered approaches to education. We illustrate what we perceive as some potential benefits that online teaching and learning provide, as well as articulating some drawbacks to be cautious of. Ultimately, we share ways to ensure students in all classes are heard, connected to their peers, and provided opportunities to engage with a rich array of texts so they can share their thoughts in multiple formats.

In Chapter 8, Reflecting Upon What Teaching Has Taught Us, we braid together the main elements of the book, writing personally about how our chosen profession has impacted our own existence—making us constantly think about what it means to be human, to engage with others, to open doors that encourage people to explore thinking in different ways. Along with the successes, we acknowledge our challenges and doubts, and return to the idea that the personal, professional, and political are indistinguishable in teachers who embrace diversity.

A NOTE ON HOW WE DEVELOPED TEXT

We came to this project as three equal partners who could offer both similar and distinct experiences. In initially developing the book, we brainstormed the rationale for each chapter and discussed its potential contents. As we are three working people and much of the writing would be done asynchronously, we needed a plan that would divide labor equally while allowing everyone to contribute to each chapter. We decided that, as practicing ELA teachers, Fran or Sarah would craft a first draft of each chapter. It would then go to the other one for additional comments and examples. Finally, it would be sent to David, who would edit and expand, adding comments, examples, and sections, as well as integrating relevant sources and references. Chapters 1–6 evolved this way. Conversely, David took the lead in crafting the Introduction and Chapter 7 on the pandemic, and organizing Chapter 8—with Sarah and Fran adding their thinking later.

We share our process, in part, to explain how we address "voice" throughout the book. We wanted readers to engage with us as embodied people rather than a disembodied text. In brief, the lead author of a chapter identifies themself and continues to write in the first person. If the voice changes to one of the other authors, it is identified in the text, for example, I

(Sarah), I (Fran), or I (David)—so the reader always knows who is speaking when personal experiences or perspectives are shared. This way, we maintained our individualized voices *as well as* incorporating sections where we use "we" for aspects of pedagogy that we all agree upon. It is our sincere hope that readers will find this choice beneficial, rather than distracting. Finally, due to changing cultural norms, we decided to use "they" as the gender-neutral pronoun for both teachers and students.

CHAPTER 1

Assessing How Students' Identities and Communities Influence Their Learning and Our Teaching

I (Fran) was teaching a course on American literature for the first time. It was my 4th year at a small public Title I high school in New York City. The lights were off and on the overhead projector was the poem "Incident" by Countee Cullen, originally published in the 1920s.

> Once riding in old Baltimore,
> Heart-filled, head-filled with glee;
> I saw a Baltimorean
> Keep looking straight at me.
>
> Now I was eight and very small,
> And he was no whit bigger,
> And so I smiled, but he poked out
> His tongue, and called me, "Nigger."
>
> I saw the whole of Baltimore
> From May until December;
> Of all the things that happened there
> That's all that I remember. (2023, p. 21)

After having a student read the poem aloud and then a second student read it again (because, as my students all know, poems always have to be read at least twice), I ask two questions: Why is that the only memory the narrator has from the 7 months he spent in Baltimore? and Why does Cullen use the "n-word"?

One student chimes in, "Because people remember the traumatic stuff. You forget the good stuff, but the bad memories sometimes never go away."

Another echoes, "Maybe he had never been called that word before, so it was kinda a shock to him, especially because it was another kid who called him that."

I ask them why Cullen uses the word in the poem and whether we should censor the word when reading or speaking the poem. What if we change it to "Black" or even "stupid"?

"That would be stupid," a student responds. "It needs to have the word or the whole memory is different."

Another student agrees, "If a little boy called him 'Black,' who cares? He's Black. If a little boy called him 'stupid,' that could be any kid talking to another kid. You have to use the n-word to show it's racist."

One last student shares, "And the fact that it's this little kid makes you think about where he heard this word. Obviously, his parents are racist too. It's this whole cycle, and that's why the little boy remembers this moment. It's when he realizes what the world is really like."

In the early 2000s I unabashedly discussed the word in class. After all, Countee Cullen was a Black man, and he chose that word, and the shameful racist history of our country is lost if I don't honor his intentions. Cullen's poem was my segue into *The Adventures of Huckleberry Finn* (Twain, 1884), a novel where the word is used 219 times. While Mark Twain was White, I would, of course, teach the novel as a satire, with Twain trying to expose the absurdity of slavery and the hypocrisy of southern slave culture.[1]

In my junior year of high school, I read *The Adventures of Huckleberry Finn* for the first time in my Honors American Literature class at my all-female Catholic institution in Washington, DC, where approximately one-third of each class was Black (the result of a special initiative in place that pushed the school to have mandated diversity to better reflect the composition of DC, rather than of Maryland and Virginia, where most of the students came from). I had read *The Adventures of Tom Sawyer* (Twain, 1876) in middle school, so the characters were not new to me. However, I have zero memory of having any conversation or lessons about Twain's diction choices. Obviously, there is the possibility that my English teacher did discuss the n-word and I have forgotten. While memory is subjective, either my teacher felt Twain's language warranted no discussion or I was unaware of the significance of repeatedly using the word "n*****" in a text.

I am not sure when the word became such a huge topic of public and White debate. In my senior year of college in 2002, I vaguely recall some White "intellectuals" discussing Randall Kennedy's *N*****: The Strange Career of a Troublesome Word* (2002). They kept saying the title, and I got the sense that they liked now having "permission" to say this controversial word openly. The decade following brought an emergence of the word in rap music, along with debates about who and how and why it should or shouldn't be used. Now, with the recent Black Lives Matter and other protest movements, I can't imagine a time where this ever won't be worthy of discussion.

Let's return to my classroom where, as the teacher, I was the only White person in the room, trying to navigate a racially charged word and book for the first time. After discussing Cullen, we read a scholarly article and moved on to discuss who has the right to use this word. Students brought up rap artists and the differences between "n***er" and "n***a." Many had mixed feelings. Some felt that Black people had the right to use the word in conversation, while others thought no one should use the word.

"So can I use it?" I ask coyly.

All eyes turn in shock. "No way, Mrs. Bittman. You're White."

I nod in understanding.

Finally, we got to Twain and my dilemma of whether the n-word should be read aloud. After much discussion, I had students vote, setting a precedent of how to handle the situation. After all, was it not my right to tell my students of color that they could not say this word? Inevitably, that year and every year following, students voted that it should be up to the discretion of the individual. From that point on, if we were reading aloud, some students chose to jump over the word, some said it, some said "n," and some just said "Black." I always read the text aloud as Twain had written it, telling myself that the racism inherent in the word was necessary to be historically accurate.

Eight years later I was teaching *The Adventures of Huckleberry Finn* again but this time in Connecticut to a classroom of mostly blond, all-White students at the honors level—the top English class that juniors could take. While I still began with Cullen, I had upped my game with the Smart Board and had a variety of resources: a CNN clip interviewing a rapper on his usage, comedian Dave Chappelle doing stand-up about the word, and even President Barack Obama sharing his thoughts on language. This time I felt like the conversation was even more important, but also really different.

Students felt very strongly about the historical necessity of keeping the word in the novel. But, when we moved on to who has the right to say this word in general, students were very split. One voiced what many felt: "Censorship is wrong no matter what. People should be able to use whatever words they want. It doesn't mean there won't be repercussions to using those words, but you can't say a word is ok for some people to say but not others."

Another student disagreed: "I don't think you can just ignore history completely. Racism still exists in our country because of the institution of slavery. That word used in anything but a historical framework validates the hierarchy in our country where White men continue to dominate all other groups."

Unlike before, I felt that these students shouldn't get to vote on whether or not to use this word. In the city with my diverse class of students, I wanted them to decide what they felt comfortable with and teach me their perspectives about race and language, as I felt like the outsider. But here with this very White population, I felt they needed some further education. They needed to hear from voices beyond their own about how people feel about race and language, because they lacked those voices in the room. So, I told students to use what they felt was right when reading this text, and while

I would reach the word and wonder painstakingly whether I, too, should bleep it, the vast majority of that class jumped over the word. I want to believe that they hoped by not speaking it they were somehow acknowledging the White privilege they and I so obviously hold.

Four years later, in 2021, my students are shocked when we come across the word in Steinbeck's *Of Mice and Men* (1937). No one even thinks to utter that word aloud, but I also make it clear that the word is not permitted to be said aloud in our classroom. One student, who is analyzing the role of Crooks in her essay, asks, "Can I use that word in a quote to show the racist treatment at the time period?" She adds, "I hate to type it into my paper." I suggest that she can star out the word so that she doesn't need to type it. I finally see how much more aware the next generation is and how important it is for educators to embrace this growth. Now I say "the n-word." Part of me looks back and is shocked that I ever said the word aloud when reading a novel or play in class. I recognize that when we silence the n-word altogether, some people may argue that we run the risk of hiding history. For example, I recently watched the HBO miniseries based on Colson Whitehead's *The Underground Railroad* (2016). Despite having read the novel when it was published, I was taken aback by the prolific use of the n-word, and wondered whether, if it was removed, the show would lose the horrific tone it set for its audience. That said, above all, I understand that the history of the word is complex and believe not articulating the word in any class, to any student, is the most respectful pedagogical choice. Justin Grinage (2013) has noted that the n-word said aloud serves as a "boiling pot" metaphor. By this he means it can have a cumulative effect, becoming potentially harmful when students hear it repeatedly over the course of a unit. He notes, "Whenever the word is said, it carries the historical and emotional temperature of White people's gruesome [past] behavior. At any point the water, which is already hot, can boil over or explode" (cited in Borsheim-Black & Sarigianides, 2019, p. 99). In sum, all three of us recognize that the n-word is a lightning rod, imbued with a history of hatefulness, and will continue to merit complex, serious discussions involving the tensions of its use (including in audiobooks). For readers who wish to further explore this topic, we have included some resources in Appendix B, which is available for download at www.tcpress.com.

WHY CONTEMPLATING STUDENT COMMUNITIES AND IDENTITIES MATTERS

Teaching the same text in two very different high schools made me realize how much the student composition of a class influences the learning that is done there, and we as educators need to be cognizant of who is in our class and what they need to learn. Student composition in classrooms across the country varies enormously and will continue to grow in that direction—something we see as an asset to teachers. Students vary in race and ethnicity, gender and gender conformity, sexual orientation, dis/ability, language proficiency (in one or more languages), and social class—not to mention in politics and religion—along with other markers of identity. Some things we've learned include that while it is important to foreground particular issues to engage with them, there really are no "single issues," as each one is impacted by other markers of identity within the same person. For example, the life experiences and worldview of an emergent bilingual Black Latina, of working-class family, immigrants from the Dominican Republic, are markedly different from those of a third-generation monolingual English-speaking dyslexic Chinese American from a middle-class family. And yet, they may be sitting next to each other in an 11th-grade ELA class in which you have to teach Toni Morrison, F. Scott Fitzgerald, Amy Tan, Junot Diaz, or William Shakespeare. Each element of a student's identity is brought forth when they engage with literature, connecting them through their own experiences and observations, linking them to things they already know while simultaneously introducing new information.

SELECTED PRACTICES

One of the most important things a teacher can do is get to know their students—who they are, what they think, their likes and dislikes, previous experiences, and so on. Here are some strategies to build relationships with students, including ways for teachers to get to know who is in their class at the start of the semester to help initiate, sustain, and deepen teacher–student relationships. In addition, we discuss some considerations relevant to teaching aspects of identity that are integral to the literature being studied, showing how students can shift their thinking through learning and connecting within classrooms.

Building Rapport

I have always found that as soon as I can set up a good rapport with students, and get students to feel comfortable with one another, their "buy-in" to the lessons and sense of classroom community helps all aspects of learning. One of the aspects of teaching that I found challenging at first, but soon came to see as an integral part of the routine, was beginning from scratch with a new class of students at the start of every semester. Knowing your students' names (and how to correctly say them) and having them know one another's names is the first step. One activity I've done is to have each student create a 1-minute Flipgrid video introducing themself and sharing 10 personal things. When I observed all the videos, they provided wonderful insights into who my students were. As I watched, I created a bingo board with one unique block for each student. For example, one block said, "Has eaten" with a picture of an alligator, and another, "recently learned to" and a picture of a skateboard. Students' homework for the weekend was to complete the bingo board and find out the unique interests of each of their classmates. This activity helped students become familiar with the names and faces of their peers, allowing them to connect with one another through similar interests (Holbert, 2015).

Requiring Students to Hear the Other Side of an Issue

In an ideal classroom full of diversity that includes varying viewpoints, the most significant aspect of expanding students' minds is not just hearing, but *understanding*, opposing viewpoints (Newell et al., 2015). One easy way I've found to do this is through introducing counterclaims in essay writing. This forces students to recognize claims from other sides. I often find students struggle to reassert their "own" side with as much conviction once they've argued against themselves, experiencing a form of internal reckoning, realizing they weren't as sure of their argument as they previously thought they were.

Similarly, in debates when students are given the opportunity to readjust their stance, rather than rigidly sticking to one side, they begin to recognize the importance of hearing multiple viewpoints—and the nuances that shade purely "yes" or "no" responses. One activity I've found effective is Philosophical Chairs (Gonzalez, 2015). In this practice, students begin the debate situated on their "side" of the question. For example, when reading Morrison's *Song of Solomon* (1977), I ask: Is Milkman responsible for Hager's death? As part of this activity, empty chairs purposefully are left throughout the classroom, so that when different peers share their ideas and evidence, students are able to physically shift their positions closer to or away from their original stance.

Modernizing and Personalizing Topics

With so many different interests, passions, and beliefs filling one classroom, allowing more student choice recognizes the importance of each class member (Williamson, 2017). Having students make connections between classic texts and current events allows these texts to come to life and for students to find their own perspectives on related modern-day issues. When reading Sophocles's *Antigone* (2005), I have students connect Creon's behavior to a modern-day leader. Several years ago, the majority of students researched and connected him to Kim Jong-Un. In 2019, a handful of my students were Venezuelan and focused on Nicolás Maduro. In 2020, almost 90% of my students researched and wrote about Donald Trump.

Student choice in projects also can promote ownership of their assessment and therefore more interest in learning. Projects permitting students to present their understanding in different learning modes recognizes their strengths and creativity. For example, as a closing project on Salinger's *The Catcher in the Rye* (2001), students' options included designing a carnival ride that reflected the protagonist Holden's experience, retelling a classic fairytale from Holden's voice, or designing a soundtrack for the novel (see Figures 1.1 and 1.2). Whether an artist, a writer, or a music lover, students had the ability to choose their own passion.

Giving Students the Opportunity to Explain Themselves

A colleague of mine shared a system she instituted a few years ago in her class, which I plan on using in the future. Every time a student does not complete an assignment, she has them fill out a short form explaining what happened that kept them from doing their homework. This has three benefits:

(1) It allows students to explain obstacles they currently are facing. For example, I have had students in the hospital attending to sick parents, others facing the pressure of training for major sports tournaments, some who have contracted temporarily disabling stomach bugs, and those overextended due to theatrical performances.
(2) It allows teachers to keep track of the different reasons used, which can be important for future goal setting and parent/teacher conferences.
(3) This form of accountability positively influences some students to complete their homework each time.

Figure 1.1. Soundtrack Option Assignment

Name: ____________________

The *Catcher in the Rye* Soundtrack

After reading *The Catcher in the Rye*, you and a partner now have the option to set our novel to a beat.

1. Choose 5 pivotal scenes in *The Catcher in the Rye*
2. Choose a song for each scene that would highlight the emotions of that scene.
3. Explain in detail the connection, using both textual evidence from the novel and evidence from the song.
4. Create a five-slide PowerPoint or Padlet presentation, where each includes:
   - Scene in *Catcher*
   - Link to song
   - Explanation of the connection (Prove the perfection of your choice = lyrics, instrumental, etc., with textual evidence)

Figure 1.2. *The Catcher in the Rye* Soundtrack Rubric

Critical Thinking: - Demonstrate an understanding of key concepts from the novel (characterization, theme, symbols, diction, etc.) - Critically interpret, evaluate, and synthesize information	/10
Creative Expression: - Generate innovative, creative ideas and products - Originality - Communicate effectively for a given purpose	/10
Textual Evidence: - Expand upon ideas in the story to help create new product - Sufficient evidence used to support product - High-level analysis of chosen evidence	/10
TOTAL	/30

These four suggestions are only a few of many approaches to getting to know students (for others, see, for example, Salend, 2015; Valle & Connor, 2019). Commonalties and differences among students that surface can be used to inform activities developed in future lessons. In a perfect world, every classroom would contain a significant level of diversity among students, all of whose voices were heard with the common understanding that all people potentially could learn from one another. Even though classrooms across the United States are now more diverse than ever, many still lean toward one segment of the community, even exclusively, and perhaps have no representation from others. So, what can a teacher rooted in a social justice disposition do in this situation? One recommendation is to make sure missing voices are heard through the literature we choose and the resources we bring into the classroom (Alsup & Miller, 2014; Hansen & Smyth, 2016). In the following section, we share ways in which students can engage, when reading texts, in discussions that explore diversity-related issues.

Gender

Thoughts about gender in the United States have changed radically since the women's movement of the 1960s, liberating many females from highly restrictive roles, guaranteeing their rights within the law, and emphasizing equality with men. While much progress has been made, significant discrepancies still exist between men and women, reflected, for example, in salary earnings, sexual harassment and assault, and professional positions of power—discrepancies that are further exacerbated by race, social class, immigration status, and so on. Interestingly, the current younger generation have contested long-established norms of gender—rejecting the rigidity of roles assigned at birth, in favor of gender being a fluid concept. As part of this movement, pronouns are no longer assumed, with people specifying their preference to be addressed as he, she, or they—changing the landscape of the classroom and workplaces (Zimman, 2019).

One year, on the first day of teaching my (Fran's) 9th-grade English class, my social studies partner and I decided to combine our sections and have students interview each other and then present their new peers in pairs. Students at my high school come from three different middle schools, so many of their classmates were complete strangers. On the day of the presentations, two students came forward to share their findings. Ryan, a shy boy with a low voice, began, "Castel comes from Longwood Middle School. He enjoys drawing anime and watching Netflix." Ryan continued presenting, using the pronoun "he." I felt my face turn red and a sense of panic run through my body, because I am looking at Castel and see a girl. I am worried Castel will start crying or run out of the room. Castel's peer just misidentified gender, and I think: *What could be more traumatic to a teenager?* I look over at my teaching partner, hoping he will have a suggestion to halt this catastrophe. As I am about to jump in and attempt to salvage this situation, I see Castel laugh at something Ryan said, although I missed what it was due to grappling with my internal anxiety. Before I know it, Ryan wraps up his presentation, and then Castel begins talking about Ryan. After class I look in our online student information portal and see that Castel is listed as a male with a note that he is transgender. Two days later the school social worker held a meeting with all of Castel's teachers to share some important history about Castel's family and his recent change, which occurred in 8th grade. Had I stepped in during that moment, I likely would have humiliated two students and myself. Once Castel laughed and Ryan continued, I saw that clearly Ryan had learned more about Castel by talking with him than I had by drawing surface-level conclusions.

Just as it is important to recognize the constructs of gender in the classroom, it also is important to unravel the gender constructs in the literature we read and the complex worlds characters inhabit (Primamore & Deluise, 2010). In every text, there is arguably a potential angle to investigate gender. Perhaps even more so if we look at the portrayal of women by men in the canon of classical, contemporary, and unconventional fiction. In what ways are they idealized, vilified, or somewhere on the spectrum in-between? How was the writing of women initially not taken seriously? Why were African-born Phillis Wheatley's (2001) poems not in the American canon for so long? Why did the female authors of *Jane Eyre* (C. Brontë, 1983 edition) and *Wuthering Heights* (E. Brontë, 2002 edition) originally have to use male pseudonyms to get published? Why did the distinguished writer of the Harlem Renaissance, Zora Neale Hurston, almost slip into obscurity until her body of work, including *Their Eyes Were Watching God* (2006), was "recovered" by author Alice Walker? How did Lorraine Hansberry's *A Raisin in the Sun* (1959) break new ground, striking a chord in America that still resonates with readers over 60 years later? In what ways did the social movements of the 1960s open doors for female writers such as Toni Morrison, Maya Angelou, and Alice Walker, who brought fresh perspectives on gender, race, motherhood, family, sexuality, and American history? How does Octavia Butler's time traveling in *Kindred* (2004) or Margaret Atwood's dystopian future in *The Handmaid's Tale* (1998 edition) expand our thinking about histories? What is it about the intersectional experiences of Ntozake Shange's *For Colored Girls Who Have Considered Suicide/When the Rainbow Is Enuf* (1997) that reveals different ways of knowing the world? How does Louise Erdrich (2008) inform us of past and contemporary Native American experiences? In what ways does Julia Alvarez's *How the Garcia Girls Lost Their Accents* (2010) and Amy Tan's *Joy Luck Club* (2006) ask us to reflect upon firsthand accounts of immigration, acculturation, and intergenerational differences? How does Edwidge Danticat's *Breath, Eyes, Memory* (2015 edition) inform us of the Afro-Caribbean diaspora and national politics? In sum, women's writing has helped redefine how we conceive of gender, asserting the need for equal representation within the curriculum. After all, women constitute 51% of the population (Statista, 2021).

Sexual Orientation

I (Fran) often begin my lessons with a brief "do now" or a "get ready," consisting of a question or quick-write for students to self-reflect, note their ideas, and put them in the right frame of mind for the day's lesson. A few years ago, as I was teaching *Romeo and Juliet* (Shakespeare, 2014 edition), I had students write about the qualities they look for in the opposite sex. As I read the prompt aloud, I noticed how my wording assumed that everyone was heterosexual. I quickly tried to reword my prompt, but the damage was done. I realized it is unfair for a teacher to make any type of assumptions about a student's sexual orientation. Often, high school is a time where many adolescents struggle to come to terms in understanding their sexual identity—whatever it may be (Mayo, 2022). For teachers to ask questions that imply one sexual orientation is acceptable, and another is not worth discussing, is a form of erasure, undercutting issues of equality that have taken so long to achieve. Using a gender-neutral term such as "partner" allows all students to participate, while leaving them the option of choosing a gender should they wish. To state the obvious, teachers should be supportive of students who identify as LGBTQ+, without making assumptions or *ever* "outing" a student, for that is a deeply personal decision left up to each individual.

However, it is always good for teachers to bear in mind that, statistically speaking, their classrooms will *always* contain LGBTQ+ students, regardless of whether students are ready to self-disclose or even accept that part of their identity themselves. In a society that can be hostile toward diversity, including sexual orientation, students may decide to remain closeted for reasons of physical safety and psychological survival. Regardless, teachers can promote a climate that is supportive, and respectful, of the LGBTQ+ population (DeWitt, 2012). One way of doing this is to create book lists with options for independent reading, or literature groups featuring different-themed categories, including those of LGBTQ+ interest. These can include classics such as E. M. Forster's *Maurice* (2005 edition), James Baldwin's *Giovanni's Room* (2013 edition), *Selected Works of Audre Lorde* (2020), or modern classics such as Alice Walker's *The Color Purple* (2019 edition), Dorothy Allison's *Bastard out of Carolina* (1992), Annie Proulx's *Brokeback Mountain* (2005), Barry Jenkins's Oscar-winning movie adapted from his semiautobiographical play *Moonlight* (2017), or Andrew Sean Greer's Pulitzer Prize–winning *Less* (2018). It is heartening that over the past few decades LGBTQ+ fiction has flourished as a subgenre of Young Adult (YA) fiction, portraying characters as valued community members living healthy lives—see, for example, Nancy Garden's *Annie on My Mind* (1982) and Jacqueline Woodson's *The House You Pass on the Way* (1997)—a far cry from Lillian Hellman's classic *The Children's Hour* (1934) in which the outed lesbian teacher commits suicide from shame. Still, for many in the United States, LGBTQ+ issues are contentious, exemplified by Emily Danforth's YA novel, *The Miseducation of Cameron Post* (2012), in which the heroine is sent off to a special camp to be "de-gayed," reminding us that these places do exist and that many people still reject the diversity of LGBTQ+ people. (See Appendix C at www.tcpress.com for more information and recommendations.)

Religion and Politics

LGBTQ+ issues remind us of how various aspects of identity can be entangled with religion and politics. I (Fran) have very strong religious and political beliefs. That is why, from the start of my teaching career, I have been vigilant in not sharing these with my students. I believe my job is to help students improve their reading and writing, to use literature as a means to evoke empathy for others, and to hone students' questioning skills. The minute I, a person of authority in the room, share my own bias, I lose the ability to be neutral. I don't want students to feel combative or dismissed if I don't align with their belief-systems. In addition, I don't want students to close themselves off from hearing other views if they feel like they're being only shown one point of view. Yet, I know it is impossible to keep politics and religion completely out of the classroom.

In 2020, more than ever before, students came in with very strong political ideas, often incensed by what was going on in the world around them. One student told me that her AP Biology teacher refused to acknowledge the January 6, 2021, attack on the U.S. Capitol in Washington, DC, the day after it occurred, pretending she had no idea what they were referencing. Students have questions about what is going on in the world, often entering the classroom with faulty information. I believe one of the most important things we can do is have students ask questions and help them find the resources to answer those questions as best they can be answered. Even when I have a student make a very controversial comment in class, especially when it is something I personally disagree with, I pose the idea to the class: "Does everyone agree with Samantha?" or "Does anyone have a response to what Kendal just said?" thereby opening up a dialogue where multiple perspectives are heard. That said, if you teach in a community where the vast majority of people think alike, that means you will need to find other sources to introduce contrasting views, usually in the form of interviews or news clips of people presenting the other side of the issue, so contrasting voices are still heard (Harris, 2021).

During the 2020 presidential election, I had students analyze different advertisements from the Trump and Biden campaigns. We talked about who the intended audience was, what marketing strategies were being used, and the overall effectiveness of each advertisement. This led to several political debates, including one in which a student shared that her family could never support Biden, even though she believed in much of his platform, because he represented pro-choice. As a strict Catholic, she said that abortion was a deal breaker, and her family had to support whichever candidate held that position above all else.

Religion also comes into play in so much literature when God is mentioned. Many students are brought up within a particular religion that profoundly shapes their worldviews. Even if family members are nonpracticing, cultural mores, celebrations, and holidays frequently are still honored. Often when literature reflects views on God and religion that sharply contrast with one's own, discussions and even full units can become strained. More than once I have had a parent complain that a given book is not appropriate for their child. However, usually a text that has God and religion as a central part of the narrative offers a rich opportunity for students to explore philosophical questions and, through discussions, to begin to understand belief systems very different than their own (Kahn, 2007). Chinua Achebe's *Things Fall Apart* (1994 edition) lends itself as a perfect example of when religions come into conflict, with the traditional Igbo religion infiltrated by Christian missionaries. Both Marjane Satrapi's *Persepolis* (2004) and Elie Wiesel's *Night* (2006 edition) center on religious characters who grapple with their relationships with God during extremely difficult times in their lives, the Iranian Revolution and the Holocaust, respectively. Finally, a plethora of modernist literature focuses on the questioning of God in general. William Faulkner's *As I Lay Dying* (1991 edition) includes 15 different narrators, many sharing their very close or very distant relationships to God and religion, begging teachers to pose the question, "What exactly is Faulkner saying about religion through these multiple viewpoints?" Rather than shy away from diversity, teachers can use all these texts as wonderful opportunities for students to share, compare, and learn about other religions and belief systems, making them better prepared for the world beyond literature.

Affluence and Poverty

Other than race, the largest divide I have seen in the various classrooms I have taught in is socioeconomic status. Simply stated, affluent students usually have more time and resources to help them succeed in school. For example, during the spring of 2020 while my school turned remote and asynchronous, my student Catalina's parents lost their jobs, leaving her to support her family with her job at a local grocery store. She went from working part time to full time. When she got home at night, Catalina had to help her elementary-age sister with her schoolwork, as both parents were not fluent in English. Catalina had so little time for her own academic work that her grades plummeted. In all good faith, how could my colleagues and I hold Catalina accountable for the work she wasn't doing? By June, Catalina had managed to pass all her classes with some extensions and help from her teachers. However, ultimately her lowered GPA hurt her college admissions, instead of revealing the maturity she embodied in becoming the primary breadwinner for her family. Catalina started her postsecondary education at a community college because, due to her lower GPA, she was not able to get a large scholarship, as some of her peers did.

In another example, during my years teaching the New York State Regent exam (when the format consisted of four essays written over 2 days), I offered extra help after school to my students once a week. The closer the test loomed, the more students would show up. The week before the exam, I had so many desks in my classroom that students had to position themselves in the hallway outside. My entire high school also held Saturday school during the month before these state-mandated exams. Hundreds of students would spend their mornings practicing exam questions and playing review games, while eating pizza to make the most of our time together. Yet, a decade later when I offered the same extra help to my far more affluent student population in Connecticut in preparation for their AP Literature exam, only four students showed up. I can only attribute this to the stronger support systems they have at home, including ingrained expectations of attending college as their parents and siblings had before them, access to cutting-edge technology, quiet/private spaces to study, and the option of tutors.

Speaking of which, a common challenge faced by ELA and social studies teachers in wealthier areas is private tutors. I have had some directly contact me about the students they're helping, to better understand what I'm asking, rather than discuss the task with their tutee. Several colleagues have looked at the Word document "edit history" of their students' essays, only to see how tutors heavily revised their tutee's papers, improving the grade dramatically. Private tutors can cost up to $200 an hour, a steep if not impossible price for the majority of the population. However, those students who have the advantage of parents who can afford tutors unjustly benefit from their position on an extremely unlevel playing field.

Similarly, if a student has a stay-at-home parent who is able to check their homework, edit essays, and help brainstorm projects, that student invariably will be able to complete their assignments at a higher level than if done alone. Yet, in the same class, a fellow student might have two parents who work multiple jobs, resulting in the student having the additional responsibility of caring for younger siblings. That same student is going to have less time and less help to complete the same assignments. And while many high schools try to set up programs to help students get these resources, it usually is not enough. Given the commonality of such extreme circumstances, we believe that teachers have the obligation to recognize—and try to address in the best ways they can—the inequities created by socioeconomic differences (Scherer, 2016).

Emergent Bilinguals

Two years ago, I (Fran) had a junior transfer student from Argentina named Marta placed into my American Literature I class. Because English wasn't Marta's first language, she was put into my "regular"-level class. After a few days, I could tell what amazing reading comprehension skills she had, and by the time she wrote her first paper on Nathaniel Hawthorne's *The Scarlet Letter* (2015 edition), I was convinced she'd been placed in the wrong class. I advocated for Marta to be moved up to an honors level class that spring, enabling her to take AP Literature during her senior year. Similarly, this year in my regular-level Short Fiction class, I had two students, Miguel and Laura, both seniors, who had just moved out of the English as a Second Language program; this was their first "regular" English class. All semester they were the strongest students in the class, consistently sharing thoughtful insights about the stories we read and pushing themselves to choose more difficult authors to study for their independent projects. Even Miguel's and Laura's writing, while sprinkled with some minor grammatical errors and occasional issues needing clarity, conveyed deep insights with an abundance of strong textual evidence to support them. I kept thinking how these, and so many other, students were held back from the higher-level classes, which they were clearly capable of understanding, simply because their speaking and writing were not totally precise. As teachers, we need to make sure we're helping these students improve their speaking and writing while also challenging their high intellects (Hastings & Jacob, 2016).

At the same time, I also see the life experiences they bring to class as valuable. For example, in one class we were discussing the immigrant experience in America, and I asked students how many of them had parents who were born in another country. More than a third of them raised their hands. All of them said they had dual citizenship, with one having triple citizenship. I encouraged these students to help give our class perspectives beyond America, as immigrants possess the unique ability to view the world through multiple lenses.

Race and Ethnicity

Racial inequalities have always functioned as the great divide in the United States, with histories that have been whitewashed at best and omitted at worst (Cuauhtin et al., 2019; Loewen, 2018; Zinn, 2005). Recently, we have seen the development of *The New York Times* "1619 Project" (H. Jones, 2019), which, in highlighting the first year that enslaved Africans were brought to America, challenged the typical history of U.S. establishments and development. Calls for the Pulitzer Prize–winning "1619 Project" to be banned from school curricula swiftly came from politicians, such as President Trump and Senator Tom Cotton of Arkansas, believing it to be racially divisive. From our own perspectives, we must acknowledge the sometimes shared, sometimes different realities experienced by people of all races. Like other historical artifacts, literature provides a door through which the past can be linked to the present, allowing the authors' thoughts to connect to the students' thoughts. Just as it is important for students to see their racial group mirrored in their teachers, they also should see themselves represented in history and literature. Featuring authors from diverse backgrounds brings experiences and insights that students may share with the author. Likewise, grappling with and teaching against stereotypes is necessary, if sometimes complicated, work. For example, in Richard Wright's *Native Son* (1940), Bigger Thomas, the protagonist, is a young Black man living in abject poverty who commits crimes, including accidentally killing his White employer's daughter. Wright's intent was to illustrate society's creation of a "no win" existence, where all the cards are stacked against Bigger from birth; a critique of "All men are created equal"; and the impossibility for many of the American dream.

New York City, one of the most diverse places to live in the world, has served as a magnet for people from around the United States and the world aspiring to the American dream. Historically it has been known as "a melting pot" for all cultures. In the 1990s, this well-known metaphor was respectfully challenged by Mayor David Dinkins for its strong implication of assimilation; he preferred the term "gorgeous mosaic" (Dinkins, 2013) to represent the city's demographics, foregrounding the importance of each individual as a distinct piece in contributing to the big, colorful picture. We raise this point as the mosaic metaphor affirms the value that differences bring, raising issues of nuances between and among ethnicities. For example, as an immigrant from the United Kingdom, I (David) arrived in New York City (NYC) with little knowledge of Latin culture. I assumed people speaking Spanish had some form of connection to Spain, as that had been my only experience to date with Spanish speakers. I was quick to learn the differences between people's preferred choice of term to self-describe—Hispanic (signaling descendants from Spain) or Latino/a (signaling descendants of Latin America). Distinctions are important, as they are imbued with different meanings.[2] For example, *Hispanic* implies a Eurocentric connection, associated with Whiteness, and *Latino/a* connotes identification with an Indigenous and mestiza (mixed) heritage. Given that for the past several decades, the largest growing ethnic group in the United States have been Latinos, it is imperative that teachers do not see students in this—or any other—category as a monolithic group and learn about their histories both within (Gonzalez, 2011) and outside of the United States (Foote & Goebel, 2017).

Over the years I became fascinated with the concept of "ethnicity," realizing *everyone* is part of one or more ethnic groups. In unpacking my own Anglo-Irish ethnicity in the context of the United States, I realized Whites rarely thought of themselves in terms of ethnicity, as Whiteness was the default position for all "others." As teachers, we have to be aware of our limited current knowledge of different cultures without making assumptions. For example, in my first year of teaching, I was initially unaware of differences between students who were Puerto Rican and Dominican. Through coming to know them, I began to recognize and respect some distinctions in cultural norms. This realization, I thought, would be similar to Puerto Ricans and Dominicans living in the United Kingdom who at first saw no difference between the English and Irish, but then came to recognize distinctions as well as similarities. The point being, recognizing our current limitations of knowledge can serve as a motivator to satisfy our curiosity (for it is a responsibility) to learn more about our students' ethnicities—as it helps us to better connect to them. Having students write about their ethnicity as part of an autobiographical assignment in the form of familial connections to other parts of the world, customs, religions, celebrations, language(s), music, food, famous people, and so on, allows students to be the experts on topics, while their classmates and teacher learn about them, through them (Bickens et al., 2013).

Dis/ability

It is worth bearing in mind that students with disabilities constitute 14% of students in public schools (NCES, 2020), which means all teachers always have students with disabilities in their classrooms. The reason we have placed a slash in the word "disability" is to call attention to how—as a label given in school—it can come to define a student, overemphasizing what a student can't do versus their abilities. Here, we begin by differentiating three responses—inclusive, technical, and cultural—to support students with dis/abilities. In terms of an inclusive response, I (David) start with the premise that "everybody belongs" (Shapiro, 2003), as it is a student's civil right to be in a general education classroom. Using Universal Design for Learning (Novak & Rose, 2016) as a framework, I have collaborated with many teachers to create classrooms that are "accessible" in terms of space, student interactions, and engagement with the curriculum. In terms of a technical response, at the start of the semester, I urge teachers to be aware of who their students with Individualized Education Programs (IEPs) are and their accommodations ensured under Section 504 of the Rehabilitation Act of 1973. IEPs and 504s let teachers know what needs to be done to support students in their learning. In terms of a cultural response, I ask teachers to consider disability as a form of diversity and a social justice issue (Gabel & Connor, 2009). As such, it should be integrated into the curriculum to (a) be shown as a natural form of human variation through positive portrayals, and (b) actively teach against limited portrayals and stereotypes that can be found throughout much of classic literature—for example; Richard III's (Shakespeare, 2008 edition) deformed physique reflecting his moral bankruptcy; the latent, unpredictable, and deadly violence associated with Lennie's intellectual disability in *Of Mice and Men* (Steinbeck, 1937); and the pitiable Tiny Tim who inspires charity in *A Christmas Carol* (Dickens, 1986 edition). I therefore ask teachers to proactively include more complex, three-dimensional portrayals of dis/ability in their own reading and that of their students, in both fiction and memoir (see Appendix D at www.tcpress.com for some further suggestions).

I (Fran) realize the longer I teach, the more I have begun to adapt many of the accommodations listed on one or two students' IEPs for all my students—because the accommodations potentially increase ways of accessing learning for everybody. For example, some accommodations I commonly see are "give visual examples," "provide a study guide," "check progress on large assignments," and "provide additional time." In addition, I think it's very important to ensure there's always an open line of communication to check in with students and confirm that you are providing them with the resources they need and encouraging them to be proactive in alerting you when issues arise. For many teenagers, self-advocacy is a work in progress, so helping them scaffold this skill is essential.

"Remedial" and "Honors" Students

Much has been written about inequalities born from tracking systems, which segregate students into different levels based on academic performance (see, for example, Oakes, 2005). And yet, although we work within these hierarchical systems, we must not let them become reified in terms of viewing students only as "honors," "regular," "remedial," and "special," knowing many students will internalize these labels for life, some feeling that their ranking of worth in society has already been determined in high school or even in elementary or preschool (White, 2021). Bearing this thought in mind, we share some observations about tracking.

When teaching regular "on-level" or remedial "below-level" classes, some teachers present less material, teach much more slowly, and use easier texts than in honors or "above-level" classes. Often, remedial classes are filled with students who struggle to focus in a school environment or just need more practice on some skills that students in higher tracks have already mastered. While teaching at one high school, I (Fran) taught the same course at regular and remedial levels. My remedial class contained six boys and one girl, all just as bright as the students in my regular-level class. A few were painfully shy, several struggled to write sufficiently, and some had trouble sitting still. If I lessened the rigor or content, I knew I would not help these students grow the skills they needed, so I did a lot more reading together in class, modeling, and interactive analyses of texts. By the end of the year, half of the students were ready to move up to the regular-level class. Had I walked into class thinking these students were incapable of the standard curriculum, I would have projected an attitude of dismissal, holding them back from achieving the level they could and did achieve.

The converse is also true for students in the honors and AP classes. Teachers can perceive those students as having a level of excellence before they actually achieve it. One of the indicators *U.S. News & World Report* uses when ranking high schools is how many students take AP exams. Interestingly, it does not use how many students earn credit from the AP exams. This has incentivized high schools to push as many students as possible to sign up for AP classes. So, while the AP classes have become more diverse around the country, students in city schools score way below average. To counteract this issue, when I worked in New York City, I had my most academically accomplished students take the English Regent exam a semester early and then used the next semester as a "pre-AP" class. This allowed them more time to prepare for the rigors of the AP class they would take the following year.

The various aspects of identity discussed in this section impact students' sense of self, including self-expectations, their place in the world, and the knowledge(s) that they possess that can be engaged with. The recognition that none of us are perfect, and that we cannot know everything, are only two of many reasons why we are lifelong learners. Bearing that in mind, we end this chapter with a couple of intrapersonal activities designed for introspection.

REFLECTION AND RISK-TAKING

Figures 1.3, 1.4, and 1.5 present some resources to help teachers to (a) think about their own (un)conscious biases, (b) reflect upon the dynamics of their own classroom, and (c) routinely elicit feedback from students that will be used to inform their craft.

Figure 1.3. Self-Reflection: Recognizing My Own Bias

Psychologists at Harvard University and the Universities of Virginia and Washington developed Project Implicit to create Hidden Biased Tests or Implicit Association Tests (IATs) to measure unconscious bias toward race, ethnicity, gender, sexual orientation, and other markers of identity. You can test yourself via the link below.

https://www.tolerance.org/professional-development/test-yourself-for-hidden-bias

Figure 1.4. Self-Reflection: Whom Am I Not Seeing in My Classroom?

- Which three students in each of your classes do you hear in discussions most? Why?
- Which three students in each of your classes do you hear in discussions least? Why?
- Which students have missed the most assignments? Why?
- Which students have been absent the most? Why?
- Which students struggle to find partners for groupwork? Why?
- Which students have the lowest grades in your class? Why?

Figure 1.5. Self-Reflection: Example of End-of-Year Student Survey

Student Surveys

- On a scale of 1–5 (one being super easy and 5 being super challenging), how difficult was English class?
- On a scale of 1–5 (one being almost nothing and 5 being a whole lot), how much did you learn in English class this year?
- On a scale of 1–5 (one being pretty bad and 5 being excellent), how was I as an English teacher this year?
- Which text did you enjoy the most/learn the most from this year?
- Which text should I cut from next year's syllabus?
- In what area/skill have you most improved this year?
- In what area/skill do you still struggle/not feel entirely confident about for 10th grade?
- What could I have done to help you learn more/better this year?

SUMMARY

The majority of teachers in America are White, middle-class, English monolingual, heterosexual women. We must be clear that there is nothing wrong per se with this demographic. However—like it or not—all teachers are in a key position in society as cultural brokers. In brief, it is easy for White, middle-class norms, values, and histories to uncritically be (re)asserted, even unconsciously, over the students we teach. Alternatively, if we use a critical lens and adopt a position that embraces diversity, we can engage—through the worlds that literature provides us with—in issues related to social equality. A major step in this direction is to recognize the diversity that already exists within one's classroom and capitalize upon it through integrating relevant issues into lessons and selecting materials that will expand students' thinking.

QUESTIONS FOR FURTHER REFLECTION

1. What are some ways that you can find out more about your students' cultures?
2. In what ways can students' knowledge of their cultural (and other aspects of) identity be used to inform your teaching?
3. How might classroom spaces (walls, bulletin boards, displays, work samples, student "statements," and so on) be structured to represent and reflect student diversity?
4. What are some pedagogical ways you can employ that require students with different life experiences and perspectives to respectfully engage with one another?
5. On admittedly busy days, what are some ways to constantly be open to reflecting upon your attempts to affirm diversity in your teaching?

CHAPTER 2

Building Relationships With Students

Normally I (Fran) wouldn't even share this story, as it makes me look like a "bad" teacher. However, I think it is so important to realize that everyone makes mistakes, even seasoned teachers. Often one action can have a reaction we weren't expecting and, unfortunately, we can't always erase or easily fix the mistakes we make.

During the COVID-19 pandemic, I logged on to my Google Meet for our virtual Wednesday. Our school was doing a hybrid model with two cohorts, one who came in Mondays and Tuesdays and the other, Thursdays and Fridays, with Wednesdays fully remote for all. As Wednesdays were the time students were all "together" on one platform, I decided that it would be a great day to do an activity that required whole-class discussion. My AP Literature class had poetry lessons every Wednesday, in which two students would teach a poem to the class. My goals were noble: study poetry for students to enhance their analytical skills; require students to take on the role of teacher, therefore learning the material more deeply; and have some class interaction analyzing the poems' themes and literary devices. So far, the first three groups had done amazingly, pushing their peers to understand challenging language and engage in interesting conversations.

Today Meg and Amanda were teaching "The Eolian Harp" by Samuel Taylor Coleridge (2017 edition). Logged in and ready to go, they took over right away. I was impressed with the level of research they had done on Coleridge and the poem in general. After providing some background, they read the poem and then began line by line, stanza by stanza, explaining exactly what each word and line meant. They lectured on and on for about half an hour before I cut them off and had students take the assessment on the poem, a set of multiple-choice questions from an old AP exam. Before students logged off, I thanked Meg and Amanda for the "very, very thorough and very, very boring presentation." I said it as a joke, kind of. I had written in my notes "boring," disappointed that they'd lacked interactivity in their presentation, especially after participating in three previous dynamic lessons by peers. In my mind I gave the criticism as a caution for the remaining student presenters to engage more with their peers, rather than just lecture about their assigned poems. I'd told them how good teachers help students understand a piece of literature, rather than tell them what it is about. Yet, when I looked at the sea of boxes on my screen after I said "very boring," instead of the humorous reactions I expected, I saw shock from the other students and embarrassment from the two presenters. Immediately, I regretted my word choice, but it was too late. To this day I'm still not sure whether my words didn't come across how I had planned because of the virtual learning environment's two-dimensionality or because of my momentary insensitivity, or possibly both.

That night, one of the two students emailed me, telling me how bad she and her partner felt and how they had tried very hard to make their lesson work and that they were already going through a lot as seniors in a pandemic. I felt a hundred times worse. I was so disappointed in myself as a teacher. I also was very impressed with my student who had the courage to stand up to me, calling me out on my careless actions. I immediately emailed both students and apologized for what I had said and how I had said it. I explained what I was trying to do, but admitted I had done it very poorly.

In class from then on, I could tell that the two presenters disliked me. While I don't think it's essential for every student to like a teacher, it definitely helps if they don't dislike you. I had broken their trust and lost their "buy-in" to my class. Apparently, my mother was right when she told me that a joke is funny only if it's told at your own expense. I worked hard to gain back the trust of those students and to make them feel supported by me as a teacher. Regretfully, my actions were not totally fixable, but I used this learning experience to become a better teacher. From that moment on, I vowed to always contemplate my students' feelings before voicing my own thoughts. In hindsight, it would have been much better to have solicited student feedback about the strengths and weaknesses of the lesson and offered suggestions for future groups on how to be more engaging.

The next year my daughter started middle school. I saw how nervous she was about switching classes, her first day of school outfit, whom to eat lunch with, and all the other anxieties that come from transitioning out of elementary school. Having observed her, I walked into my own classroom full of 9th-graders and realized that my English class was probably the last concern on their list of priorities. Instead of just stressing the importance of my class on the first day, I emphasized the importance of community building and began some ice-breaker activities (shared later in this chapter). I also asked whether they had any questions about their schedules, our very large building, or life in general. One student asked me to print out a copy of her schedule, as she had already lost it. Another asked me about going off campus for lunch. A third wanted to know how to get a computer, as she had transferred from another district and now didn't have one like the other students.

As teachers we have epiphanies every year. We learn from our mistakes and improve our craft. While I already knew how important building relationships with students is, that unfiltered moment reminded me of how important not tearing them down is.

WHY RELATIONSHIPS MATTER

As the story above shows, relationships are everything. One of the enduring lessons from the COVID-19 pandemic has been the impact of trauma on students. The trauma students experienced reminded many teachers that Maslow's (1943) classic hierarchy of needs is still relevant in the present[1] (Crosby et al., 2020): Students cannot learn until they feel safe. Trauma experts talk about how students are forced into having "survival brain," a space where they are so consumed with navigating threats that it inhibits deeper learning from occurring. While a teacher's ability to meet students' food or housing needs is limited (although we can print out schedules and even provide snacks), teachers can address students' psychological needs through building relationships that make them feel safe, valued, and seen. This can be as simple as, when touching on a character's religion or language or traditions, having students do a quick go-around where they share some aspect of their culture. For example, when students read about Okonkow's celebration of the New Yam Festival in *Things Fall Apart* (Achebe, 1994 edition), we discussed our favorite aspects of our own cultural holidays. This gave all students an opportunity to share different traditions. The quality of these relationships is what helps students' brains become receptive to learning. As relationships deepen, teachers can form alliances with students, becoming the "warm demander" (Bondy & Ross, 2008), an ally and coach who can push students to greatness as they take academic risks.

SELECTED PRACTICES

While we prioritize discussing building and maintaining quality relations with students, we also want to include other people who make up the students' world, such as parents, other family members, and caregivers, along with members of the school community at large. Likewise, to ensure that we—as professionals—feel an integral part of the school, we include ways to build relationships with teaching peers and other colleagues.

Developing Relationships With Students

When a student walks through your door on day one, you can't assume much about your future relationship, other than that in order to make it successful, they have to "buy into" your class. Some of the ice breakers I've used include a three-pronged "Getting to Know You" activity (Figures 2.1 and 2.2) designed to have students (a) generate questions and interview one new classmate in depth, (b) create a short presentation about the person, to be evaluated with a basic rubric (Figure 2.3), and (c) provide enough information about everyone that I can create an in-class quiz about who is in our class.

Figure 2.1. Ice-Breaker Activity

Getting to Know You

Questions—When you first meet someone, you want to learn about them. Start by writing down at least 10 questions you could ask someone you have not met before that would lead to you having a fuller understanding of them.

Interview—You will be assigned one person with whom to work. Ask your partner your questions, and follow up based on the responses they give. Record things that you feel are particularly important to the class's understanding the person you are interviewing.

Design Element—Once you have completed the interview, and also answered your partner's questions, it is time for you to design a presentation (either electronically or on paper) that will help us remember the person you will be presenting. Possible design elements include . . .

- Newspaper article with visuals
- Poem with a picture of your partner
- Rap/Song
- Additional presentation styles are allowed, just make sure to get them approved first

Presentation—On Tuesday you should come to class prepared to introduce the person you interviewed to the class. The presentation should be between 30 and 60 seconds. Please use Figure 2.3 to understand how you will be graded on this presentation.

Once you've gotten to know your students over a period of time, there are so many reasons why they might buy in, including love of the material, respect for the teacher, fear of low grades, or a desire to impress their peers. The reason doesn't really matter, but the impetus to learn must be there. After this initial buy-in, the student–teacher relationship (and student–student relationships) must be grown and nurtured, evaluated and adjusted. Ideally, this ongoing work means students eventually will feel safe with you and in your class—looking to you for guidance, and understanding that the classroom is a supportive and stable environment (Gillen et al., 2011) in a world that can seem filled with uncertainty for teens.

One thing that immediately breaks down the wall between teacher and students is sharing with them. Telling an anecdote that is directly tied to something you are teaching, or even sharing a highlight from your weekend, can really humanize you to students. Along those lines, learning about students helps teachers make more connections. Asking them informally what they did over the weekend, how their games went yesterday, or what they plan to do over the holidays can go a long way in establishing and maintaining rapport. Of course, teachers are not best friends or substitute parents—a distinction many new teachers initially may struggle to make. Indeed, figuring out how to build relationships can be a largely personal journey. Some

Figure 2.2. Model for Presentation. Example Fran Shared of Her Coteacher

Mr. Schopick

1979
40 years ago TOMORROW
the great Neal Schopick
sandwiched between two sisters
a nurse mother
a lawyer dad
in Connecticut

2004
the great Neal Schopick
teaching history
infusing his journeys
—Iran and North Korea—
into his lessons
at Greenwich High School

2019
the great Neal Schopick
traveling to over 100 countries
South Korea, Papua New Guinea,
and Japan this summer

New York City
Home
Favorite place
Despite his wanderlust

Find him bicycling for 3 hours
Without any water
A camel
Awaiting his next adventure

teachers offer to help edit essays; some make an extra effort to reach out to parents; some have snacks provided during after-school activities; some take students on trips to museums, theaters, and sports games, and spend social time with them. Apart from sharing examples, we can't prescribe actual ways that will always work, as the best moments are usually spontaneous and informal, influenced by a teacher's personality. These moments may happen at any time of the day. It is also worth noting that what may appear to a teacher as a typical or incidental interchange with a student can be entirely memorable for that student.

While we have emphasized informal interchanges with students as being integral to building relationships that feel organic, we also can outline

Figure 2.3. Introduction Presentation Rubric

Information shared: - Specific - Interesting - Important	/10
Creativity of format	/5
Presentation: - Clarity of speech - Organized delivery - Eye contact	/5
TOTAL	/20

some practices and systems teachers can use to positively influence relationship building in a more formal way. As with many aspects of teaching, good student–teacher relationships are not something teachers should hope will happen "magically" (Milner et al., 2018), so purposeful planning and consistency of both words and actions are key (Parker, 2019).

For building relationships with students, day one (or even before, if possible) is the best place to start. In the fall of 2020, after almost 6 months of pandemic lockdown, I (Sarah) started the school year wondering how to better come to know students I'd previously met only in the virtual world of Google Meet, students who also had likely experienced the most traumatic year of their lives. As my first assignment, I decided to have students reflect on the previous year and their hopes for the upcoming year in an "emotional free-write" (Figure 2.4). These purposefully open-ended questions elicited a wide range of information from students—some light-hearted, some heartbreaking, and everything in between.

The information I garnered was so rich that I created a spreadsheet to track it, a document I reviewed before class in the first month so as to better ask Maria how her parakeets were doing or to schedule a meeting with Jasper to see whether his Internet started working again. While this practice was a great way to notice things I'd have picked up on had we been in person, it is an opening routine I now continue using in in-person instruction. This initial check-in, although some may think it somewhat superficial, actually provided basic information about students and their cultures, highlighted any "red flags" for immediate intervention, and was a jumping off point to build

Figure 2.4. First-Day Emotional Check-in

1. Pick two words to describe your experience during the pandemic. You may choose from the list or pick your own. Take 5 minutes to free write about how the past has informed your selection of these words. (This will be read by Ms. Bickens, but not by anyone else unless there are immediate concerns about your safety.)

2. Pick two words that describe how you feel about this coming year. These could relate to school starting, senior year, or upcoming events in your life. Take 5 minutes to free-write about your selection of these words and how they connect to your fears, hopes, dreams, and/or obligations for the upcoming year. (This will be read by Ms. Bickens, but not by anyone else unless there are immediate concerns about your safety.)

3. Please fill in the blanks for each statement below.

- ➔ I am "from" . . .
- ➔ The pronouns I prefer to use/be called by are . . . (please indicate other preferences around using pronouns publicly, with parents/guardians, etc.)
- ➔ When I am happy I . . .
- ➔ When I am sad I . . .
- ➔ When I am angry I . . .
- ➔ If I am struggling with school I . . .
- ➔ The best way to help me if I seem to be falling behind is . . .
- ➔ The best way to get to know me is to ask me about . . .
- ➔ The best book I ever read was . . .
- ➔ Two things (silly likes, serious values, cultural background, neighborhood, people I love, etc.) that make me who I am are . . .

real relationships in the coming months. Daily or biweekly SEL check-ins (like pick the Internet meme that describes how you're feeling, or argue the tastiest type of junk food) can continue relationship building, and versions of this more formalized check-in can be repeated throughout the year.

Despite a teacher's desire to make steady progress in teaching the curriculum, teachers also must set some time aside for continued "formal" relationship building. Daily or biweekly social and emotional learning check-ins can continue as part of relationship building. We believe SEL is integral to a student's general well-being. It has a substantial history (see Figure 2.5) and a body of evidence to support its effectiveness (Durlak et al., 2016), despite a desire to ban it by conservative commentators (Strozewski, 2022).

Check-ins can take the place of a "do now" or "get ready," and can be as simple as students picking a SpongeBob meme to illustrate how they feel or—in a more academically focused attempt—creating a simile or metaphor about their mood. Silliness often reigns, but there's room for it as an ingredient of a safe and relaxed classroom environment: You may learn more about your students as they argue the perfect "done-ness" for a piece of toast or what wins the title of "best junk food" than you would trying to have a serious conversation.

Figure 2.5. Spotlight on Social and Emotional Learning

The concept of what has come to be known as social and emotional learning within education in the United States has exised for decades. It can be traced back to James Comer and the Yale School of Medicine's Child Study Center, where he conceived of, created, and piloted a program in the late 1960s called the Comer School Development Program. In "Educating Poor Minority Children" published in *Scientific American*, Comer (1988) asserted that "schools must win the support of parents and learn to respond flexibly and creatively to students' needs. A successful program developed in New Haven points the way" (p. 42). Comer worked with schools that were predominantly African American, and had both low academic achievement and attendance rates, to create collaborative management teams that included the school principal, teachers, parents, and mental health workers. The team focused on academic and social programs with a view to changing procedures and practices that negatively impacted students' behaviors. Using this model, Comer found student academic performance rose significantly as problematic behaviors decreased.

With a partnership between Yale University and their public school system, New Haven became the site of increased research between 1987 and 1992, developing a Social Development Program for K–12 classrooms (Weissberg & Shriver, 1996). At the same time, the W. T. Grant Consortium, which focused on youth development and efforts to prevent school failure, put forth a framework for incorporating social and emotional learning in schools, articulating skills for the development of emotional competence. These included, for example, students self-identifying, labeling, evaluating, managing, and expressing feelings—along with greater understanding of how to control impulses, delay gratification, and reduce stress both inside and outside of school.

In 1994, the Collaborative to Advance Social and Emotional Learning (CASEL) was established (https://casel.org), contributing to formalizing the concept through research, conferences, and publications. Professional publications such as the Association for Supervision and Curriculum Development's *Promoting Social and Emotional Learning: Guidelines for Educators* (Elias et al., 1997) helped broaden interest in SEL among educators around the country. Additionally, SEL entered the lexicon of popular culture through Daniel Goleman's provocatively titled book *Emotional Intelligence: Why It Can Matter More Than IQ* (1995), which was translated into different languages. In 2001, the board members of CASEL changed its name to the Collaborative for Academic, Social, and Emotional Learning, thereby formally incorporating academics as central in SEL. Since then, the organization has continued to advocate for SEL to be an integral part of all teacher education programs.

In sum, a goal of SEL is for students to develop a sense of self-awareness, including understanding their strengths and areas of need. Moreover, SEL aims to help students understand how behaviors influence relationships, the power of decision-making, and the importance of conscious self-management. For readers interested in SEL, there are resources listed in Appendix E, available at www.tcpress.com.

Other purposeful means of building relationships may be more systemic. For example, "drop in" lunch periods, formalized extra help or office hours, or one-on-one writing conferences inside or outside of class all show students that you're willing to spend time with them. In the end, what matters is consistency (on top of those informal relationship-building exchanges we discussed earlier). It is, admittedly, easy to subconsciously let relationship building decrease in priority when state exams loom or a marking period rushes to a close. The important thing is to understand that relationship building is a foundational aspect of learning, rather than a nice "add-on" only if time permits. Once these relationships are built, students will be much more comfortable participating in class and taking risks in their work. Recently students were encouraged to write thank you notes to their teachers for teacher appreciation week. Many of the letters I received specifically thanked me for creating an environment that made students feel comfortable to participate and not be judged by their peers.

Adding student choice into the curriculum is another specific and explicit way to build relationships and learn more about students in your class. Let's face it, most people don't like to be told what to do, especially teenagers. Giving students choice empowers them in small but significant ways. For example, you can let them choose their own partners, their own seats (sometimes), their own essay topics, or their own project format. You can let the whole class create the list of topics that will be debated, or vote on the next book or the next fieldtrip. Choice also can be used in tandem with community building. Students may each be given a day to choose the (school-appropriate) song that accompanies everyone walking into class or may vote on a class mascot or motto. Having students feel like they have a voice in your class will greatly increase the buy-in and will help you learn more about their likes, dislikes, and—importantly—how they learn best.

When a difficulty does arise, whether it's about behavior or work produced, the relationship that you've already built with the student is key to negotiating any conflict. A one-on-one meeting in private often can do wonders. Sometimes students just need to be alerted to the issue, and sometimes they simply need to know that you actually care enough to save them from destructive behaviors. Offering extra help sessions also has many benefits. Even if students don't take you up on the help, knowing that they can seek out extra help makes many students less stressed about larger papers and projects. Finally, try to find strengths in all students. The human brain isn't fully developed until one's mid-20s, so these students are still growing and need to be nurtured accordingly.

Just as important as having a strong relationship with your students is to create an environment in which students also have strong and respectful relationships with one another. A few years ago, my social studies partner and I (Fran) combined our classes for student presentations. As a very passionate and sometimes overzealous but very endearing student was giving her presentation, I noticed three girls in the front row giggling and rolling their eyes. I gave them the "death" stare, and they immediately stopped, but I felt terrible for the girl presenting and was so disappointed in the three students, whom I really liked. I pulled the three girls aside the next day and spoke to them about how much I liked them all and how disheartened I was to see them treat a peer that way. They immediately apologized and never acted like that for the remainder of the year. Often students don't realize how they come across to others, whether their teachers or their peers. A teacher's role includes providing opportunities for students to work together effectively and respectfully in their classrooms, so they can develop skills that serve them in the future as coworkers and responsible citizens.

Building Relationships With Coworkers

There are many wonderful things about being a teacher, including the fact that no day, week, month, and year are ever alike. There's constant change and flux, and we all agree that it never gets boring. Another wonderful thing is coworkers. They are the only people who truly understand the stamina required for teaching and are always there to celebrate, comfort, and commiserate. Coworkers often end up becoming some of your closest friends. I (Fran) recognize my bias, but I have found teachers to be some of the most kind, moral, and intelligent people I have ever encountered. Recognizing the importance of coworkers as supports, sounding boards, and allies, it is essential to build strong relationships with as many people as possible.

While it's important to have a good relationship with your principal and other administrators, it's even more important to connect with the teachers in your department, especially those with whom you plan curricula each year. These colleagues are going to be the biggest assets in maintaining your equilibrium and getting your creative juices flowing. Case in point, I eat lunch with my two closest colleagues almost every day. On reflection, I spend more time with them than with my noneducator friends (and sometimes, when times are busy, more than with my own family). We talk about everything, from a lesson that disappointingly didn't go as planned, to a student that we are trying to reach, to our personal concerns about our spouses and children.

When starting off as new teachers, we were warned (often by administrators) to "avoid the teachers' room at all costs." Unfortunately, there are some popular stereotypes of teachers being burned out, constantly complaining, or lazy. However, all you need to do is spend 15 minutes in a school to find the astounding passion with which most teachers approach both their subject matter and their responsibility to educate young people. Seeking out these impassioned, seasoned teachers can guide you in many ways, including structuring lessons, planning a curriculum, and generally understanding the culture of a school. We have all found experienced colleagues to be welcoming of peers who wish to informally observe how they teach, including ways they motivate and engage students, and the dynamics of teacher-to-student and student-to-student interactions, and to assess the learning taking place. If you are assigned to a new course, find out who has taught it previously or who is the master teacher in that domain. Usually, colleagues are flattered that you want to access their expertise and they usually accept an invitation to have coffee, soda, or a beer. During these informal meetings, it's fine to ask probing questions about the class and brainstorm ideas together. If you are lucky, your colleague may be willing to share some units of study with you that you can, with customization based on your own interests, preferences, and needs of students, make "into your own." If you happen to be a seasoned teacher reading this, and have had reservations about "sharing your recipes," we encourage you to be generous in sharing your time and lessons freely. We all remember how challenging our first year of teaching was. Any time someone asks us about a course or a text we've taught, we all have a similar disposition to share everything we have. Why not? It is gratifying to watch another teacher use a project, teach a lesson, or use a curriculum that you've developed. Even experienced teachers love knowing what colleagues have done before them, using that as a jumping off point for their thinking. In many ways, it's an integral part of our profession to see what other people created, use what we like, and then customize by building from there. For seasoned teachers, the same applies. Often new and younger teachers have expertise to share as well, especially new technological platforms that seasoned teachers may not have encountered before.

Another valuable time saver is having a planning partner. Last year when I was assigned to teach Short Fiction for the first time, one of my coworkers also was slated to teach the course. First, she and I asked every teacher we knew who had taught this course for any texts and authors they recommended and any suggestions for how to structure the course. Every teacher we asked shared something, many their entire curriculum. Then we met together a few times to brainstorm what we liked, what we wanted to add, and what we had to do to make the class engaging for our students. Finally, we divided the work up and began reading and planning. By the time school started, we had an outline of what we would be teaching and how we would structure our units. As we taught each unit and class, it was so helpful to have a mutual sounding board so we could ask each other: What worked? What didn't? How might we change certain things for next year? We also shared project ideas, activities, and worksheets, and by the end of the semester, I felt like we had really developed a solid curriculum and was proud of our hard work. I know for a fact that working with a colleague makes the planning a more dynamic, creative process and more enjoyable than thinking through everything solo.

Generally speaking, having good relationships with your colleagues makes life easier. My golden rule is to always say yes—if possible—when a colleague asks for a favor. For example, if someone asks you to cover their study hall while they leave early for a doctor's appointment, say yes. If, every Friday, your office orders out lunch but needs someone to pick it up and you happen to be free, volunteer. Maybe your coworker is having a birthday party for her 2-year-old, and you have a bouncy house; ask her if she'd like to borrow it. While all of these examples are generous things to do, they also create a form of collateral goodwill. So when you need someone to cover your homeroom or lend you a sump pump when your basement floods, your colleagues eagerly step up.

In addition to your peers, it is also important to build a strong foundation with administrators, the people who rate you, have the ability to facilitate your tenure, and possibly can fire you. I have learned to put in 110%, especially when you are at a new school where your colleagues don't yet know you. Once you have a solid reputation as a good teacher, if something goes awry, as it inevitably does in an imperfect world, the administration will brush it off. However, early on, you have to earn your new boss's and colleagues' respect. Tenure at my present school takes 4 years to earn. I recall one of the mentor teachers saying to me, "New teachers should act like they are interviewing for the first 4 years." While that thought is challenging for any new teacher who already has so much on their plate, having the support of your new colleagues as you navigate the system can help enormously.

What any new teacher, and even many seasoned teachers, fears the most is the "pop-in," unexpected visit of an administrator. A snapshot of maybe 5 or 15 minutes of a lesson is never a true representation of what a teacher is capable of or what a class is really learning, yet unannounced observations are very common. No matter how many years teachers have taught, it is understandable that they have fears and anxieties of being unfairly judged in an unanticipated visit. One way to accept—and even embrace—the idea of being observed at any time is to have an open-door policy and invite administrators in. Rather than waiting around for administrators to notify you of a formal visit or to pop in unexpectedly, reach out to them when you would like them to see what you're doing. This could include introducing a unit, having students engage in a Socratic seminar, or presenting interesting projects. Another way to hone pedagogical skills is to make video-recordings of yourself while teaching. This method allows you to focus on one particular aspect of practice (e.g., asking questions, facilitating discussions, making transitions between activities, etc.) or holistically self-evaluate your current strengths and areas to develop. While the value of this approach has been documented (Baecher, 2019), it is important to note that these recordings must be for self-use only, and guidelines about including students in the frame vary among states. In brief, regardless of your method of choice, your administration will likely be pleased with your initiative, and it gives you input into observations of teaching and the opportunity to share some of your best work.

Finally, we acknowledge the value of constructive feedback and the importance of being open to it. None of us is perfect, and it's unrealistic to think that we are. One of the great things about teaching is that it allows us to actively be lifelong learners. There's always new content information to learn, literature to engage with, technology skills to maintain and update. There's also the pressure—which we have all learned to manage—of being the best that you can be in any given moment. But we know, too, that all teachers fall short most days. So, in any post-observation conferences, while it may momentarily feel bad to be made aware of less well-developed aspects of our pedagogy, we have found that most criticism is designed to support an educator's professional growth. Sometimes we can't see what's right before our eyes because we're too close to it, including both the everyday "good stuff" we do as part of our teaching as well as some areas that could be developed. In fact, our experience has shown that formal observations can be extremely helpful for our professional growth. Part of the administrator's job is to ensure that students are receiving a quality education through teachers' efforts. If you are ever unsure of any aspect of feedback provided by an administrator, it's good to ask clarifying questions and be open to their viewpoints. At the end of each year, you can always ask your administrator/evaluator if there is something more they would like you to be doing. This approach precludes getting to the end of a tenure track position and being told you fell short in some ways. It's good for teachers to want to know where administrators think they can improve. Even if they might not always agree with the administrator's assessment, it's important to at least ask.

Creating Relationships With Students' Parents, Other Family Members, and Caregivers

While parents, other family members, and caregivers usually play an active role in children's education, by high school there's an increased chance of them fading into the background. It is not uncommon for a teacher to form relationships with the few adults who support the most challenging students, but never see those who've raised high achievers. Teachers also may risk falling into the "squeaky wheel gets the oil" habit of engaging with the most demanding parents, going above and beyond to avoid escalation to the administration or superintendent's office. Of course, all parents are ideally partners-in-learning, and teachers must form relationships with parents not only to better help students learn but also to deepen the teacher–student relationship itself.

One key to maintaining productive relationships with parents is to be both proactive and responsive (Ferlazzo & Hammond, 2009). Many schools require an introductory email the day school begins, introducing yourself and your class. If you are a monolingual teacher, a translation program can be used to send it in Spanish and any other languages commonly spoken by families in your school community. Often this small gesture can calm nervous parents and show that you are respectful of their cultural background. As part of the opening email, asking parents questions such as, "How does your child learn best?" or "What can I do to best support your child?" can frame them from the start as partners-in-learning, rather than potential adversaries fighting with you to raise their child's GPA.

Student grades are always part of parent interest and concerns. This is understandable, as so much is at stake, including the desired goal of earning a high school diploma, the assumed foundation for future success, and the required key to attending college. Making all grading transparent is therefore essential to supporting healthy parent relationships. This can be facilitated by having clear rubrics, for all major assignments, that are reviewed with students before they begin the task, and shared with parents so they can better understand the targeted skills and concepts that are being taught within a specific assignment. That said, we also acknowledge here, as we have elsewhere, that teachers must be sensitive to the fact that not all parents are able to support their children in this specific manner, for a variety of good reasons such as time limitations (many work multiple jobs), language abilities (some are monolingual or emergent bilinguals), varying levels of privilege or education, or simply differing cultural beliefs about their role in relation to the teacher (Cioè-Peña, 2021). Rubrics can be generic for tasks like constructing an essay (see Figure 2.6) or more specific, such as when the class is studying the book *Things Fall Apart* (Achebe, 1994 edition) (see Figure 2.7). They also serve as an informal contract of sorts, namely, students know exactly what they're supposed to do, and for parents to understand what is being asked of their children.

It is therefore clear to see why, in middle and early high school, it can be beneficial to send emails home when major assessments are due and to encourage parents to motivate (and if we are honest, sometimes push) their children. Grading on a timely basis also helps students and parents know where they stand at any point during the semester, avoiding "grade shock" at the end of a marking period. To be consistent, I try to input a few grades per week so that it is always clear how a student is performing. On that note, if a student is struggling or habitually not turning in work, I know it's best to waste no time in reaching out to the student to chat and, if need be, in consulting with the guidance counselor and parents. Waiting for parents to contact you or for the end of the term to share unfavorable news about grades potentially can cause a problem to deepen. Without a doubt, if we are being realistic, some parents can be unreasonable. We have found that it's best to talk in person or over the phone, using a translation service if necessary. Often, dissatisfied people write emails that are far more severe than they normally would communicate. Sometimes, help from an administrator

Figure 2.6. Example of Generic Rubric for Constructing an Essay

Name: ______________________

Animal Farm [Orwell, 2004 edition] / **Macbeth** [Shakespeare, 2003 edition] **Essay**

Thesis Paragraph: /15
- Broad opening
- Thesis
- Preview: two specific examples in the text

Body Paragraph #1: /30
- Topic sentence: Introduces the first example
- Thoroughly explains the example
- Concluding sentence ties to thesis

Body Paragraph #2: /30
- Topic sentence: Introduces the second example
- Thoroughly explains the example
- Concluding sentence ties to thesis

Concluding Paragraph: /10
- Restates thesis (in new words)
- Reviews evidence
- Final comment: something new

Mechanics/Clarity: /15
- Grammar
- Spelling
- Clarity of language

TOTAL: /100

is needed, whether a department head, counselor, or principal. Having two voices of reason in a difficult situation is beneficial. Finally, as always, the focus—as much as possible—has to be on the positive characteristics of the student and on seeking a productive outcome. For example, if a student misses a homework assignment and your grading policy does not allow a make-up, consider what this student can do to bring up their grade. Or, if a student has been disruptive in class, what is a positive behavior you've witnessed from them that you hope ("know") you will see again?

Beyond this form of negotiating with parents, teachers also should simply engage with them as resources for learning and community building (Gestwicki, 2015). For instance, invite parents to speak for career day or to share a talent with the class or school community. Depending on the topic, they may be resources for class research or interview projects. In addition, parents and other family members may be invited to attend a celebration of cumulative work, such as a publishing party. As parents' participation in enriching the classroom grows, they trust the teacher more. And as teachers grow relationships with parents, they potentially can learn more about their students, deepening this bond as well. Cowhey (2022) suggests teachers do a

Figure 2.7. Example of Specific Rubric for Essay on *Things Fall Apart*

	Exceeds Expectations (A)	Meets Expectations (B)	Needs Improvement (C)	Unsatisfactory (D/F)
Purpose and Insight	Skillfully establishes and maintains a clearly articulated purpose and a thorough understanding of the task; exhibits originality, embraces complexity, and persuades with logic.	Demonstrates a clear sense of purpose and understanding of the task; exhibits originality, embraces complexity, and persuades with logic.	Demonstrates a sense of purpose or understanding of the task. Ideas are simple and safe but persuade with some logic.	Purpose may be unclear and/or task may be misunderstood. Ideas are simple and/or illogical.
Evidence, Support, Development	Thoughtfully provides logical and meaningful context for the task; skillfully develops specific, concise, and convincing ideas; smoothly embeds illuminating details, evidence, and explanations.	Provides logical context for the task; develops specific, concise, and convincing ideas; embeds details, evidence, and explanations.	Provides context for the task; attempts to develop ideas with details, evidence, and explanations.	Does not provide context for the task; ideas are not developed with details, evidence, or explanations.
Organization, Focus	Organization is exceptionally sound; features a consistent, unified, and cohesive structure; and uses a variety of purposeful transitions. Topic sentences skillfully reflect the author's purpose and determine the function of the paragraph within the broader context of the piece.	Organization is effective, features a unified and cohesive structure, and typically varies its transitions. Topic sentences reflect the author's purpose and determine the function of the paragraph within the broader context of the piece.	At times, organization is incoherent, structure may be inconsistent and only occasionally uses transitions. Topic sentences attempt to reflect the author's purpose and the function of the paragraph within the broader context of the piece.	Organization is incoherent and lacks structure. Topic sentences neither reflect the author's purpose nor determine the function of the paragraph within the broader context of the piece.

Clarity, Fluency	Articulates ideas clearly and effectively; word choice is precise and effectively tailored to the audience and tone. Well-developed and varied sentences engage and further the reader's understanding.	Articulates ideas clearly and effectively; word choice is appropriate to the audience and tone. Varied sentences further the reader's understanding.	Ideas are not articulated clearly; word choice may not be appropriate to the audience and tone. Sentences are repetitive and/or awkward in structure.	Ideas are unclear; word choice is imprecise and/or inappropriate to the audience and tone. Sentences may confuse the reader's understanding.
Conventions, Mechanics	Piece has been carefully proofread before submission. Demonstrates mastery of proper syntax, mechanics, spelling, and formatting. Consistently adheres to appropriate MLA guidelines.	Piece has been proofread before submission. Demonstrates proper syntax, mechanics, spelling, and formatting. Most elements adhere to MLA guidelines.	Piece reflects some evidence of proofreading before submission. Occasionally demonstrates proper syntax, mechanics, spelling, and formatting. Some elements adhere to MLA guidelines.	Piece has not been proofread before submission. Does not demonstrate proper syntax, mechanics, spelling, and formatting. Does not adhere to MLA guidelines.

close analysis of "who participates and who doesn't" in various school events, ranging from parent/teacher conferences to PTA meetings to school fundraisers. She notes that often families might not be engaging in school–home activities due to work constraints, lack of child care, or language communication. To counter this phenomenon, she recommends school administrators and teachers not only take a close look at who is missing, but also help reach out to those families to ensure all students' caregivers are able to feel connected to their children's schools.

While it is important to reach out, and be available, to all parents and caregivers, many parents of students with disabilities historically have expressed their dissatisfaction with school–family interactions. For example, parents have expressed concerns about how IEP meetings are conducted, citing them as intimidating because of imbalances of power. Usually, they are outnumbered by a group of educated professionals who have already decided their recommendations for the child, before hearing the parents' input and perspective (Valle, 2009). These power dynamics can be exacerbated further if parents have children who are multiply minoritized, such as having a learning disability *and* being a student of color (Harry & Klingner, 2006). There is still much work to be done in the area of supporting diverse parents in schools. In Figure 2.8 we highlight four recent texts for readers who wish to engage deeper in this area.

Fostering Relationships in the Larger School Community

While academics, no doubt, are the main focus of schooling, the social and emotional needs of students also have been recognized as invaluable. Creating opportunities for students to explore, benefit from, and contribute to the larger community is also possible. While what students learn in schools is important to help them grow as learners, take required examinations, and become prepared for the world after school, they often have interests beyond what schools offer (Jones & Hill, 2016). Many students value the things beyond the classroom more than their coursework, so providing opportunities to foster engagement with the whole school community—and beyond—also contributes to a rounded education.

In the larger school community, for example, teachers can dedicate some time to after-school or weekend events, such as moderating a club, attending performances by the school band, facilitating a Friday night school dance, cheering a basketball or baseball game with another school, or supporting students at local track events (Mendenhall & Bartlett, 2018). (Note: We are wary of encouraging too much volunteering in case teachers become spread too thin. Depending upon the school district, many of these activities can come with financial compensation.) Volunteering in these ways also allows you the opportunity to interact with other teachers and with students who may never set foot in your classroom. Furthermore, encouraging your

Figure 2.8. Books Exploring Ways to Engage Multimarginalized Families in Creating Strong School-Home Relationships

Affirming Disability: Strengths-Based Portraits of Culturally Diverse Families by Janet Story Sauer and Zachary Rossetti (2020, Teachers College Press).

The authors challenge historically deficit-based perspectives of both students with disabilities and their families (often of color, recent immigrants, monolingual non-English speaking). The book features narrative portraits of six immigrant families and their children with disabilities, encompassing their cultural histories and personal perspectives of schooling, including all aspects of the IEP meetings (assessment, identification of disability, placement, recommended instruction, and so on). The text calls upon teachers to practice cultural humility (Nomikoudis & Starr, 2016) in order to foster family engagement, and to reject deficit-based perspectives of students and families.

Meeting Families Where They Are: Building Equity Through Advocacy With Diverse Schools and Communities by Beth Harry and Lydia Ocasio-Stoutenburg (2020, Teachers College Press). The authors look at how the forces of classism, racism, and ableism have shaped how children of color with disabilities and—by extension—their families are perceived in our culture. To counter this, they offer a working model of advocacy, coconstructed to work across all families. Again, the theme of cultural humility is present, as teachers are asked to both unpack the origins of their assumptions about "normality" and rethink how to understand human differences in equitable ways.

Families With Power: Centering Students by Engaging With Families and Community by Mary Cowhey (2022, Teachers College Press). Award-winning teacher, writer, and community activist, Cowhey culls from her considerable experiences, featuring stories that illustrate ways to connect with students' parents, caregivers, and family members. In looking critically at the school she loves, the author identifies areas in which educators can come to know, better support, and demonstrate care for students' families through home visits, bilingual family math nights, morning math clubs, financial literary projects, information about events for immigrant parents about how schools work, cultural organizing, and collaborating with other organizations.

LGBTQI Parented Families and Schools: Visibility, Representation, and Pride by Anna Carlile and Carrie Paechter (2022, Routledge). Although UK-focused, the authors illuminate issues that are both parallel to those in and pertinent for U.S. schools. LGBTQI parents and their children often experience prejudice within their local communities. Sharing both LGBTQI parent perspectives, and their children's, the authors suggest what educators can do to be catalysts for change by creating inclusive classrooms, schools, and communities.

students to get involved in the broader school community—and visibly supporting them by your presence—can make them feel more connected to the school and their peers.

Taking advantage of opportunities beyond the school community is important too. Of course, the places to go with students vary based on the context of the school. For instance, I (David) saw how much students enjoyed being out of the school environment, and in the community at large, as a break in the routine. Living in New York City, there is an abundance of resources. In particular, for ELA classes, I saw the value of taking students to see plays that were in the curriculum, such as *Fences* (Wilson, 1986) or *Macbeth* (Shakespeare, 2003 edition). I also noticed that students loved performances in general, particularly dance and its universality to all cultures. Moreover, to watch a Brazilian dance troupe perform Candomblé—including martial arts–like movements—captivated students and served as a basis to discuss the Afro-Brazilian cultural and religious experiences as part of the African diaspora. There are also some wonderful organizations such as Community Works (see Figure 2.9) that coordinate affordable performances and cultural events for public school children and youth—with a purposeful eye on both sharing contributions from local cultures familiar to students and introducing them to international performances.

One thing I noticed is that locals may not know enough about the cultural riches that their cities, towns, and regions offer to be able to take advantage of them. For example, when I took students on trips via the subway to certain neighborhoods in the city, they'd ask, "Are we still in Manhattan?" Among other things, going out helped integrate a better sense of local geography and show students that they could travel successfully from A to B. I (Fran) have a colleague who teaches sociology and takes his students to ride trains and buses through different neighborhoods, where they then walk, visit venues, and eat together in local restaurants. We agree with the premise of exploring different neighborhoods, even the idea of cultural tourism helping local economies (Loukaitou-Sidens & Soureli, 2011), while being mindful that trips should be educational and interactive rather than voyeuristic.

Visiting museums can be an educationally satisfying experience, but as with plays and cultural performances, it is always best to preteach what to expect and what is going to be seen. This way, students have a context for what they observe, which should make greater sense to them than if they saw things "cold." Whether it is an institution like the Museum of Natural History with its dinosaur skeletons, representation of species, and planetarium, or the Metropolitan Museum to see an Egyptian temple, medieval armor, Native American masks, or contemporary fashion, students appreciate seeing things "in the flesh." Most museums have an education department that is eager to work with teachers—from coming to classrooms and having a pre-show and discussion of selected works to be viewed, to providing customized guided tours, to sharing museum-based resources with teachers. For example, I (Fran) have taken my students to an art museum for a tour, and afterward students had an art class at the site where they reproduced some of the painting styles they'd seen.

Figure 2.9. Spotlight on Community Works

This organization is an example of a local resource that teachers can take advantage of.

Although resources vary across the states, there are usually some available in every region.

Community Works started as a small, grassroots organization and became one of the largest providers of literacy, arts, and mentoring programs to schools and community groups around New York City. Collaborating with a network of community-based artists and organizations, Community Works serves over 150,000 public school students and community groups yearly through live performances, exhibitions, workshops, mentoring, and other programs.

For example, the Theater Connections program provides affordable multicultural performing arts events to over 65,000 students in pre-K to 12th-grade classes every year. Both established and emerging artists perform music, dance, and theater for students and community residents. These groups present dynamic, highly interactive, professionally produced performances, ranging from African storytelling to Shakespearean plays, Latin jazz to Afro-Haitian percussion.

Theater Connections workshops provide mentors to public schools and neighborhood centers around the city to train young people in music, theater, dance, and the literary and visual arts. Exhibitions focused either on history or the visual arts are presented in schools and community centers throughout the city. For instance, the Long Walk to Freedom honored unsung local heroes of the civil rights movement, highlighting contributions of 16 civil rights activists; *Harlem Is . . . Celebrating the Living History of Harlem*, a publication documenting concert performances of the same name, celebrated 30 Harlemites whose contributions to the fields of education, music, art, politics, sports, and community service have defined the neighborhood's rich and diverse cultural legacy (https://www.harlem-is.org).

Community Works' Theater Connections program takes place at four major sites: the Kumble Theater for the Performing Arts in Brooklyn; Hostos Center for the Arts & Culture in the Bronx; Pace Downtown Theater in Lower Manhattan; and Riverbank State Park Theaters, as well as many smaller venues throughout the city.

(Although this organization is NYC based, we have included a selection of others in Appendix F, available at www.tcpress.com).

Teachers also can take the initiative and request tickets from organizations amenable to making donations. I (David) was able to take students to see a variety of events ranging from Radio City Music Hall's *Christmas Spectacular* to a New York Yankees game in the Bronx. Staying with the theme of trips on a shoestring budget at best, zero budget at worst, there are ways to get creative with walking tours. I'd often combine a museum visit with nearby places of interest. For example, after first going to the Museum of Modern Art, in winter I'd take the students to see the holiday tree at Rockefeller

Center and St. Patrick's Cathedral on Fifth Avenue, and in summer to Central Park and the zoo. These trips were satisfying as students were able to combine "high culture" and local sights, while socializing with one another. Regardless of where you are, there are always opportunities to explore the cultural and natural assets of the local area.

In addition to visiting places of interest, students also can work part time in the community via a variety of auspices. For example, some schools have community service requirements or options, which can mean working for blocks of time in elementary schools, nursing homes, libraries, nonprofit organizations, animal shelters, food kitchens, museums, and community centers. Teachers also can encourage students to donate their time outside of school to work in places of worship, serve in charity shops, or help deliver food to those in need. All in all, there are a lot of opportunities for teachers to support student participation in their communities (Markos, 2022).

The Hard-to-Reach Student

We have focused in this chapter on the importance of ways to initiate, establish, and cultivate professional relationships, particularly with students. But what happens when a student resists our attempts, making them hard to reach? This situation is inevitable and can lead teachers to have feelings of frustration and self-doubt. When finding ourselves in these situations, we have responded in various ways. The first is to acknowledge that if a student is completing their work, and is somewhat detached on a personal level, that just may be their personality. It's also important to note that not all students will want to talk with you formally or informally, or even like you as a teacher, in every class of your career. However, a student trying to be "under the radar" in terms of having a low profile, should become "on the radar." When this was the case, I (David) would make some additional efforts to connect with the student. I wanted to know whether the underconnectedness was due to shyness or lack of confidence, or they were a struggling learner or simply disinterested in the subject of ELA, or there was another reason I was unaware of. Some approaches I used, included observing student behaviors with other students and teachers, both in and out of classrooms; chatting with them in natural versus forced ways; analyzing their work; seeing whether they had an IEP; reaching out to parents; and speaking with their former teachers to compare notes. All of these ways enabled me to find out more about the student. In turn, once the reason for their reticence to connect was known, I could respond accordingly with individualized support, providing options for demonstrating their knowledge (paper or oral presentation?), planning groups for specific student combinations, talking with the student at key times, giving them space when needed, and so on (Crosby et al., 2018). These efforts can take time, and teachers have to be consistent, patient, and flexible in their approach. Once the student comes around, trusts the teacher more and knows they're "on the student's side," class is more comfortable for both.

All that said, occasionally there may be a student who resists every attempt made by the teacher to engage them, even refusing to work. As in many situations in teaching, there's no magic bullet. However, speaking to a student in private in a genuinely curious, nonconfrontational, unhurried way to find out why they resist engagement and work can lead to meaningful conversations (Danforth & Smith, 2004; Kohl, 1995). Students often open up to teachers who express concern and care. It may take several conversations and check-ins, but patience and persistence usually pay off. I've found that students sometimes need acknowledgment that they're having a difficult time, they're depressed, they're bothered by something in school or angered by events outside of school, or are unable to compartmentalize and manage their feelings. Some students simply need what they're dealing with to be acknowledged, before being encouraged to focus on the importance of the present as it relates to their future.

If these approaches are taken, and students still resist learning (and perhaps disrupt the learning of others), it's important to reach out to other professionals and perhaps family members with a view to resolving the issues. Collaborating with, and being an ally of, the school counselor is one way to better understand the actions of a student. Likewise, talking with a former teacher to see whether there is a consistent pattern of behavior, or there has been a significant change, is important. Seeking advice from a senior teacher and/or an administrator are other possibilities. All three of us also have had experiences with case conferences in which several teachers meet to discuss what plan of action is to be collectively taken to get a struggling student back on track. Parents also can be brought into these conferences and used as resources to share learning patterns or past academic struggles and successes. Ideally, classrooms are places where students can enjoy learning and have a good rapport with their teachers. However, some students may experience personal crises in their families or personal lives and/or develop various behaviors, including negative feelings about learning and school. It's imperative, whatever the circumstance might be, that, as teachers, we do not let deficit thinking and student blame cloud our work. Our goals are always to help each student as much as we can. As we've established, teacher–caregiver relationships are also key, so working closely together with families often motivates the student to do better. At times, if the home environment is part of an immediate problem, it can be more effective for school personnel, such as administrators and/or counselors, to first address the situation. A moral of the story is: Teachers cannot do it all alone. It is a strength, not a weakness, to recognize our own current limits if a student is permanently disengaged, and then reach out to a network of colleagues with the aim of best supporting that student collectively.

SUMMARY

Teachers must invest in creating and maintaining positive relationships with students. This can be done from the first day in a variety of formal and informal ways. While always being focused on students' academic needs, teachers also must plan to provide support for students' emotional and social well-being. Strong relationships occur through investing time in creating a good rapport with those we teach and providing them with a safe environment. In addition to students, teachers should work toward developing mutually supportive and respectful relationships with peers, as this makes the work more intellectually stimulating and socially enjoyable. Likewise, teachers can develop open communication with parents, as well as a good rapport with administrators, as all relationships are essentially in the service of supporting students through quality teaching. Finally, teachers can also broker relationships between local institutions to provide cultural experiences that broaden learning.

QUESTIONS FOR FURTHER REFLECTION

1. Recall your own high school experience. How well did your teachers "know" you? If you had a strong relationship with a teacher, why do you think that was? If you did not have these strong relationships, what could have happened to better "reach" the younger you?
2. Were most aspects of your identity represented in the ELA curricula you were taught? If so, how did this benefit you? If not, what do you wish had been included? Why? How often were you exposed to racial and/or ethnic groups different than your own? What knowledge did you take away from engaging in texts about people who were demographically different than yourself?
3. Recall a teacher you respected from your own education. What were some of the things they said and did to make sure you felt recognized, were treated fairly, and enjoyed coming to class?
4. What strengths do you feel you already possess in terms of building strong relationships with students? Which characteristics do you think you'd like to improve? What are your less well-developed areas and what can you do about them?
5. What are some benefits of cultivating professional relationships with peers? What may be some drawbacks?
6. Why do you think it is valuable, as Harry and Ocasio-Stoutenburg assert, to "meet families where they are"?

7. What do you think and how do you feel about the idea of receiving ongoing feedback from administrators?
8. In what ways can working on community projects potentially expand students' knowledge of diverse members within communities?

CHAPTER 3

Creating a Balanced Curriculum

The student approached my desk quietly, her purple-dyed hair flowing behind her. Rachel was a Korean American senior, an outspoken student, the type who raised her hand, but then tilted her head to more deeply consider her response before verbalizing her answer. She hovered above me in a long, flowered dress and bright-green face mask, clutching a bag of Cheetos and her phone, as I (Sarah) hit send on the email I had been composing.

"Ms. Bickens? I've been thinking about something," she opened. I nodded and looked up. "I'm a senior, and I've never read a book by an Asian American author—or any Asian author really." The statement sounded like a question, a confusion more than an accusation.

I paused and chose my words carefully. "Hmmm." I mentally reviewed what I knew of our school's English department curriculum in my head. "Yeah, geez, I guess not."

"Why do you think that is?"

"Umm. I don't know. It's a tricky one." I decided to take the mea culpa path of pure honesty. "Really, I think it comes mostly from my own ignorance. I was never really taught Asian authors as a student, so I don't always feel confident teaching them. Plus, and this speaks to bigger issues of racism in our country, there aren't a lot of novels written by Asian American writers that are popular choices for high school English classes." I looked up at her apologetically, knowing this answer was inadequate but, at least, my truth.

Seeing an opening, Rachel rightfully pushed the issue. "I mean, we read books by almost all other races. We really should read at least one Asian book. You should change it for next year."

"You're right. I should change it. I'm going to think and do some research, look for a good book, okay?"

Rachel nodded, a waterfall of purple hair briefly obscuring her face. "Yeah, for sure. Let me know what you pick. Thanks, Ms. Bickens." She spun slowly on her heel and left me to my thoughts.

I wish I could say this was a moment from a decade ago, of awareness for a young, White teacher, educated in a very White, male, Western canon. In reality, this conversation happened in the spring of 2021, into year 2 of a global pandemic, and at the peak of a reckoning around the value of not just

Black lives, but Asian American lives as well. This was not, however, a conversation that was new to me. Every few years, a student of Asian American Pacific Islander (AAPI) descent would approach me, asking why books by people like them were not in our curriculum. Or an English department meeting would touch sheepishly on the fact that we rarely teach any authors of Asian descent outside of maybe *Kite Runner* (Hosseini, 2003) and the occasional short story. My answer would be similar to what was described above: guilt about this unrepresentative curriculum and promises to change it in the future. I would buy selected books from Amazon, do some summer reading, and look for a fitting choice. Then, the summer would end, with no new unit planned, and my well-intentioned self-promises to focus a unit around an AAPI author would fizzle out with the August heat.

In 2021, this promise felt different, less empty and abstract, more substantial and urgent. Across the country attacks against Asian Americans were on the rise, including in New York City. The Atlanta spa shootings (Fausset et al., 2021) had been recognized as a hate crime, and the often "silent minority" of AAPI people were calling for the same justice rightly demanded by Black Lives Matter protesters during the previous spring. Even if only a handful of my students were of Asian descent, our city and country were made a "gorgeous mosaic" (Dinkins, 2013) in part because of the AAPI community. Even if many of my students were not directly affected by anti-Asian violence, they could be educated to speak out against this racism, could be motivated by the humanity in literature to see the inhumanity in some of us as an attack on all of us. Isn't this why ELA teachers love books, why I became a teacher? After years of empty promises to "do better," this time I really would.

WHY A BALANCED CURRICULUM MATTERS

A balanced curriculum is a multifaceted thing and, therefore, can be challenging. However, when in doubt, it is always useful to keep anchored in the term "balanced" in its broadest sense. We also know that the list of factors to consider when balancing an English curriculum could fill pages. Generally speaking, we may consider: race, ethnicity, gender, culture, religion, (dis)ability, sexual orientation, gender identity, geographic location, time period, genre, writing style and period, not to mention the general topic of the text. Books must be by different people, on different topics and genres, written in different ways, with different points of entry and challenge for students. We want students to read dystopias and memoirs, poems and speeches, modern fiction and ancient tragedies, fun short stories and challenging epics. We also want them to learn about the horrors of historical and ongoing oppressions while also seeing the brilliance of agency within marginalized groups and their accomplishments despite pervasive inequalities, foregrounding positive representations and offering hope for further change (see, for example, Hernandez-Armesto, 2014; Kayyali, 2005; Muhammad, 2020; Zia, 2001). Additionally, we want students to be exposed to the almost infinite variety of experiences contained within literature. But there are only so many books or units one can squeeze into a year (or 4 years of high school), so decisions—sometimes difficult ones—inevitably must be made. Moreover, with only a half dozen or so texts through which to inspire learning in a given year's curriculum, these decisions *must* be purposeful and balanced.

There are so many factors to consider as one plans the texts for a curriculum, a series of adjustments for student population, the current state of the world, and the evolution of what we consider a "good" literary education to be. However, in general, teachers should ensure students have a balanced view of people both like and *unlike* themselves in a text. A long-existing metaphor from Dr. Rudine Sims Bishop (1990) of looking at literature as "mirrors, windows, and sliding glass doors" (p. ix) has received deserved newfound attention as educators seek to make their classrooms more culturally responsive and engaging, and use literature to support social–emotional skill building. Writing about children's books, Sims Bishop centers literature as a path to adventure and new worlds, a window into the previously unknown. She argues that some books must embrace and affirm the identities of the young people reading them, for "when children cannot see themselves reflected in the books they read, or when the images they see are distorted, negative, or laughable, they learn a powerful lesson about how they are devalued in the society of which they are a part" (p. ix). Recently, there has been much talk about Black (and Indigenous and Latinx and Asian American and LGBTQ+ and Muslim) lives mattering, and students from these groups begun to learn that they count *within* literature, recognizing they are important when they see themselves in the narrator of a novel, the hero of a play, or the subject of a poem.

We believe that a diverse range of books benefits *all* learners. Sims Bishop (1990) posits that children from dominant social groups "need books that will help them understand the multicultural nature of the world they live in," meet people unlike themselves," avoid a "dangerous ethnocentrism," and appreciate their "connections to all other humans" (p. ix). Despite our country—and world—becoming more diverse, schools remain segregated by race (Breyer, 2022) and social class (Spring, 2016). It appears that the dangers of ethnocentrism are very much alive more than 3 decades after Sims Bishop presented her warning. And while many people strive to understand and embrace a range of identities and cultures, our country remains largely divided into relatively homogeneous communities and schools. This segregation can facilitate a dehumanization of those who do not reflect expectations and cultural norms, making them into "the other," viewing a stranger as an enemy rather than a person with a shared humanity. Indeed, in their book *Letting Go of Literary Whiteness*, Borsheim-Black and Sarigianides

(2019) make a convincing argument for teaching an "anti-racist" literature curriculum to majority-White student populations, arguing that teachers must act from an "anti-racist perspective" to avoid "perpetuat[ing] racism through the texts in our book rooms and the ways we teach them" (p. 4). Literature can be, if not a cure, a salve for the divisions of our country and an entree into important antiracist work, allowing all children, and White children especially (who may exist in a world that still assumes Whiteness as the norm), to see the beauty in different cultures or empathize with the experiences and struggles of diverse people.

This celebration of difference may seem obvious to many, especially younger teachers of a new generation, but it should not be taken for granted, especially in the fraught post-Trump culture wars of the 2020s. For example, an older, White generation of educators and administrators may fear the changes that come from diversifying curricula, seeing it as an eschewing of tradition and even a dangerous shifting of values. The conservative perspective often seeks to preserve the White, Western canon, a drive popularized by E. D. Hirsch's (1988) push for "cultural literacy," which currently is manifested in suburban school boards that prescribe texts to preserve this canon, viewing it as unproblematic. Recent attention has come to these school boards and state legislatures, tightening their grips on reading lists, spurred by a fear of critical race theory (CRT). Largely misunderstood from its origins in law, CRT focuses on illuminating cultural practices within structures and systems that uphold historical inequalities and their impact on marginalized groups, with a view to what can be done to better understand and redress the situation (Crenshaw et al., 1996). A theory taught primarily in doctoral-level programs, and in some master's-level programs (Ladson-Billings, 2021), it has been seized upon by largely Right-wing media that purposefully define it as anti-White and seek to use it as leverage to ban any and all conversations about race in schools as racist (Carlson, 2021). Tucker Carlson went as far as to propose that teachers wear cameras to monitor that CRT is not being taught, an idea welcomed by at least one teacher to call attention to how footage would show the overwhelming successes and honest struggles of what actually goes on in classrooms, making the point that members of the media are out of touch with real teachers' lives. The teacher also stated that if CRT would be a helpful teaching tool to better understand the complexities of teaching race, then it actually would be welcomed (Kearny, 2021).

As we write, it seems that CRT likely will remain the hot potato it has become, catapulted from the margins of academia to everyday conversations on television. What we can deduce from this debacle is that *any* discussions of race in U.S. classrooms are feared by a sizable number of the largely White population. A moderately progressive teacher who may wish to shift from Ernest Hemingway to Zora Neale Hurston, or from Oscar Wilde to Junot Diaz, must feel grounded in their choice and steady in their conviction that the curriculum has to both reflect the students and provide them with windows to see other worlds. Embracing diversity does not mean replacing White authors. It means, rather, ensuring that authors of diverse backgrounds who are part of our country's history (or any country's history for that matter) and contemporary society have a right to sit at the table. Teachers can actively enable this form of equality. On a positive note, there has been widespread pushback at the idea of banning books and discussions of race (Backus & Salvanto, 2022).

In many ways, highly conservative efforts via school board membership to influence which texts constitute the curriculum can be interpreted as a form of pushback against the efforts of liberal groups who also see the crucial value of texts as a means through which important knowledge is gained. Urban districts and Left-leaning suburbs, bolstered by groups like #DisruptTexts, *Rethinking Schools* (https://rethinkingschools.org), and the Zinn Education Project of Teaching People's History (https://www.zinnedproject.org), as well as larger social justice movements as a whole, see the books by diverse authors that students read as a means to address systemic racism reflected in society in ways that traditional texts do not. These groups argue that the White (male, cisgender, heterosexual, Christian) focus of a traditional reading list is not merely old-fashioned and preserving certain limited values, but serves—whether wittingly or unwittingly—as a tool of White supremacy and oppression.

Indeed, many teachers will find themselves in the middle of the fundamental dilemma of what should constitute the curriculum where they work. On one hand, there may be school boards, parents, or administrators who are reluctant to change long-cherished reading lists. On the other hand, there may be families, students, and teachers that value diversity and wish to modify what they perceive to be an oppressive canon (Dyches, 2017) (also see, for example, Figure 3.1, which discusses teaching classics.

Borsheim-Black and Sarigianides (2019) stress that texts by authors of color should not be "supplemented in" or relegated to special months but instead be "full-length titles" (p. 43) in a new and more representative canon. While we agree with this philosophy, we also recognize the reality of many teachers' school landscapes. It may be hard for a teacher, especially a novice to the profession, to forgo *The Great Gatsby* (Fitzgerald, 2004 edition) and instead teach *Bodega Dreams* (Quiñonez, 2000). Power structures and politics within school can be slow to change, and on a practical level, school budgets often are stretched too thin, influencing the purchase of new sets of books. However, although teachers may lack autonomy around the books they teach, they can always advocate for the addition of more varied viewpoints in the curriculum. Those who are disempowered from choosing full novels still can incorporate diversity in multiple ways that go beyond engaging in a futile fight to change an existing reading list. In the next section we suggest practices to help balance a curriculum, many easily integrated in a way that allows teachers to maintain some degree of autonomy while keeping school boards, administrators, and parents satisfied.

Figure 3.1. How to Teach or Not to Teach a Classic Text

Many classic texts may appear unproblematic to some teachers, while being highly problematic to others. There is a greater awareness that plots, storylines, characters, scenes, settings, diction, and so on, from another time, which once may have been seen as innocuous to the majority of readers, are now subject to different interpretations. Teachers' perspectives toward texts also can change over time. For example, some teachers may no longer choose to teach widely known classics they once taught, such as Conrad's *Heart of Darkness* (2021 edition), its colonial racism having been debated for decades (Denby, 1995); Twain's *Huckleberry Finn* (1884) with its frequent use of use of the n-word; or Steinbeck's *Of Mice and Men* (1937), for a variety of reasons, including a murdering protagonist, gratuitous animal killings, limited portrayals of women and African Americans (Kenney, 2013), and stereotypical tropes of people with disabilities (Lawrence, 2020).

We come to this debate wishing to recognize the different realities of teachers. Some teachers have a choice whether to teach a certain book. Others have none; they must teach texts required in their school's curriculum. Our point here is: If an educator is teaching a classic text, it can be done critically, thoughtfully, and sensitively—when engaging with the elements of the story. Take, for example, Harper Lee's *To Kill a Mockingbird* (1960), a popular staple of the high school curriculum since its publication, yet also critiqued for its featuring rape, incest, limited racial depictions, and racist slurs—along with its White savior narrative (Jablon, 2022).

Set in a small town in Alabama during the 1930s, the core element of the story is a court case in which Atticus Finch, a White lawyer, defends Tom Robinson, a Black man accused of raping Mayella Ewell, a White woman. Although innocent, Tom is found guilty because of racial mores of the time, despite evidence clearly pointing to Mayella's advances toward Tom and abuse by her own father, Bob Ewell. Fearing for his life from an enraged mob, Tom tries to escape from jail and is shot dead. Seeking revenge for smearing his name in court, Bob Ewell attacks Atticus's children, who are saved by their reclusive neighbor, Boo Radley. In the tussle, Bob Ewell dies, and the sheriff decides it was an accidental death from a self-inflicted knife wound. The entire story is told through the eyes of Scout, Atticus's young daughter.

In his essay "Troubling Atticus: Letting the Mockingbird Fly Away," Griffith (2021) describes how, after he developed a deeper sense of critical consciousness, he shifted his stance of keeping *To Kill a Mockingbird* on a pedestal for many years while teaching. Over the years he came to see Atticus as overly epigrammatic, a Jim Crow liberal who persuades jurors to swap prejudices from not believing poor Blacks to not believing "white trash" and women. Atticus also believes in a slow approach to dismantling systemic racism, an approach that negates the urgency to do so. Griffith further noted that what he once thought of as a tool for antiracism actually barely features voices of Black characters. In sum, with a critical read, the lines demarcating good and evil, morality and immorality that engender a deep love of this book in the American consciousness may not be as clearly drawn as readers once thought. We think of this perspective not as "spoiling" the book by taking away a nostalgic innocence, but rather as complicating what often is presented as a neat and tidy picture.

(*continued*)

Figure 3.1. How to Teach or Not to Teach a Classic Text (*Continued*)

In problematizing *To Kill a Mockingbird*, Griffith suggests other texts encompassing similar themes that possibly could be taught alongside the book, or even replace it. These include Witi Ihimaera's *The Whale Rider* (1987) with a young female protagonist who resists situational influences; Mildred Taylor's *Roll of Thunder, Hear My Cry* (1976), set in the South during the same time period as *To Kill a Mockingbird*; and Bryan Stevenson's *Just Mercy: (Adapted for Young Adults): A True Story of the Fight for Justice* (2018) about a lawyer's dedication to disadvantaged clients.

In brief, a premise of this book is that what were once considered classics *can* be replaced, where there's need, opportunity, and desire to do so, with texts that diversify the curriculum. For the many educators who have limited or no say in the books they're required to teach, we recognize that "problematic" classic texts can still be taught with a critical lens and understood as artifacts of their time that illustrated important issues that are still significant today. Additionally, the classic text can always be compared and contrasted with other texts about similar themes by diverse authors.

SELECTED PRACTICES

In this section we examine practices that can be used to varying degrees to achieve a "balance" in an English class curriculum. As we've acknowledged, many teachers may not have much control over texts, so we consider approaches that may be used both with full teacher autonomy and as an addition or enrichment to an established curriculum. Many of these practices are organizational approaches centering multiculturalism and diversity identities rather than actual instructional methods. In Chapter 4 we dive into how shifts in teacher practice—the *how* you teach rather than the *what*—can deepen cultural responsivity in a classroom.

Know Your Students Well

Although we have already discussed ways to build relationships with students earlier in this book, it bears reemphasizing that a large part of relationship building is knowing the nuanced identities and cultures within your classroom, the source material through which teachers may create their balanced curriculum. Put simply, if you want to better align your curriculum to the students in your class, you have to first know who they are. For teachers who *do* have autonomy to select texts and build reading lists across grade levels, a deep knowledge of students' cultures and identities is key to picking those books that can serve as both "mirrors and windows," showing students characters both like and unlike themselves. While some English teachers may prefer to view themselves as professors of knowledge, purveyors of wisdom, and interpreters of literature, a high school educator is so much more. They are relationship builders and connectors—of teacher to student, of student to student, and of students to literature. We cannot sugarcoat the challenge that it is hard to get to know each student well in a class of over 30 teenagers. We also cannot assume that they automatically will like us, trust us, or believe our motives for what and how we choose to teach. That has to be earned by constantly being, among other things, well prepared, academically engaging, consistent in routines, flexible in teaching methods, fair in ensuring equity to everyone being taught, and—last, but not least—genuinely interested in who students actually are.

"Official" school data often misrepresent the whole student. The reduction of complex human beings with complicated histories to numbers in the form of statewide standardized test scores or in-school evaluations is very limited and often inaccurate. Such representations obscure the nuance of 3 years spent living in the Dominican Republic, a mother who navigates the world in a *niqab*, after-school family duties of caregiving to infants and elders, or living in a group home or temporary shelter. It is important to remember that no identity is a monolith or etched in stone; great diversity exists within all ethnic labels, including in majority-White classrooms whose students may differ in religion, home language, socioeconomic level, sexual orientation, gender identity, geographic region of origin, and so on (see, for example, Bukowczyk, 2017; Connell & Pugliese, 2019; Lee & Casey, 2007; Lensmire, 2017).

As the year continues and relationships with students develop, teachers must work to learn the nuances of each student's culture (Lalas & Valle, 2007). Again, this goes beyond a pie chart of basic racial identities to deeper aspects of culture. Activities to allow teachers greater access to students' experiences and knowledge can be woven throughout a school year. When discussing setting, a teacher may ask students to provide a "tour" around their neighborhoods or to point out a space in their community that has helped shape them. In a lesson analyzing how values shift from one generation to the next, students may interview an older family member about their perception of these changes. While teaching folktales or looking at folklore (a valuable piece of background for teaching *Their Eyes Were Watching God* [Hurston, 2006 edition]), teachers can have students recount folktales from their own cultures to learn the value and challenge of recording oral tradition (see Figure 3.2).

As pandemic schooling has made teachers and students more adept at using digital technology, many of these tasks are well-suited for video or Flip Grid. Students may post their neighborhood tour videos or elder interviews (with permission), and these digital platforms allow sharing to take on a more community-building purpose as students create the very windows their peers (and teacher) may "look through" as they learn about cultures different from their own. Of course, while these activities provide teachers with valuable

Figure 3.2. Example of Activity—Be an Anthropologist: Oral Tradition, Dialect, and Folklore

- This activity can be used as preteaching for a text that relies on oral tradition, folklore, and dialect, or can be used in conjunction with a section of a text that focuses on these techniques. I (Sarah) typically use this activity before starting to read *Their Eyes Were Watching God* as a way to highlight Zora Neale Hurston's work as an anthropologist, specifically one who sought to preserve Black and Indigenous stories passed from generation to generation.

1. Students read an example of a folktale, preferably one that attempts to mimic the dialect and spoken traditions of oral language. (For Hurston, students read "The Son Who Went to College" from *Mules and Men* [2008 edition].)
2. Students read the text (which can be challenging in its use of dialect and nonstandard grammar and spelling) twice and discuss the use of dialect. They consider why Hurston recorded this story in this way and analyze how the story would be changed if the elements of dialect were not included.
3. Students work in triads. One student thinks of a story that is told often in their family—preferably a folktale or other story that presents a moral, but really any story that can be "energetically" told will work.
4. The student storyteller tells their story to the rest of the group. This can be done in person (with the student telling the story twice if necessary) or via a video (on Flip Grid or posted on Google Classroom). The rest of the group attempts to record the story to "preserve" the oral language on the page. This may include informal language, nonstandard grammar and spelling, or other techniques of dialect.
5. Students reflect on the experience of "being anthropologists," hopefully appreciating the skill behind Hurston's use of dialect as she preserved folklore and oral tradition.

information to match a curriculum to students' needs, they also allow students to make connections to the texts and feel a sense of belonging in the class, which leads to increased engagement and higher achievement (Anderman, 2002).

Independent Reading

Incorporating independent reading into classroom practice is an important way to foster a balanced approach to teaching literacy that incorporates individual reading, direct instruction, and groupwork. Independent reading allows students to venture off "on their own," build confidence, and find joy in their ability to dissect a text. Teachers still play an active role in purposefully differentiating texts, based on reading levels, that challenge but do not frustrate students. For the purposes of a representative curriculum, independent reading allows teachers and students to co-select texts (Allred & Cena, 2020) that may connect with a student's identity that is not addressed in texts read by the entire class. When a teacher is able to build a diverse library, students may pick texts that connect to their cultural backgrounds and/or their personal interests. To create an independent reading routine in a class, teachers should consider:

- **Purpose:** The broader purposes of independent reading are outlined above. However, depending on the larger unit of study, the more specific purposes may differ. For example, perhaps a teacher who plans to start memoir writing in an upcoming semester will select memoirs and autobiographies to read and ask students to track "brilliant" uses of language that may inspire their own future writing. Maybe a teacher who is focusing on the "habits of good readers" (see Figure 3.3) and wants students to practice "visualizing" will select books with vivid imagery. Independent reading also can be a way for students to read books connected with a historical time period, or broader themes, linking to concurrent or upcoming units in history or English. Independent reading also can serve simply to encourage students to build a positive relationship with reading and hopefully to continue loving books. Whatever the primary purpose, student choice is key and therefore a feature of teacher–student conferences.
- **Student Accountability and Assessment:** It can be challenging to hold students accountable for reading in class and assess them when each one may be reading a different book. To be mindful of not "over-assessing," teachers should approach independent reading as a practice that is designed to be largely pleasurable. That said, low-stakes writing tasks, such as three-sentence journal entries or scaffolded discussions, can provide teachers with assessment data, while emphasizing for students that writing and discussing are integral to understanding what's been read. Depending on the teacher's purpose, students may keep personal or dialectical journals, or may annotate the text (either directly or through sticky notes). To promote discussions, teachers may pair students who are reading the same book or thematically similar books, or may rotate one-on-one conference times to talk to students about their books. Independent reading also can infuse creativity into class, as students can have the option to draw pictures, make collages, or write songs about what they have read.
- **Scheduling:** Teachers should establish their purpose in scheduling independent reading and ensure it is a routine that students know and expect. For example, some teachers may allot the first 20 minutes of class to reading in a double-period. Others may use 15 minutes at the end of Tuesdays and Thursdays. Or, one entire class a week may be devoted to independent reading.

Figure 3.3. Seven Habits of Effective Readers

These seven habits, which all share the same purpose of making connections, appear to be intuitive for some readers but often need to be explicitly taught to others who may struggle in one or more areas. The questions listed under each skill can assist teachers in explicitly modeling these skills, with the idea that students eventually can internalize them.

1. **Visualizing** means readers can picture in their mind's eye what is happening in the text they're reading, as if a film were playing in their heads. This allows them to get a stronger sense of the setting, characters, and events—helping them to make connections.
   - What can you see in the scene?
   - What do you imagine the scene to look like?
   - What places does the scene remind you of?
   - How does seeing the scene help you understand it?
2. **Activating Prior Knowledge** (sometimes called "schema") helps readers to make multiple connections to relevant information they already know. These connections can be in the form of text-to-self, text-to-other-text, or text-to-world, and help the student remember what they have read.
   - What does the text remind you of?
   - What about the text can you connect to yourself?
   - What about the text can you connect to other things that you've read?
   - What else about the world can you connect the text to?
3. **Questioning** ideally occurs before, during, and after reading. Asking ongoing, different types of questions throughout the text helps to understand it. Also, if a reader is not understanding a text, they should return to the place they lost their understanding and use a strategy to help reconnect to the text.
   - Is the answer to a question right there in the text?
   - Is the answer to a question in your (the reader's) mind?
   - What are the clues needed for you to find the answer?
   - What are you curious about? ("I wonder why . . .")
4. **Inferring** is what a reader does to comprehend what is not explicitly written in a text. Students can draw conclusions by actively connecting previous knowledge possessed with what has been read in the text.
   - What do certain details suggest to you?
   - What are some details to support inferences you make?
   - What do you know by "reading between the lines"?
   - What has been read previously in the text (or elsewhere) that points to the inference you made?
   - What can be predicted in the text based upon what you already know?
5. **Determining Importance** happens when a reader decides which information is most valuable to the story being told. This skill helps foreground what knowledge is crucial to better understand the narrative.
   - What's important in the section you've just read?
   - What are the key parts of this story?
   - How can you describe the importance of specific events in the text?
   - How might you summarize what's happened?

(*continued*)

Figure 3.3. Seven Habits of Effective Readers (*Continued*)

6. **Monitoring for Meaning** is when readers periodically stop to check for understanding, to see whether they are understanding the story being narrated, allowing themselves to go back to the text if they're unsure of something, and to understand connections being made throughout.
   - What's happening?
   - Why are things happening?
   - What's the main idea/topic/themes?
   - What is the author trying to show us?
7. **Synthesizing** is when students are able to take information from various parts of a text and show they are able to understand the text's meaning, usually through citing evidence.
   - How can I summarize this text?
   - How can I put the story in my own words?
   - What is the overall message of the text?
   - What do I think about the author's ideas, and why?

Note. Adapted from *Seven Strategies of Highly Effective Readers*, by E. K. McEwan-Adkins, 2004, Corwin Literacy.

Literature Circles

Literature circles—small student groups reading and discussing a shared text semi-independently—are an efficient and effective way to add more balance to your curriculum (Moeller & Moeller, 2016). Rather than read one text together and, say, learn about Dominican culture through *The Brief, Wondrous Life of Oscar Wao* (Diaz, 2008), students may read books from a variety of Latinx backgrounds, with groups focused on, for instance, Puerto Rican, Chicano, or Cuban authors, such as *When I Was Puerto Rican* (Santiago, 2006), *The House on Mango Street* (Cisneros, 1991), *Dreaming in Cuban* (Garcia, 1993), and *Dominicana* (Cruz, 2020). Literature circles often are focused around a common theme (identity, immigration), historical event (the Holocaust, the American civil rights movement), or a common genre or technique (dystopian, memoir) so as to provide opportunities for students to compare and contrast texts and to allow for whole-class analysis and gathering. Literature circles simply provide teachers the opportunity to teach more texts, and thus include a variety of identities of students (mirrors), while also exposing students to a greater diversity of experiences (windows/sliding glass doors).

While literature circles can be a unit of focus on their own, they also can be integrated into existing units that may be more writing-focused and thus do not include a singular prescribed text. For example, I have used literature circles in conjunction with a unit on writing a research paper, allowing students to choose from a selection of nonfiction books about social justice issues. Students read books such as *The Laramie Project* (Kaufman, 1994), *Undocumented* (Padilla, 2016), and *Between the World and Me* (Coates, 2015) to explore issues around LGBTQ+ rights, immigration, and race, respectively. As they read and met biweekly, students also began research for a paper around their respective issues. In a 9th-grade class, I (Fran) used literature circles as students wrote their own multigenre autobiographies. Students met weekly to analyze writing techniques in memoirs and autobiographies, such as *When I Was Puerto Rican* (Santiago, 2006), *I Know Why the Caged Bird Sings* (Angelou, 2009 edition), *The Glass Castle* (Walls, 2006), and *The Color of Water* (McBride, 1995), to support their own creative process as they wrote about their lives.

In all honesty, a successful literature circle experience requires a lot of work from the teacher when beginning the unit. It is all about developing routines and building habits that come with accountability in the first weeks. The process becomes much easier for teachers as students learn to manage their own groups, developing skills in self-monitoring as they engage deeper with the student-centered nature of the task. There are many different ways to run a literature circle unit in middle and high schools (Hill & Noe, 2003; Moeller & Moeller, 2016). In addition to a unified purpose or theme in the literature circle unit, the top priorities in planning should be to:

- **Select books that students can navigate independently (at least most of the time).** Literature circles with admittedly worthwhile texts such as those of Leon Trotsky (1993 edition) and Ralph Ellison (1995 edition) are rarely successful, as students need more intense teacher guidance to understand these books. Similarly, teachers should create a reading calendar, as this is great practice for navigating a college syllabus, with *realistic* reading assignments for each group meeting. I typically assign 20–30 pages a night for high school students, although this can be modified for individuals or groups if need be. For students who are emergent readers, or who are dyslexic, an accompanying audiobook can be made available.
- **Survey student preferences.** Provide students with brief overviews of each book or allow them to skim covers and the first few pages. Use a Google form or simple paper survey to allow students to indicate their first, second, and third choices for books. This is where I also ask students whether there is currently another student with whom they absolutely *cannot* work, thereby being proactive in creating functional groups.
- **Create groups purposefully.** This is again where knowing your students comes into place. Ideally groups should be a mix: higher-level readers with less-developed readers; vocal leaders with more reflective students; the super-organized teenager with the one carrying the chaotic backpack; a variety of races, social classes, students

with disabilities, and emerging bilingual students. As literature circles should be dedicated predominantly to student discussions, having diverse perspectives improves these exchanges.

- **Consider student roles.** If we view literature circles as the coming together of diverse student voices and skills, we should consider how to nurture that by giving students a variety of tasks or lenses through which they may analyze a section of reading. Using "role sheets," which let everyone understand they have a "job to do," is one way to ensure that students see themselves as an important piece of the larger puzzle of making literary meaning. Typically, students complete one role sheet (really a focused worksheet) for each reading assignment. Then, part of the literature circle meeting time is devoted to sharing out pieces of the role sheet work, a process that allows students to better understand the text as they consider a section of reading from multiple angles. Roles may vary depending on grade level, unit focus, or final assessment. In 9th grade, students may select from a "thematic sleuth" (looking for themes), "word wizard" (focusing on challenging words), "questioner" (looking for points of discussion), and "figurative finder" (identifying and explaining figurative language). In upper grades, these roles may become more advanced, with focuses on Common Core standards or culturally responsive sustaining education topics such as relevance or criticality. In a recent 12th-grade "social justice" literature circle unit, my (Sarah's) role sheets were more rigorous, aligned to Common Core standards around inferences, language use, theme, and author's purpose (see Figure 3.4). Students may select a different role weekly or stick with one focus throughout. Of course, the teacher can help guide these decisions if necessary, matching student strengths to roles.

As mentioned above, teachers should adjust the literature circle role sheets to fit the needs of the class. Students may stick with a focus for the entire unit or mix it up each week. Similarly, students may complete a sheet for each reading, or teachers sometimes may assign readings and then assess through other means such as "group quizzes" (a quiz in which all group members work together to answer questions), "discussion sheets" (a worksheet that asks students to pull 2–3 quotes and create a group discussion question), or "multimedia connection sheets" (students pull quotes and connect thematically with a current event, TV show, movie, or song).

- **Develop (and stick to) a routine.** Depending on whether literature circles are enriching a larger unit (such as a research paper or an autobiography) or are the sole focus of a unit's work, you may devote, for example, Tuesdays and Thursdays to literature circle

Figure 3.4. Example of Literature Circle Role Sheets

Below is an example of a role sheet. I (Sarah) would have students complete these role sheets twice a week.

Name:_________ **12th ELA—Social Justice Literature Circles Role Sheet**
PURPOSE PURSUER [Role]

REMEMBER! *Role sheets are due (checked) on Tuesdays and Thursdays and will be part of your group share on Tues/Thurs. ALL role sheets will be submitted at the end of the unit in your literature circle folder!*

Date: ______________ Pages Read:___________

Brief summary of pages read:

____

____

____

⊙ ***What was the "author's purpose" in this section of reading?***
Consider: What argument is the author making? What idea or opinion did they want to convey? What emotions did they want the reader to feel? What did they want the reader to realize?

____

____

____

⊙ ***Support your claim!*** *What two QUOTATIONS support your understanding of the author's purpose?*

Quote 1: ______________________________________

Quote 2: ______________________________________

⊙ ***ANALYZE!*** *Based on the textual evidence above, do you think the author was convincing in making their point? If yes, what information, rhetorical techniques, or other aspects of the section of reading made it particularly persuasive? If not, what information was missing, vague, or confusing? Or, what about the writing rhetorical techniques made the section unconvincing? If YOU were writing this text, what would YOU have done to better serve the section's overall purpose?*

____

____

____

____

discussions and then have students spend the other days writing the research paper or prepping for the mandated state exam. If your unit is entirely literature circles, consider a routine focus for each day. For example, with seniors, I typically devote Tuesdays and Thursdays to independent reading after conducting a mini-lesson that focuses on reading at the beginning of each session. Then, Mondays are for group quizzes and sharing out role sheets; Wednesdays are for student-created questions and discussion; Fridays are for "multimedia connections," where students bring in current events, songs, movie clips, and so on, that connect to conflicts and themes in their books. Students share and discuss these connections and then may use them to "teach" their book in the summative assessment project (see Figure 3.4).

- **Determine accountability procedures.** As student work in literature circles may be only loosely supervised, teachers should ensure there are ways to hold participants accountable for actually doing the *work*. There are several approaches to this. First, the aforementioned role sheets may be collected and assessed by the teacher. (There also may be days when the teacher visually checks some role sheets, collecting a sample to gauge student understanding, but not always grading all sheets carefully.) All role sheets also should include a way to simply hold students accountable for doing the reading. This may include a space to summarize the reading or a quote and discussion question generated from the reading. Weekly group quizzes are also a way to hold students accountable for reading. In this scenario, students work together and use their role sheets to respond to questions, either specific to the section of reading or more general (e.g., describe the three most important events in the reading). Students also may be given individual quizzes, but the group quiz format underscores the collaborative nature of their collective literature circle work (see Figure 3.5). As students discuss in their groups, teachers can require them to take notes and/or synthesize the most important points made in the discussion. Finally, students must be reminded that their work builds toward the final assessment.
- **Build toward a summative assessment.** My preferred means to assess literature circles is by having each student group plan and teach a lesson about their book (and its themes/conflicts) to the class. Students can use quotes from their role sheets, current events from multimedia connection sheets, or best questions from their discussions to plan their lessons. This culminating project helps students build teamwork and speaking skills, while also allowing them to demonstrate their deep knowledge of their text, as the students become the teachers. However, if time doesn't allow for

Figure 3.5. Example of Literature Circle Presentation Requirements

9th-Grade English—Literature Circle Lesson Presentation Requirements

Aim (all group members)
This should be a question that relates to the theme, topic, or major conflict in your book. The lesson should focus on this question and should give your classmates the information they need to answer this question at the end.
Ex: How does racism affect a child?

1. Do Now (all group members)
   - Design a creative do-now that asks your classmates to write for 5 minutes.
   - The topic should have classmates write about an issue in their lives that will later relate to the text.
   - The question should be more than just a yes/no question.
   - The question should not require any knowledge of the text to answer.

Ex: Have you ever been jealous of someone else? Explain.

2. Overview of book (one person)
   - Provide an overview of the book.
   - This may be in the form of: a 1-page typed summary, a poster, a comic strip, a skit, a book review.
   - Provide the basic details of the book: characters, setting, plot, themes, conflicts.
   - DO NOT give the ending of the book away.
3. Creative element (one or two people—only after all other jobs have been taken)
   - Bring in something that creatively relates to your book and use it to give your classmates more information about the background of the book.
   - Options include: a movie/television show, a song, photos, an historical excerpt, a website, a PowerPoint presentation, a piece of art, a poem, etc.
4. Reading excerpt with questions (one person)
   - Select a 1–2 page excerpt of the book for your classmates to read.
   - Provide a brief context for the background of the excerpt: Where does it fit with the rest of the book?
   - Create five or more questions that go with the excerpt to check that your classmates understand.
5. Reading activity (TWO people)
   - Create something for your classmates to "do" with the reading.
   - This may include: looking for literary terms, analyzing themes, having a discussion or debate, drawing a picture/comic, making a predication, characterizing a character, creating a skit or dialogue, creating a bio poem, writing a creative piece in response to the reading, etc.
6. SUMMARY (all group members)
   - Summarize the main point(s) of your lesson. You can do this in several ways: Post-its, ask your classmates to answer the aim, play or brief game, etc.

(*continued*)

Figure 3.5. Example of Literature Circle Presentation Requirements (*Continued*)

What do I have to DO?

- Submit a rough draft of the lesson on **TUES, 12/9**—see handouts for requirements.
- Submit a final draft of your lesson part **the day before your lesson**, including a brief description of the work that went into your planning.

Present your lesson part on your assigned day: *When I Was Puerto Rican* [Santiago, 2006], M12/15; *Caged Bird* [Angelou, 2009 edition], T12/16; *Color of Water* [McBride, 1995], W12/17; *Black Boy*, [Wright, 2023 edition], F12/19; *Kaffir Boy* [Mathabane, 1998], M12/22.

If you will not be here for your group's date, you MUST tell me NOW!

this, students may do a science fair–style event with tables about each book to share more informally when groups visit one another; write a final essay analyzing the book; or create a piece of artwork or performance connected to the book.

- **Be open to selecting new books for future literature circles.** Read widely to plan for future literature circles or supplementary texts by using resources such as Disrupt Texts (https://disrupttexts.org). One obstacle to creating a literature circle unit is the admittedly daunting task of reading several books a teacher has never read (or been taught before). Even if you are not currently a classroom teacher, start to read books you may not be "naturally" drawn to, whether they are books about characters unlike you, books in genres you typically avoid, or something you wish you had read in high school. Each summer, I like to pick two or three self-assigned "homework" books that I always meant to read or books that I wouldn't necessarily read for pleasure. Dividing this work up with a colleague is another great way to build your textual repertoire and may even lead to some valuable coplanning. Try to read a diversity of "smaller" texts too—articles, poems, or short stories (social media, Twitter especially, is great for this). Create folders for future possible units or themes. When you encounter a text that is intriguing, put it in a digital folder (I like to email texts to my work email and then organize them in folders in my email inbox) to use for upcoming lesson planning, even if it's for a hypothetical unit several years in the future.

Supplementary Texts

For the teacher who lacks control over the books in their syllabus, adding supplementary texts is a final, if admittedly imperfect, way to balance a curriculum and add a greater diversity of texts. In such problematic situations, we must recognize that not allowing teachers some control over texts is a form of marginalizing already marginalized authors. These situations do, however, provide an opportunity to discuss what the canon is and why it exists, as well as to read traditionally canonical texts with a critical eye (Borsheim-Black & Sarigianides, 2019). Therefore, to counter a rigid curriculum, teachers may add current event readings, poems by diverse authors, or short stories. In a type of mini literature circle, teachers may jigsaw these texts, having smaller groups read (or select) a text to share with the class. For example, in a unit on *The Great Gatsby* (Fitzgerald, 2004 edition), students can read a variety of perspectives on the American dream to fuel a larger debate and hone their argumentative skills (Fierke, 2020). To enhance a unit on *Othello* (Shakespeare, 2004 edition), students can read a variety of the Bard's sonnets (Shakespeare, 2006 edition), but then also read variations on the sonnet from Gwendolyn Brooks (2005), James Weldon Johnson (2000), Langston Hughes (1995), and the *Mexican-American Sonnet* of Iliana Rocha (2019). As background on dystopias for *1984* (Orwell, 1961 edition), students can read short dystopian stories by Margaret Atwood (1998) and Rebecca Roanhorse (2018), or independently selected companion pieces such as *City of Ash and Red* (Pyun, 2018) or *The Day the Sun Died* (Lianke, 2018). In this way, students can still read to expand their worlds and to see themselves in texts, despite the original curriculum having a limited reading list.

While we wholeheartedly advocate for literature circles to become a staple of ELA classrooms, we also think it worthwhile to look at the significant benefits of their close cousin—book clubs—which can serve students in different and important ways. Jody Polleck (2022), a colleague of ours, has sought to provide safe literacy spaces for students both inside and outside of traditional ELA classrooms by creating and facilitating adolescent high school book clubs. In Figure 3.6, we shine a spotlight on extracurricular book clubs.

CODA

That summer, I was true to my word. I scoured online lists of AAPI fiction and ordered a bunch of books on Amazon. I read *Typical American* (Jen, 2008), *Native Speaker* (C. Lee, 1996), and the novella *Hunger* (Chang, 2009). However, I ultimately picked *The Woman Warrior* (Kingston, 1976), a book I had used in literature circles over a decade ago with which students had struggled. Not to let an initial failure hold me back, I created an engaging unit, mixing students' own personal writing for the college essay with ideas around truth and memoir in Kingston's text. In the end, I think it was a success. Several students of Asian descent told me they were so happy to finally read a book with people like them in it. Moreover, the themes

Figure 3.6. After-School Book Clubs

Spotlight on Extracurricular Book Clubs

Ostensibly resembling literature circles, extracurricular book clubs are quite different in that students *elect* to be part of a group, *decide* what book or books are to be read, and *choose* the issues to collectively explore. The teacher's role morphs from instructor to facilitator, acting more like a guide-on-the-side, to ensure a group runs smoothly, usually "getting out of the way" (Polleck, 2011a, p. 79) to create a space for student-led conversations as the norm. Many of the texts chosen in Jody's extracurricular book clubs were from the genre of Young Adult fiction purposefully designed to appeal to adolescents. As Jody observes, extracurricular book clubs can equally support students' academic *and* socioemotional experiences—promoting personal and social growth that, in turn, enhances peer relationships and friendships.

Taking place outside of classes, extracurricular book clubs usually occur after school, during free periods, or during selected lunchtimes within libraries, vacant offices, or classrooms. As an extracurricular activity, they also offer a potentially greater sense of freedom to discuss subjects and explore topics than many students experience in an ELA classroom. For example, characters in YA literature reflect the lives and experiences of readers who are not always equally represented—such as young women of color—within classic and modern classic literature. Jody shared that when she facilitated extracurricular groups of young women of color, some of the major topics they wished to talk about included romance, dating, changing relationships with same-sex peers, bullying, and family relationships. The self-selected texts they engaged with throughout the year spanned *The Earth, My Butt, and Other Big Round Things* (Mackler, 2003), *The True Meaning of Cleavage* (Fredericks, 2004), *Upstate* (Buchanan, 2006), and *Push* (Sapphire, 2021). One of the many things Jody notes about book clubs is that, as a book's content increasingly resonates with participants' personal experiences, the participants develop and deepen intragroup social relationships—in some instances, so much so that participants commonly offer advice to one another about similar shared life situations. In sum, she writes, "Their understanding of the text, the self, and each other, is profoundly affected by the actual social nature and context of the book club itself" (2011a, p. 78).

One thing that struck us in reading Jody's research was how much book clubs can be places in which students feel a greater sense of *belonging* than they usually do in schools. Among other things, book clubs provide a nurturing environment in which everyone is encouraged to participate equally. The ritualized, highly personal social dynamics created by participants allow many to increase their self-confidence. Moreover, book clubs also provide opportunities for facilitators to encourage critical conversations among participants, with each member developing a healthy, questioning stance toward whatever content is being read. For some students, book clubs also serve as a space in which they feel more comfortable than in classrooms to openly discuss issues of race, social class, and gender. Topics that are sensitive and complex, yet are still an integral part of young people's lives—such as colorism and intraracial discrimination—can be explored in a collectively determined way at an agreed-upon pace.

(*continued*)

Figure 3.6. After-School Book Clubs (*continued*)

In another year-long book club Jody facilitated (Polleck & Epstein, 2015), she describes how the young women participants read texts such as *Zami* (Lorde, 1982), *God of Small Things* (Roy, 1998), and *Dirty Girls Social Club* (Valdes-Rodriguez, 2003), illustrating a balance of YA and modern classic texts. Of great interest are Jody's follow-up meetings with the young women after they graduated from high school, then at the end of their first year in college. She noted that all former participants "unanimously agreed that the book club was a critical forum that was safe, allowing them to address issues that were important to them" (Polleck & Epstein, 2015, p. 99). Students spoke of being less shy in college classes, feeling more confidence responding thoughtfully to questions, being able to appreciate multiple perspectives, and possessing the ability to reflect upon characters' behaviors. Jody concluded, based on the evidence provided by the young women themselves, that book clubs are important spaces outside of standardized tests and mandated curricula to support the growth of "cultural literacy, positive identity, agentic and academic development of young adolescent women of color" (p. 100). In sum, book clubs can be considered a form of "bibliotherapy" (Polleck, 2011b, p. 104) because discussing the self-selected texts in depth not only increases socioemotional development and enhances self-concept but motivates students to be habitual readers. One participant even said, "You know what would be mad hot? If we could do this in English" (p. 21).

Questions to ponder:

1. Based on the student's comment above wishing book clubs were part of English classes, what aspects of extracurricular book clubs do you think could be integrated into literature circles? Or, as Cherry-Paul and Johansen (2019) have argued, should book clubs also be an integral part of ELA classes? Why or why not?
2. What may be your hopes and reservations about facilitating an extracurricular book club? What norms would you seek to establish?
3. What are some other groups of students who may benefit from exploring their history, society, and cultures in extracurricular book clubs?
4. What are some considerations and implications for teachers from dominant cultures as they develop extracurricular book clubs for students with marginalized histories?
5. Is it important to keep whatever's said in an extracurricular book club in the book club (unless, of course, a student discloses information you are mandated to report)? Are there meaningful ways to share in classrooms and/or the larger community some of the things learned by groups of students in extracurricular book clubs?

of immigration, female empowerment, and mother–daughter relationships really struck a chord with many of my students. For their final projects, students used found lines from *The Woman Warrior* to write their own short memoirs or poems, and all found connections between their own lives and the book. This unit really cemented that idea of literature as mirrors for students. Even if a character or theme seems removed from some students' lives, the universality of so many human conflicts and desires will, in my opinion, always allow all students an entree into a text.

While Rachel, the student who started my search for AAPI literature, graduated before this new unit came to be, her curious questions led to so many more students—Asian American students and students of many other backgrounds—benefitting from a broader range of representation in my classroom. This reminds us of the importance of relationships, of creating a classroom where students feel comfortable asking a challenging question. It also reminds us to listen with humility to students. They are often the best resources for ideas of how to improve our teaching, so we have to make sure we are open and listening. (For a list of Asian American and authors of various other ethnic backgrounds to consider, see Appendix G at www.tcpress.com.)

SUMMARY

The majority of traditional U.S. schools were first created for the White, Christian, cisgender male children of the men who conceived of them. These schools were predicated upon students "seeing themselves" in the texts they read as a key element of a good education; the thinking was that seeing your own leadership in a powerful narrator could make *you* a future leader, or seeing your own flaws in a tragic hero's struggle could make *you* a more empathetic human. Fast-forward to the 21st century, where many schools' reading lists have not kept pace with the diversification of the school system, where an increased number of students learn from books in which they rarely see themselves depicted (Koss & Paciga, 2020). Former teacher and adolescent literacy expert Kylene Beers (2002) has linked educational theory to practice by demonstrating that if students are able to make text-to-self connections, activating schema and visualizing a text through even partial connections to their own lives, they are able to better understand more-challenging texts. Diversifying the texts we read, affords all students these important benefits while making a rigorous literacy education possible for all. Moreover, as our world inevitably becomes more multicultural, having all students exposed to the diversity of the world better prepares our young people to navigate a globalized 21st-century reality.

QUESTIONS FOR FURTHER REFLECTION

1. Think about your relationships with students. What students have you connected with as an adult? How did these relationships form? What students do you feel you didn't reach? Why do you think

this was the case? If you could go back to when you first met these students, what would/could you do differently?

2. Practice having a "difficult conversation." Imagine a parent, coworker, student, or school board member challenged a book you chose to teach that was "outside" of the traditional canon. How would you defend this choice (perhaps using the window/mirrors/sliding doors ideas)? What "pushback" do you anticipate this opposing person might give? How could you frame the educational benefits of your choice?
3. If asked to discuss the importance of balancing texts in your curriculum with a coteacher, what might be some of the primary points you'd articulate and why?
4. What are some ways that you can think beyond the limitations of a small number of books being in the curriculum? What options and choices might you offer students to read books in literature circles, book clubs, or independently?

CHAPTER 4

Developing Cultural Responsivity and Culturally Sustaining Practices

As I (Sarah) began my first year of teaching 9th-grade English at a Boston public charter school, this important beginning also marked the first time I had spent my day around a majority of people of color, the first time my Whiteness felt conspicuous, like an ill-fitting dress or awkward haircut I pretended not to notice. Having been raised in a very White suburb, with a very White friend and family group, I did not want to talk about race, didn't know how to even begin, and perhaps didn't even realize I should want to attempt to tackle what felt—to me—like a volatile and uncomfortable subject. While my readings around race in college made me aware of the flaws in claiming that I "didn't see color," when I looked at the sea of Black and Brown faces in my classroom, I did rest comfortably on a color-evasive adjacent idea—the foundation of a "common humanity." We were all people; we would learn and grow together.

In my English class, students gamely played along, writing poems about Homer's *Odyssey* (1997 edition) and drawing pictures to learn tricky vocabulary words. However, one morning, the limits of shared humanity became glaringly obvious. It was time to present characterization skits from *Of Mice and Men* (Steinbeck, 1937). Students had worked diligently for 2 days, crafting a scene outside of the novella while remaining true to one of the unique traits of their selected character. I explained the rubric, what the audience of peers should look for, and ended with what, in the moment, seemed like a throw-away line: "You can clap when the group is done, but don't go crazy. Just do, like, a church clap. We don't wanna get too loud." Twenty-seven sets of eyes turned to me, 54 eyebrows raised. Three Black 14-year-olds in the front row seemed to silently debate with one another, asking, "Should we tell her?"

A comic pause. Sweat began to form on my brow.

Then, "Bawwwwwwww. This lady thinks that's a church clap?!!!" Feet stamped with laughter, several students banged on their desks as tears rolled from their eyes with delight.

"A church clap?!?" Karen mimicked the golf-like movement I had just demonstrated. "Miss? Please." Her nose scrunched up like she had smelled something funny.

"Miss—what church you go to?" Ronald asked, half rhetorically, half out of genuine interest.

I hadn't attended any church for a long time. My memories were of quiet, mostly White-attended Unitarian gatherings spent in reflective contemplation, coupled with scenes from movies—mostly with White casts. I did, however, have a glimmer of an idea of gospel choirs and the African American religious tradition, but this was so distant from my own lived experience that it barely entered my consciousness.

"Cause at my church, we clap like THIS." Eva stood up, hands above her head, swaying from side to side, clapping her hands and yelling, "Praise Jesus!" in ecstasy.

I was so taken aback by this moment, I didn't even know how to respond. I murmured, "Ok, Ok, settle down. I just meant to be sort of quiet." At the time, it felt like a failure of discipline. I counted down from 10, hoping the energy would lower with the numbers. After reaching "one," the students were quiet and characterization skits began.

After class, I reflected on this moment. I felt like a foreign exchange student, accidentally using the wrong expression to say good morning. I began to see the holes in my "shared humanity" approach to my students, the limits to the "good teaching reaches all" style. Yes, teachers had to value the humanity of their students and work to give them good teaching, but this had to be the starting point, not the end accomplishment. I also began to see that *the work was on me*, as the adult—and only White person—in the room. I was, although I was loath to admit it, a stranger in the (mostly) shared cultural community of my students. In many ways, the foreign exchange analogy was an apt one. I was the outsider. The onus to do the work to bridge the gap was my responsibility. Later, I engaged with my mentor Kiera, an African American woman not much older than I, in a conversation about this moment. While even then I was aware that she had no responsibility to "explain Blackness" to me or fix my own racial shortcomings, I was grateful she took the time to lend a critical ear.

First, Kiera laughed. "Ha! They really played you!"

I grimaced in response.

"See, that's okay, Sarah. You have to let them see you fail. That's the first thing. It's a step to making you seem real. But you also have to know who they are too."

"Well, maybe you can give me ideas, ways to reach them?"

Her eyes strained to control their desire to roll with derision. "Well. You can't be me. They'll see through that immediately. You have to really, really learn your students. You need to learn their cultures, which, by the way, are not all the same, even if they all have brown skin. Ask them questions. Talk to them after class. Chat with their parents at pick up. Visit their neighborhoods. KNOW them. Not just the facts or the data, but know them as people and as people of color. They know you care in a general sense already. But you have to show them you care about who they are and where they come from, that you'll highlight and celebrate that in the classroom."

"Alright. I can try to do that," I responded with determination. And I really did mean it. I wanted to do better. I taught more diverse books, adding *I Know Why the Caged Bird Sings* (Angelou, 2009 edition) and *The House on Mango Street* (Cisneros, 1991 edition) to the curriculum. I added an autobiography component, eager to draw out my students' personal experiences. I invited parents to come see their children read chapters. I "did" all the things my mentor had explained as important, truly believing too that they were important. As a result, the sense of community in my classroom did improve as I got to know my students.

WHY CULTURALLY RESPONSIVE AND SUSTAINING PEDAGOGIES MATTER

However, looking back, much of this work I did as a first-year teacher to build community feels superficial. While in retrospect I was doing many things right—teaching diverse authors, building relationships, trying to share the "realness" of my flawed self, and engaging families—I didn't really know *why* they were so important. I still hadn't fully wrestled with the idea of true cultural responsiveness and my role in it as a White woman teaching majority BIPOC students. Moreover, the idea of "sustaining" this culture or fostering "criticality" (Muhammad, 2020) in my students was a long way off.

Culturally responsive and sustaining pedagogies have grown to be a focus of 21st-century education, especially in urban centers. The notion of culturally responsive teaching originated in the work of scholar-educators such as Gloria Ladson-Billings (1994) and Geneva Gay (2018) and is based on the solid foundations of multicultural education, a tradition that has existed for decades, established by a constellation of scholars that include James Banks (1993), Sonia Nieto (1992), and Christine Sleeter and Carl Grant (1987, 1988). Over the past decade, culturally responsive teaching has gained traction, as it explicitly calls for teachers to engage directly with the cultures of students they teach in order to successfully engage them in learning (Hammond, 2014). More recently, the concept of culturally responsive and sustaining (CR-S) pedagogies also has resonated with many in the educational community, with its goal to sustain the cultural practices of communities of color who face historical and systemic racism—Black, Latinx, Indigenous, Asian, Pacific Islander, and immigrant students—purposefully maintaining them rather than yielding to forms of assimilation/eradication through White, middle-class, normative processes of schooling (Paris & Alim, 2017).

The push for culturally responsive and sustaining education has become codified in state and local educational policy. In 2018 New York State created a framework for CR-S pedagogies. The New York State Education Department (NYSED, 2018) explains that the goal of their framework was to "create student-centered learning environments that affirm racial, linguistic, and cultural identities; prepare students for rigor and independent learning; develop students' abilities to connect across lines of difference; elevate historically marginalized voices; and empower students as agents of social change." In many ways this movement is also a response to a previous history of superficial "band aid" approaches to cultural relevance: teach *Raisin in the Sun* (Hansberry, 1959), celebrate Hispanic heritage month, have a step team at your school—and you can cross cultural relevance off your list. It is also a response to the "deficit model" of thinking about the divergent achievement levels of Black and Latinx versus White and Asian students, a way to push back against the standards-based movements of the early 2000s that frantically focused on "catching up" Black and Brown students so they could be "as good" as their White and Asian peers. While the drive to "close the gap" can be a noble and necessary one, this goal can have unintended consequences, harming the very students it seeks to uplift. As Hammond (2014) explains, a byproduct of deficit thinking creates "dependent learners," relegating BIPOC students to an education of rote memorization and test prep, and isolating them from the critical thinking skills that are so vital for success in our modern economy.

Of course, the racial disparity in educational achievement levels is still a major concern. For example, the National Assessment of Educational Progress (2019) notes that "scores in reading in 2019 averaged 230 for White fourth graders, while Black and Hispanic students scored 204 and 209 respectively." This difference continues into high school, when the average total SAT score is 1123 for White students, 946 for Black students, and 990 for Hispanic students (NCES, 2018). While arguments about the fundamental biases of these exams in general are well-founded, differences in college readiness and high school completion rates remain of concern: "Slightly more than half of Black and Latino (51.5%) students earned a degree after six years, compared with nearly 70% of White students" (Education Trust, 2017). Educational attainment, then, corresponds to poverty rates as adults. According to a 2019 Census report, the poverty rate for Blacks was 18.8%; for Hispanics, it was 15.7%; for Whites and Asians, it was 7.3% (Creamer, 2020).

As teachers, we see education as opportunity. For many, myself included, we entered this profession in part as a larger mission to right the injustice of poverty and racism in America. However, these numbers, relatively unmoving in the past 50 years, and exacerbated by a technical divide during the 2020–2022 pandemic, lay bare how ineffective our educational system has been for the majority of Black and Brown students. While an infusion of multicultural literature is a commendable place to start, this "quick fix" of multiculturalism is not enough, nor is soullessly trudging through "drill and kill" test prep. We have to address systemic racism and cycles of poverty that perpetuate racial inequity in America, and we have to fundamentally rethink how Black and Brown children are educated. Culturally responsive and sustaining pedagogies are part of addressing this urgent need. While practices around CR-S pedagogies have long been embraced by many educators of color, this greater focus both seeks to shift instruction for a majority-White teaching force and, in a broader sense, works to reframe how we conceive of our educational system—a system created largely within the very White supremacist structures CR-S pedagogies strive to disrupt. This is an urgent focus for White teachers, such as myself, but is also an important larger "conceptual revolution" that requires the attention and work of teachers of all races and backgrounds as we dismantle structures of oppression and rebuild the American educational system to truly support the thriving of students of all identities.

SELECTED PRACTICES

In this section we take a look at four different aspects of CR-S pedagogies illustrating ways of putting theory into practice: (1) learning and reflection to do the work on yourself first, (2) sampling some CR-S teaching techniques, (3) building criticality in students, and (4) maintaining relationships and building community.

Learning and Reflection: Do the Work on Yourself First

In the past few years, I've begun to look back on this critical "church clap" moment. My New York City public school has spent considerable time having "courageous conversations" about race, reflecting on our "racial autobiographies" and having "knee-to-knee" conversations about formative racial experiences (Singleton, 2005). In knee-to-knee conversations, two people sit facing each other with knees literally touching, with one person talking about a critical race issue while the other listens for a sustained period of time without responding. Then, the two switch and ultimately reflect on the experience. This type of exchange is valuable because simply raising the issue of race with a parent, partner, or friend can help teachers—especially White teachers who may have lived with the privilege of being able to avoid uncomfortable race conversations—practice facility in talking about race when it comes to sharing with students or broaching more challenging issues of racism.

This self-reflection has worked in tandem with self-education. My colleagues and I have dissected Hammond's (2014) ideas of the "4Rs" of culturally responsive education, looking at how we can build relationships and show the "realness" of ourselves in a classroom while maintaining academic rigor and cultural relevance. We have traded ways to build "alliances," meaningful partnerships with students, through a mix of academic coaching and social–emotional learning that can work to break students' patterns of dependent learning. I've had book groups with peers to apply Christopher Emdin's *For White Folks Who Teach in the Hood . . . and the Rest of Ya'll Too* (2016) to our work with AP students. More recently, we've brainstormed ways to include Gholdy Muhammad's "criticality" (2020) in our lessons and celebrate Black brilliance alongside narratives of oppression. These pillars of CR-S pedagogy are invaluable; I recommend them as required reading for any educator, but especially for White teachers who work with mainly BIPOC students.

Reading and reflection about CR-S pedagogy is, indeed, an invaluable first step. The life of a teacher is busy, and there is barely time to add a Beyoncé gif to the slide show, let alone keep a journal reflecting on your biases. However, I encourage teachers to do just this. The time is precious, but the benefits are exponential. For example, take 10 minutes a week to journal about an issue around race that arose over the course of the week. Think about key moments from your own childhood or college years that may still inform your explicit or implicit biases about race. Go back to moments with students that challenged your assumptions around race. I've begun to do this work, examining, for example, volunteering as a senior in high school to tutor Black 1st-graders in an impoverished town near my home, and how this well-intended experience actually served to frame a biased, deficit model of how I thought about educating Black students in the past. In fact, the "church clap" memory came back to me as part of this reflective practice. I've found that work around CR-S teaching has not been easy and requires honest—and really continual—self-reflection. It also entails, as Singleton (2005) emphasizes, "acceptance of non-closure," in other words, being okay with the messiness of half-conclusions and the raising of further questions rather than finding neat answers (see Figure 4.1). As a teacher, a "type-A" personality, a caretaker, and a White woman, I have to resist the urge to tie up my thoughts—even if they're just for me to read—in a nice bow and pat myself on the back like I've just solved racism. This work doesn't always feel good, but, in the end, it will make us stronger teachers and better humans in general.

Truly Culturally Responsive Teaching Techniques

Zaretta Hammond writes extensively about culture in *Culturally Responsive Teaching and the Brain* (2014). Without wishing to oversimplify, she argues that a culturally appropriate education will engage students' brains more fully than traditional models and result in true learning. She describes the idea of "deep culture," the "tacit knowledge and unconscious assumptions that

Figure 4.1. Questions to Consider in Self-Reflection Around Race

1. What is your first memory of race? When did you first become aware of race? Was this a positive or negative moment?
2. When do you first remember a conflict around race? How did this make you feel?
3. Is your personal "world" racially homogenous? If yes, how does this make you feel? If you live in a diverse community, how do you feel about this diversity? Was this a purposeful choice or an "accidental" result of other choices or life forces?
4. What is a time when teaching that you felt like you handled an issue around race poorly? Why? What would you do differently if you could go back?
5. Consider a recent current event that exposes racism. How did you react to this? Why? How could you bring ideas raised by this event into your classroom?

Note. Inspired by and adapted from Glenn Singleton's *Courageous Conversations About Race* (2005)

govern our worldview" as the "roots" (p. 23) of the cultural tree that sustains any learner. While cultures in a classroom almost always vary, considering cultural archetypes can be a useful way for teachers to offer students choice that will more fully speak to their roots.

Two cultural archetypes that lend themselves well to the practicalities of lesson planning and engaging students of color are collectivism (Guiffrida et al., 2011) and oral tradition (James, 2000). Many ethnic groups in the United States, especially more recent immigrants, as well as cultural groups outside of the United States and Europe, have valued working together, sharing ideas, and building knowledge as a group, the antithesis of the "every man for himself" ethos that was valued by the White founders of America. Collectivist teaching practices privilege these same ideas: collaboration, teamwork, and interaction as education. Oral tradition complements ideas of collectivism. Valued in cultures with strong preliterate emphasis on performativity and storytelling, oral tradition grows when a culture embraces shared work and knowledge building. While I often offer choices that include both more traditional individualistic and written tasks as well as collectivist and oral tradition–based tasks, the traditional approach is what I've always done. Pushing myself to think about how to include communal work and tasks centered on orality in the process of learning that takes place in my classroom is one way I try to shift my focus to CR-S practices. Often this work involves deconstructing the White, Eurocentric views of individuality and meritocracy that shaped my own education and teacher preparation programs. For White teachers especially, CR-S lessons can feel scary or even illicit, like you're rebelling against the "rules" of what you were always told school should be like. Admittedly, pulling back from these assumptions can be challenging, but purposefully framing learning around pedagogies that embrace cultural models relevant to your students will ensure that deeper, more meaningful learning takes place.

Collectivism stands in contrast to individualism, and my collectivist lessons run the gamut. They may be as simple as starting the class with everyone calling out one adjective to describe how they feel, or by creating an ice breaker that has students work together to silently build the highest paperclip tower as an exercise in strategic teamwork and leadership. I often use group activities in an inquiry-based approach to activate and share initial knowledge at the beginning of a unit (see Figure 4.2).

My shift toward collectivism also includes, of course, lots of groupwork. My students participate in literature circles with rotating roles and shared quizzes, depending on one another to excel and build knowledge. They discuss articles using the "save the last word for me" protocol from Facing History and Ourselves (https://www.facinghistory.org), which has a student share a quote and then listen to three peers debate it before they can put in their two cents. Students dissect a heated Shakespearean argument using a "freeze frame" skit structure (see Figure 4.3) and write a newspaper "edition" with each person tackling an editorial role.

Finally, students work together to process knowledge, especially at the end of a unit. They work in groups to write poems in the style of the Romanticists and then analyze one another's work. In addition, students

Figure 4.2. Mix and Mingle Human Scavenger Hunt

This activity is best suited for the beginning of a unit when students may read different texts and benefit from sharing ideas from them to build a common knowledge.

1. To open our Harlem Renaissance unit, student pairs each read two Harlem Renaissance poems, annotating for theme and literary devices and discussing their meaning.
2. Students are given a "bingo card" that lists different qualities of the poems: Find a poem that has a simile, references Africa, has an image of hope, describes oppression, uses a formal rhyme scheme, is stream of consciousness.
3. Students then get up and find another pair, taking their "bingo card" with them. They have a conversation with the other pair, trying to find at least one square of their card to check off. Students may read part or all of one of their poems to show the quality.
4. Students then rotate (mix and mingle—teachers also may provide music during the transition time and turn off the music when it's time to pair up again, musical chairs style) and find another set of partners, making a new group of four.
5. Students repeat conversations in groups until they either fill the whole card, or get "bingo," depending on how much time there is for the lesson.
6. Finally, students return to their seats. The lesson closes by pairs reviewing the knowledge they learned from their classmates and drawing larger conclusions about the Harlem Renaissance (largely that there was great diversity within this poetic movement) based on their discussions with classmates.

Figure 4.3. Freeze Frame Skits

This activity works best for a scene in which two or three people are arguing or having a heated debate. I have used it for *Othello* (Shakespeare, 2004 edition), *Macbeth* (Shakespeare, 2003 edition), *A Raisin in the Sun* (Hansberry, 1959), and *Fences* (Wilson, 1986).

1. For *Fences,* I focused on the argument between Troy and Rose when he admits to his extramarital affair. To prepare for the lesson, students already read the entire six-page argument, and I divided it into six smaller sections for groups.
2. Each group of three receives a photocopied page of the fight scene so they can annotate the scene.
3. Students decide on a person to play Rose, one to play Troy, and one to be the freeze frame narrator.
4. Students read the scene together, annotating for characterization and making notes about how to act out that characterization through tone, diction, and gestures/movement.
5. Students discuss why they think the two characters are fighting. They work as a group to pick two or three places to "freeze" the scene and have the narrator explain why the two are fighting. Students work together to write this additional "subtext" for the scene.
6. Students practice, making sure they know when to freeze and unfreeze the scene and giving one another feedback on how they are conveying the characterization of the characters.
7. Students present their scenes, with the audience providing feedback on the characterization and freeze frame pieces. (At the end, students will have seen the entirety of the important scene presented, with explanation from the freeze framer.)

write essays as a group (see Figure 4.4) and plan lessons to engage the class in the focus of their social justice literature circle group.

A caveat: Groupwork can be messy and loud. Teachers often hesitate to rely too heavily on it for fear of management issues or out of concern that administrators will poke their heads into the room, not quite understanding the "chaos" they perceive. Some teachers, myself sometimes included, may shy from groupwork because it strikes them as unfair; often one student appears to be doing most of the work, while the others appear to goof off. However, this fear stems partly from the bias of White teachers (and the White-controlled American education system, where grades are still individual) to privilege individualistic work as the "best" way to demonstrate learning. I encourage teachers to shift their mindset and see how building skills around teamwork and cooperation (which are so valuable in today's business world and in life in general) should be given primary emphasis in the classroom (Cropanzano et al., 2011). Groupwork requires, for sure, clear expectations, roles, rubrics, and timelines. Students need exemplars and constant check-ins—framing the teacher as coach—in order to do well. Indeed, this is a place where relationships between teacher and student are

Figure 4.4. Group Essay Writing

While this can be used at any time in a unit or year, it is most useful when students are beginning to learn new ways to approach writing body paragraphs. This may be when moving to a new, more rigorous grade or when learning to write in a new analytical style or for a new audience.

1. Students read a text together, typically a poem or an AP prose essay prompt.
2. Students analyze the text in groups of four, annotating and identifying key elements connected to a thesis or prompt.
3. Student groups are given a "part" of the text as their focus. This would correspond to a body paragraph focus for the entire essay. For example, one group may look at the opening two paragraphs of a short story.
4. Students read the text again, discuss their focus section and agree on 2–3 quotes that will be most important to include in the body paragraph.
5. The teacher reviews the essay body paragraph structure: topic sentence, context and evidence, close reading/literary device analysis, broader thesis analysis.
6. Each student in the group takes a "part" of the above as a focus and brainstorms ideas using the quotes the group has selected.
7. Then, following the order of the paragraph, students write the paragraph collectively. The person who has the topic sentence starts, thinking aloud as they write the topic sentence and then reading the final product to the group. The group suggests edits and then passes their shared paper to continue with the context/evidence, continuing these steps until the whole paragraph is written.
8. Finally, groups swap paragraphs and edit one another's work. The teacher then collects, edits, and shares the entire essay with students as an exemplar. The group earns one, shared grade.

vital. Hammond (2014) presents the idea of "alliances" of teachers being allies to students, encouraging them to take risks and become independent rather than dependent learners. If teachers truly commit to a focus on "collectivist work," grades may be exchanged in favor of qualitative feedback or may be based partially on demonstrating cooperative skills. Finally, as with any new activity or routine, teachers must remember that students also get better over time; teachers who do one group project a semester should not be surprised that students don't know how to "do" groupwork. Like any classroom practice, this type of cooperation and collaboration must be practiced and supported over time. However, the benefits of groupwork are clear and go beyond the soulless rhetoric of "career and college readiness." Hammond (2014) explains that in being culturally responsive, collectivist teaching activates the brain more deeply and results in more profound learning that lasts. Collectivist cultures have used storytelling and cooperative practices for thousands of years to process knowledge and still use these practices in religious and home settings. Including these practices in teaching ensures that "neural pathways are primed to learn" (Hammond, 2014, p. 48) and students of color are more likely to succeed. Moreover, a "collectivist philosophy" in the classroom creates the community I tried to build way back in my first year of teaching. Students and teachers work together to create and share knowledge, taking risks and building a shared skill set in the process.

A second major tenet of culturally responsive and sustaining education is an emphasis on oral tradition (Columbus et al., 2004). While most White, European cultures value written traditions, many other cultures emphasize oral tradition and spoken narratives. Hammond explains this as a second example of "deep culture" and, like collectivist teaching, a way for teachers to address cultural archetypes familiar to students of color that will, in turn, stimulate neural pathways and deepen learning.

As with groupwork, including oral tradition in teaching must be done thoughtfully, must provide clear guidance, and must be incorporated regularly. You may have seen videos of some charter schools having students shout out answers to state exam questions in unison. This is *not* valuing oral tradition (and it allows the students who may most need help to hide in a sea of voices) as much as an extension of "drill and kill." Similar to the prior caveat about collectivist activities, teachers may need to reframe their expectations about what a classroom looks like; students need not always write a formal response to prove their knowledge. A verbal argument, creative skit, spoken word piece, or emotional performance may take the place of their more traditional work and can demonstrate mastery of skills and content just as well. As with groupwork, clear exemplars, rubrics, and modeling must be used to make this routine a successful, consistent classroom practice.

While oral tradition is a term that incorporates many ways of communicating verbally, in the classroom I like to consider several "categories" of this culturally responsive practice. One way to include oral tradition is through activities that depend on verbal spontaneity. While students can and should prepare for discussions and debates by reading and taking notes, I've seen way too many class discussions where students "debate" by reading their notes, word for word, from a paper of prepared remarks. Oral tradition includes a type of spontaneous response—a thinking on the fly—that is part of traditions such as "playing the dozens" that have existed in Black culture for generations. To encourage spontaneous oral participation, I have students support their physical placement along a yes/no continuum in response to text-related debate questions in a Power Shuffle or Four Corners activity (see Figure 4.5). In another "spontaneous" activity, students riff off of a deep knowledge of characterization in trial activities, playing Polonius from *Hamlet* (Shakespeare, 1992 edition) or Janie Crawford from *Their Eyes Were Watching God* (Hurston, 2006 edition), defending their actions against lawyers and witnesses at trial. Groups review vocabulary by creating stories on the fly to illustrate a word they choose from the review bag, with bonus points for the funniest response.

Figure 4.5. Power Shuffle/Four Corners

This is a variation of an activity we introduced in Chapter 1. I (Sarah) often use this activity at the beginning or the end of a unit so students can see how they compare with their peers in reference to a key idea. I've used it to anticipate ideas about guilt in *The Kite Runner* (Hosseini, 2003), to synthesize ideas about memory in *The Farming of Bones* (Danticat, 2013 edition), or to make connections to modern race issues in *Native Son* (Wright, 1940).

1. Students are presented with a general topic (guilt, memory, racism in America). They write a yes/no statement about it on a slip of paper (they may do this in pairs) and give it to the teacher. Students may not agree with the statement (for example, a good leader is cruel), but may write something they think will be provocative.
2. The teacher shuffles through the statements, grouping some statements and possibly adding their own to enrich the selection.
3. For POWER SHUFFLE, the center of the room must be clear, with "yes" on one side of the room and "no" on the other. For FOUR CORNERS, each corner of the room must have a clear path to it, with the corners labeled: "Strongly Agree," "Agree," "Disagree," and "Strongly Disagree."
4. The teacher (or a student leader) reads the statement. For example, for a war unit, a statement may be: "War is never necessary."
5. Students pick a place on the yes/no continuum (Power Shuffle) or a corner (Four Corners). Give students a moment to examine the distribution of responses.
6. Tell students to think of a defense for their "placement." In Four Corners, the students in corners may discuss this as a group. In Power Shuffle, students may share in pairs with the person near them. Or, students simply may think of a response on their own.
7. Select several students to defend their responses, allowing a variety of points of view to be shared.

Another way to look at oral tradition in the classroom is by encouraging performative aspects of language, whether through body movement, choral reading, poetry slams, or dramatic vocal usage. Some of these—such as in trial activities—also may include elements of spontaneity, while others may be more planned, but allow students to celebrate the creative sides of their voices. Group poetry presentations ask students to use physical motions, music, and shared voices to emphasize themes (see Figure 4.6). Students are asked to create dance and musical theater versions of key scenes from plays. These scenes are performed with differing emphasis on words, a lesson in diction that plays out in real time. As with the collectivist activities, these oral tradition lessons engage cultural archetypes, engaging the brain in more meaningful ways than traditional teaching methods. Moreover, as students work, laugh, and open themselves up to dramatic verbal emotion, they build the classroom as a "brave space," a place where learning can be fun, but also include taking risks and trying new things—a key component for deep, independent learning.

Figure 4.6. Group Poetry Presentations

The first time that students do this activity, the teacher should provide several examples (perhaps with her own short poem). However, after students become familiar with the structure, they may be given more creative freedom (and fewer instructions) to complete the task.

1. Students are given or select a favorite poem from a unit of study (for example, Harlem Renaissance or Nuyorican Poets). Students should work in groups of 3–6.
2. The overall instruction should be to "prepare to read the poem in a way that reflects its meaning, key themes, and conflicts, with an emphasis on significant literary devices."
3. Students may be given more specific guidelines to:
   a. Include at least one gesture or movement done by the whole group.
   b. Include two different volumes of voice or emotional tones.
   c. Include at least three different combinations of voices reading (1 person, 2, 3, etc.); consider where one voice would be effective versus multiple voices (stanzas may be broken up or even lines may be broken up word by word).
   d. Include at least four key words that are emphasized (diction).
4. Students annotate their poems to show their creative presentation decisions. This work may include a writing component that requires students to explain the rationale for their choices or students simply may explain them after performing.
5. Students practice as a group (this typically takes at least a full period!).
6. Students present.

Criticality and Dismantling the System

Another essential side of CR-S pedagogies is the idea of building criticality in students. While culturally responsive teaching techniques can lead to deeper and more lasting learning for students of color, criticality includes building skills in students of all backgrounds to critique and ultimately change unjust systems in the world. Gholdy Muhammad (2020) explains that teaching criticality means asking, "How will I engage students' thinking about power, anti-oppression, and equity in the text, in communities, and in society?" (p. 131). She values criticality as it "begins to give students the tools to respond to injustice in and around the schools" (p. 119). Criticality involves encouraging students to—not surprisingly—be critical. This means students question the texts they read, rather than being passive consumers of knowledge, and particularly question texts around issues of race and other forms of (in)equity. This is, of course, a tall order. Students must learn to question narrative perspective and bias, to consider structures of power, and to consider whose story is told and whose story is left out.

Teachers first should model any skill they wish their students to learn. This practice takes a level of bravery that comes initially through doing reflective work and building relationships with students, to make classrooms communities of trust. Teachers, all teachers, but especially White teachers, have to name race and call out racism. We have to be willing to say Black Lives Matter and to name aspects of education, even within our current classroom reality, that are still oppressive or sustain inequity. This may include looking at the philosophies behind state testing systems or examining why the AP English exam focuses on the authors it does (and excludes others). Teachers may take time from the day-to-day curriculum to address key moments in race relations, such as George Floyd's murder or the exoneration of Breonna Taylor's killers. Full disclosure, these types of honest conversations still make me (Sarah) anxious. I always begin them by using Glenn Singleton's (2005) "isolate race" tenet of naming my own race and addressing the perspective through which I am approaching the event: As a White teacher, I am processing this from an intellectual stance, thinking about the systems of oppression that led to this injustice. These conversations never wrap up neatly, as "nonclosure" is part of tough race conversations, and I often feel that I said something not quite right. And possibly most embarrassing, I have to let go of my urge to "get through" the curriculum. Trauma-informed pedagogy has taught us that students won't learn if they feel anxious and angry about the state of the world; taking the time out to work through key events around race ultimately will make the classroom a more productive place (Brunzell et al., 2019). Moreover, if students see their teachers use this critical lens, they can use this model to start applying it themselves. One way to do this is to write a classroom mission statement—what Muhammad (2020) calls a "preamble"—that puts criticality at the forefront: In this class we name oppression, question whose story, look for who was left out, create alternative perspectives, and fight for equity. While this could be a powerful first-day activity, this mission statement can be revisited and revised as the class culture grows and develops its own definition of criticality.

In addition to a general culture of criticality, a curriculum must include examples of looking at rebellion or brave critics of culture in the form of historical figures such as Toussaint Louverture, the leader of the Haitian Revolution, and fictional characters, such as Sofia in *The Color Purple* (Walker, 2019 edition), who refuses to be dominated by anyone. These examples can allow students to begin identifying ways of being critical and to question how to enact these "rebellions" themselves. Examples of critical actors from texts can be a great starting point for students to practice these skills. Students may write skits in which Sofia responds to President Trump's Proud Boys comment, "Stand back and stand by," when asked if he rejected White supremacy, or research challenges to governmental injustices today.

A critical curriculum also should address where criticality is missing from texts. Students may research what is missing from historical accounts, such as looking at various forms of segregation that have existed, or Indigenous peoples' perspectives of the "discovery" of America, or examining the contributions of Puerto Rican soldiers in World War I (when Puerto Rico became a U.S. colony in 1917 and its soldiers were overrepresented among the killed) and of Black GIs participating in, and returning from, World War II. They also can dissect literature from a critical perspective, naming the racism in the depiction of Othello and showing Othello responding to Iago's racist epithets (Shakespeare, 2004 edition), or writing a final scene for *A Raisin in the Sun* (Hansberry, 1959) that shows the discrimination faced, and responded to, by the Younger family in their new neighborhood. Critical text responses also can come in the form of looking for joy in identity when stories of oppression or suffering may be the mainstream narrative. Students may create alternative versions of stories where BIPOC characters are encouraged to celebrate who they are, or may research artifacts of joy or triumph that may have been left out of traditional history. Many of these examples of criticality also provide opportunities for CR-S activities, permitting students to work collectively and use verbal performances to critique their texts.

Finally, a critical curriculum must be relevant, with frequent connections to current events and realities of students' lives. This may include bringing in readings about systemic racism in the news, whether protests or less publicized racism in health care or education. This may not always seem like an obvious link, but if criticality is at the center of your curriculum, the commonality should always be clear. For example, I (Sarah) was remotely teaching *1984* (Orwell, 1961 edition) when the protests against the killing of George Floyd started. While a dystopian novel written in the 1940s by a British social critic may not seem a straight link to race, students were able to make connections to ideas of protest, surveillance, violence, attempted suppression, and speed of social change. They read news articles and created final projects using ideas from these links to argue whether America was or was not approaching the level of dystopia portrayed in the novel. These links need not be entirely news related, and can include personal connections as well. After reading *Native Son* (Wright, 1940), students read excerpts from *The Fire Next Time* (Baldwin, 1992 edition) and *Between the World and Me* (Coates, 2015) and used the letter structure to write to their future child or the future generation about race in America today. As students practice the skills of criticality and learn that this type of questioning is accepted and encouraged in the classroom, they begin to challenge what they learn and, as a result, engage with it more personally and deeply.

It's Still About Relationships and Building Community

All of the work around culturally responsive and sustaining pedagogies comes back to relationships and building the community of your classroom. This starts by a teacher reflecting and sharing her authentic self, or "realness." Collectivist lessons that frame students and teachers as teammates and coaches, working together to build knowledge, help build these relationships as they hold students accountable for rigorous performance tasks. Activities that emphasize oral tradition and performative language build laughter and risk-taking into a curriculum, while criticality furthers this idea of risk as students question their education itself and form lessons of relevance they will take with them beyond the classroom. Teachers have to know their students, and students have to know their teachers; an "allyship" must be forged. These components of culturally responsive and sustaining pedagogies support this vital community building. As it turns out, my instinct as a first-year teacher to learn about my students and make my classroom a welcoming place was not incorrect. It was, in fact, perhaps the primary goal of any successful learning environment. I just needed the tools to do this work in a way that was truly culturally relevant and sustaining, and, 20 years later, I've begun to figure out how to do just this.

I (Sarah) end this chapter reflecting upon how many critical moments in my teaching practice happened a few years into the profession—in that time when a teacher is still developing but has their act together enough to begin realizing exactly where they have to grow and learn, that point where you begin to "know what you don't know." The "church clap" moment, however, happened in the first few months of my teaching career. In some ways, the fact that this occurred so early is not surprising as this critical event involved race. As has been made even more apparent recently, race is something that is hard to dodge, especially for White people like myself who may have had the privilege of ignoring it when it was not convenient, hiding under early taught platitudes like "not seeing color." Since I was a White teacher who chose to work in schools with a majority of minoritized students, it was a critical realization that inevitably would come sooner rather than later. These moments of realization never stop, even as I am in my 20th year in the profession. The world changes, highlighting injustices that are as unseen by some as they are obvious to others. Just as biases are spotlighted in our society, so too they become noticeable in ourselves, even as we do the work to be better. And, although it can be a slow-moving dinosaur, the American education system evolves, moving ever so minutely toward inclusivity. However, a teacher's work is never done. We must pause, critically reflect, and creatively and purposefully "reattempt" what we may have once thought was good and done (see Figure 4.7). I did this at 22 in the "church clap" moment, and I still do it today, growing as both a person and an educator.

SUMMARY

Culturally responsive teaching may not come easily at first to some teachers. However, we believe it to be in the best interests of students—and teachers who serve them. Growing as a teacher means constantly looking inward,

Figure 4.7. Suggestions for Practicing Culturally Responsive Pedagogy

1. Review the questions for personal reflection on race. Pick one to answer once a week. Then, after a month, read your responses and reflect on trends of larger themes you see.
2. Most people, but especially White people, often avoid talking about race because they never really had to and therefore lack the vocabulary to do so. Have a conversation about race with your inner circle. Singleton emphasizes the "knee-to-knee" conversation. Ask a friend about a Black Lives Matter protest; watch the excellent movie, *Dear White People* (Simien, 2014); read Yaa Gyasi's intriguing book *Homegoing* (2017) and talk with your personal circle about it. Start in a "safe space" so you build those critical muscles to talk about race in the classroom space.
3. Visit other teachers—either in real life or online. Look for teachers at your school who do "collectivist" practices or oral tradition well. Or find them online. Many districts have vast video libraries that show good teaching. While you shouldn't try to take on the persona of a person whom you aren't, looking at successful CR-S practices can build your own confidence to try them in your classroom.

being self-reflective on issues of culture and race (and how that becomes complicated as those issues intersect with other markers of identity). Using cultural archetypes to inform pedagogy makes for engaging, active, stimulating classrooms in which students collaborate and learn from one another. Cultivating a sense of criticality within students provides them with the tools to analyze the complexities of society and explore ways of responding to inequities and injustices. Ultimately, the relationships we build and maintain with students, including respecting their cultures and rejecting deficit-based assumptions, sustain us in expanding and deepening our practices.

QUESTIONS FOR FURTHER REFLECTION

1. What are some instances of cultural dissonance that you've experienced? How did you feel at the time? What did you learn from these experiences?
2. Why is it important to build a pedagogical repertoire that encompasses all students in your classroom?
3. It has been said that it is not enough to acknowledge systemic injustices in society, but we must work toward dismantling them. What are your thoughts about a teacher's role and responsibility in acknowledging and addressing injustices?
4. Different cultures emphasize collectivism over individualism, interdependency over independence. What are some implications for your pedagogy?

CHAPTER 5

Confronting (Dis)comfort Zones

"Miss?" Tatyana turned to me, a not entirely earnest glint in her eyes. We were sitting on the bleachers as I supervised a gym class run by college volunteers, squeaks of sneakers and echoes of basketballs reverberating through the large gymnasium. I turned to her, ready to field a bathroom request or time check. "What are you?" she asked me.

"What do you mean?"

"Like, what are you? What's your race?"

"I'm an old, White lady. Isn't it obvious?" I replied, half joking, half serious as I was only 25 at the time.

"You sure you don't have some Spanish in you?" Tatyana looked skeptical.

"Huh? Why would you say that?"

Finally, a bit of sheepishness crossed her face. It did not, however, keep her from saying, "Well, your ass. You got a Spanish ass." She made a curvy sculpting motion with her hands.

It might have been the most inappropriate thing a student ever said to me, but also one of the funniest. I let out a loud, "Haaaaaaah!" and, thankfully, the bell rang before I had to attempt diving into the issues of race, identity, gender, sexuality, and general teacher-student appropriateness boundaries of the exchange.

Over 15 years later, I look back on this conversation and cringe. I was young, perhaps too informal with some students, yet more uncomfortable broaching topics of race and identity than I am now. Nonetheless, this incident emphasizes the soul-baring nature of teaching, the scary risk of standing in front of a room of 30 young people and sharing "what you are." This sharing nearly always begins in discomfort, awkwardness, and if we are honest, even fear. As relationships are formed, comfort grows, but with its rewards this comfort also brings new insights and healthy challenges.

WHY CONFRONTING (DIS)COMFORT MATTERS

At the heart of much (dis)comfort for teachers is this question that was asked of me over 15 years ago: What are you? As we've highlighted throughout this book, the near-infinite aspects of identity inform all teaching as we bring our past experiences to the classroom. You may share many things with your students, from race or religion to liking 1990s hip-hop or country music. However, especially if you are a White teacher in an urban school district, there inevitably will be areas of difference with the majority of your students. Many of these differences often lead to exhilarating—and humorous—moments of learning and growth, but differences also can lead to misunderstanding, discomfort, or even conflict. Of course, being cognizant of one's biases and assumptions is important, along with culturally responsive and sustaining practices, as we have addressed in Chapter 4. However, comfort can be a critical place as well. Teachers easily can gravitate toward students similar to themselves and topics with which they personally identify, a dangerous (and, frankly, boring) place to be. When teachers work through the discomfort of sharing themselves and their messy identities with students, the reward is a greater sense of comfort. Comfort can be a joy, a result of a classroom culture in which teacher and students are able to be the truest version of themselves. Still, the dangers of complacency are real; ironically, places of comfort provide the best opportunities to push oneself into the best type of discomfort, a place where teachers can grow and challenge themselves and their students.

When considering this type of productive discomfort, it can be useful to think of the classic Vygotsky (1987) "zone of proximal development," a developmental concept typically reserved for students that emphasizes the value in stretching past one's comfort zone. However, as we have emphasized throughout this book, teachers are never "done," as we are always striving to become better pedagogues. The true secret to longevity in this profession is to take risks, do new and possibly scary things, things that may go against your identity as a "shy person" or call into question any kind of privilege you may have. Although often terrifying, risk-taking matters, as it may be the only way for the still very traditionalist profession of teaching to address diversity and demands as it continues to grow in the 21st century.

Comfort in the classroom cuts both ways. As relationships are built, and comfort is nurtured, the classroom becomes a genuine community. A teacher who feels comfortable can more fully be themself, adding a level of authenticity to a classroom. A student who feels comfortable is more excited to learn, more willing to try difficult tasks, more honest in sharing when and why they may be struggling. That said, comfort also needs interrogation, as it can build complacency; the routines that teachers have, or their frameworks for presenting material, that are comfortable simply may be those that come most easily to them or the ones that they experienced as students themselves. It is healthy to continually reflect on even the most basic of questions, such as: Why do I choose these books? Why do my tests look like this? Why are my desks in this arrangement? Teachers may feel more comfortable with students of the same race, gender, or other identity marker. This raises issues of bias and equity and, especially for White teachers, requires more specific reflection about issues of race and culture (Howard & Banks, 2020) (a topic we explored in more depth in Chapter 4). To which students do I give an empathetic second chance, and to which students do I jump to annoyed accusation? As brutal as this sounds, it is well-documented by research that a teacher's disposition and responses to students impact many aspects of classroom life, including the formation of in-class peer relationships (Mikami et al., 2012), the increased likelihood of punishments, and, sadly, even suspensions (Tajalli & Garba, 2014). As with much of becoming an effective teacher, a lot of the work begins with the teacher themself. Journaling, reflecting, and discussing with critical teacher friends can help identify unseen problematic areas you may view simply as being "comfortable." Simply put, just because something is comfortable, doesn't mean it is best practice.

THE PEDAGOGY OF DISCOMFORT AND THE IMPORTANCE OF (DIS)COMFORT ZONES

We have used the term "(dis)comfort" in this chapter because of the ambiguity involved in teaching, particularly topics and practices that may cause some teachers, students, and community members unease. There's also an implication that discomfort can diminish gradually and, conversely, that what comforts some people, when critiqued, can cause discomfort. These observations suggest that we perhaps oversimplify what can be complex issues into binary ways of thinking, making them appear right or wrong, good or bad, worthy or unworthy, "better left alone" or "imperative to address."

There is an emotional component to teaching and learning that is not sufficiently recognized or faced if pedagogy is conceived of largely as a technical endeavor that covers an unquestioned prescribed curriculum. In this chapter, we acknowledge the emotional component of teaching by taking a look at what can be gained through challenging the existing comfort zones of ourselves and our students. Before we dig deeper into this topic, we believe it's worthwhile to look at the origins of the "pedagogy of discomfort," along with the possibilities it brings into classrooms.

Megan Boler introduced the pedagogy of discomfort in her book *Feeling Power: Emotions and Education* (1999). Her initial motivation arose as she explored the responses of her students toward the 1991 Persian Gulf War. She notes that students' reactions were largely of disengagement with media coverage to the point of tuning it out, in essence, denying the war. Boler interpreted students' desensitized responses as feelings of powerlessness to create change, going as far as to see their numbness as a survival response.

She theorized that silences reflected their shut-down feelings about important issues, blocking out discomfort, and effectively distancing themselves from human connections with disadvantaged people. This form of silent isolation from social inequalities actually "widens the gap and reinforces power differentials" (Bheekie & van Huyssteen, 2015, p. 2). In a world that can feel overwhelming, it is important to note that any one of us is also capable of this response. Fran and Sarah have noticed that some students, including some students of color, have detached themselves from a justice system that disappoints them, making them feel powerless. And in another example, many also have disengaged around issues of COVID-19. As Boler notes, to be disengaged is actually a choice. However, as Bheekie and van Huyssteen observe, "without informed options for alternatives, numbness may be the inadvertent effect of cultural literacy with respect to translating emotions into knowledge and action" (p. 2). In other words, students need to be provided with opportunities to acknowledge their silenced emotions and ignite exploration of different ways of interpreting, and acting within, the world.

Broadly speaking, pedagogical discomfort is the feeling of unease when we teach in ways that challenge beliefs about certain knowledge—knowledge that perhaps is cherished and considered stable—and the assumptions we carry about the world based on that very knowledge. This teaching practice holds the potential to encourage students to move outside of their comfort zone, questioning their trusted beliefs and customs. We realize that questioning anyone's current beliefs can be somewhat destabilizing and perhaps provoke an emotional reaction. However, creating spaces in classrooms to engage about complex issues, and the ambivalence, unease, and discomfort they may bring, is a form of teaching that can reach students in powerful ways. As described by Zembylas and McGlynn (2012), "pedagogically, this approach assumes that discomforting emotions play a constitutive role in challenging dominant beliefs, social habits and normative practices that sustain social inequities and in creating possibilities for individual and social transformation" (p. 41).

In the following sections, we take a look at some of the benefits, for both teachers and students, of using the pedagogy of discomfort, as well as acknowledging teachers' fears, offering some cautions, and illustrating ways it can be used in practice.

Some Benefits for Teachers

As teachers, we consciously adopt the role of being lifelong learners, always expanding and refining our craft. We're also limited by our experiences to date, informed in certain ways by a version(s) of our country's history, our local culture, our families, the canon of literature, the (un)official curricula of our own educational experiences, and so on. While we carry extensive knowledge, to state the obvious, we can't know everything. Also, our human limitations mean we often don't know what we don't know. Part of teaching is accepting our limitations and vulnerabilities, hopefully with views to expand our knowledge—and that sometimes comes with risks.

We want our classrooms to be interesting for students, full of rich experiences that stretch and challenge them. Engaging with—and across—differences contributes to a stimulating curriculum, as considering differences informs us about the human experience. Having students from diverse backgrounds, customs, and cultures, who may act and think in different ways both interculturally and intraculturally, expands possibilities for classroom conversations that dissolve binary ways of thinking, challenging both teacher and students to examine what they've been taught to see and not see. The role of teachers is not to be the source of all knowledge, but rather part of the collective community in pursuit of knowledge that is born from contradictions, contrasts, and ambiguities. When these tensions are examined, issues of social justice surface because one of its goals is to reveal and question the emotional core that shapes our daily practices, routines, and the degree to which we are complicit in upholding injustices.

We contend that discomforting feelings are a necessary component in challenging dominant beliefs of our normative daily practices and routines that sustain social inequities. Furthermore, these feelings create openings for individual growth and social transformation. In a lesson, for example, that challenges any stereotypical representation—of race, gender, sexual orientation, religion—in literature and/or contemporary media, there will always be levels of unease, for, as Zembylas (2015) notes, "discomfort is inescapably tied to others; we always live in discomfort in this sense" (p. 170). In brief, as it is unavoidable, we can recognize the value of discomfort and approach it in earnest and respectful ways.

The pedagogy of discomfort also raises questions about both the teacher's comfort level as well as the students' comfort levels. What might it mean for a Black or Native American teacher to teach *Red Scarf Girl* (Jiang, 1999) to a class of predominantly Asian American students? A White or Latinx teacher to teach *The Fire Next Time* (Baldwin, 1992 edition) to a class of all or predominantly Black students? An openly gay or closeted teacher to teach *Angels in America* (Kushner, 2013)? A disabled or able-bodied teacher to teach *My Left Foot* (Brown, 2014 edition)? A male or female teacher to teach *The Women of Brewster Place* (Naylor, 1983)? A war veteran or pacifist teacher who must teach *All Quiet on the Western Front* (Remarque, 1928)? We ask these questions as we know each educator has varying degrees of control about their curriculum, and each teaches differently—informed by their experiences, knowledge, beliefs, and identity. Each instance listed above may cause levels of discomfort in the teacher for a variety of reasons, and yet, despite this unease, a pedagogy of discomfort is rooted in the hopefulness of possibilities that can arise from the intersection of students' and teacher's knowledge in classrooms.

Understanding the purpose of a pedagogy of discomfort allows teachers to be proactive in their decision-making, including the selection of texts, topics to analyze, activities to craft, and opportunities for creating spaces for students to listen to one another, as they link issues they read about in ELA class to past and present concerns.

Some Benefits for Students

The notion of the classroom being a "safe space" for students to be, and express themselves, is important. At the same time, we assert that a safe space does not mean the absence of discomfort. To the contrary, a classroom environment that is supportive of students' views, experiences, questions, and wonderings is one that encompasses—along with many other things—times of unease. When teachers do engage with students about what they think and feel, students unpack their worldviews and leave comfort zones. The possible (some may say inevitable) dissonance experienced, can be seen as a form of critical rigor. Such dissonance is useful as it can be harnessed to penetrate what initially looks like student apathy or indifference, moving beyond to help students and teachers engage in new ways with others. As contradictions arise, they can be viewed not as deficiencies, but rather as opportunities for engagement, exploration, and possible transformation. In brief, as Bheekie and van Huyssteen (2015) note, embracing contradictions and the ambiguities they yield, is "often considered the hallmark of mature thinking" (p. 11), and therefore can be a tool for developing critical thinking skills for students.

Another benefit for students and teachers is the acknowledgment that emotions can be a generative aspect of instruction. Students tend to read, write, listen, and speak about what they like and what moves them—things that they have an emotional response to. Of course, there are also emotional responses to what is feared, misunderstood, avoided, or challenges their worldview. And then there are different types of emotions. Boler (1999) notes how our dominant culture reinforces emotions that are either acceptable or unacceptable, observing that teaching institutions are based on these ideas, namely, not allowing emotions that are considered bad or wrong in the classroom. It almost seems like emotions in general, and selected ones in particular, are discouraged within institutional settings.

Scholar-practitioners have written about emotionality in classrooms and how emotions such as anger often are policed and discouraged by White teachers (Matias, 2016b), even as the curriculum students experience can be deeply problematic for them, such as when marginalized groups are omitted or misrepresented (S. Jones, 2020). Even attempts at embracing social–emotional learning, the goal of creating classrooms as safe spaces welcoming of difference that support student success, often have been co-opted as a new form of regulation to deny certain emotions, such as righteous anger—an emotion that has fueled civil rights movements (Kaler-Jones, 2020). As explored by Kay (2018), meaningful conversations about race—ones that acknowledge emotionality—can occur through creating a classroom ecosystem that values safe spaces, a dialogic curriculum, specific ways of talking, and being grounded in a purpose.

When emotions are acknowledged, classrooms become places of exploring emotional responses to various issues. Prebel (2016) actively urges examining "uncomfortable emotions that we (and our students) might otherwise resist or deflect" (p. 12). These can be manifest in what Boler (1999) describes as "defensive anger, fear of change, fear of losing our personal and cultural identities" (p. 2), along with discomfort and guilt felt when we are forced to question our own beliefs and the assumptions they rest upon. In teaching college students, Prebel (2016) has found that when she uses discomforting emotional responses as starting points, her classes are able to examine how the status quo has shaped people's ways of accepting or rejecting social inequalities. And, to challenge inequitable social norms means we must be open to "changing our emotional relation to them; that is, seeing the consequences of these norms as either gain or loss. . . . Any understanding of social justice requires the fundamental recognition of the integral role of emotions in reifying or disrupting injustices" (Zembylas & McGlynn, 2012, p. 43). In other words, the role of emotions cannot be extracted from the pedagogy of discomfort, as emotions indicate feelings that can cultivate empathy, which, in turn, can lead to action.

A classroom that acknowledges the emotional impact of difficult, sensitive, or controversial issues is one in which the effective realm of education is valued. Discussing multiple perspectives is not meant to impose one opinion over another. In fact, teachers should be proactive in cultivating not "taking sides," something we address later in this chapter. Rather, as Kevin Kumashiro (2015) explains, after teaching a class of high school students in which one student differed in opinion:

> The student was not learning that my progressive view was the better view or that all views and practices were equally valid or equally oppressive; rather, the student was learning that views and practices had different implications in different situations, and that determining an anti-oppressive course of action required assessing these differences. (p. 29)

Teachers want their students to be able to think critically by evaluating information and to realize the complexities involved in making reasoned decisions that can impact social change (Schieble et al., 2020).

Addressing Some Fears

Teachers often worry about what can and can't be taught, what's allowed and what's not permitted. In developing her pedagogical theory of discomfort, Boler (1999) noted that institutions actively maintain silences and actually proliferate discourses that Bheekie and van Huyssteen believe "deny effective learning, thereby determining what can and cannot be felt or expressed by those who work and learn within these institutions" (p. 3). As can be seen across the country, there are districts and schools that may forbid any mention of race, sexual orientation, and other topics—even if they directly pertain to the literature being taught. On the other hand, there are districts and schools that actively strive to center and celebrate all forms of diversity. We understand that readers of this book will have specific circumstances that influence how they conceive of how to teach diversity through literature. Regardless, we think there are several areas that are of potential concern to all teachers, including assessing the risk factor for students, providing accurate representation of people and issues, and striving to create a balance in classrooms that are open, fair, and respectful of multiple perspectives.

In creating classrooms that confront (dis)comfort zones, teachers must weigh the ethical implications of putting some children (even temporarily) in a challenging place. This is not a goal of the pedagogy of discomfort and should be avoided. All students, along with the teacher, should feel safe enough to express themselves. The teacher has to monitor issues of risk, comfort, responsibility, and vulnerability related to topics that come up in explicit or implicit ways, as they play out through teacher-and-student and student-and-student interactions. It can be argued that while there is some objectivity in teaching, being human is about our subjectivity. Negotiating the tensions in this forever-fluctuating space can be tricky for teachers. Teachers learn to "read" classrooms, including types of silences, coupled with body language, and can shift the direction of questions and conversations accordingly, or choose to linger and wait for what's said. Silences can mean anger, embarrassment, fear, lack of confidence, confusion, reticence, or simply the time needed for students to gather and form their thoughts. Regardless, any of these scenarios can still result in a meaningful discussion.

When teaching any text and examining issues of diversity, social justice, or inequity, teachers may be concerned about teaching historical and contemporary figures that are different from themselves and their own experiences. In doing so, they must consider the sources of knowledge presented. What additional artifacts are used? Who is speaking for themselves? Who is speaking for others? How is diversity among all people represented? Teachers have to decide how much they're willing to share about their own experiences and perceptions of society, history, and culture—without imposing their own values (Grant & Agosto, 2008). We know the degree to which we open up about ourselves can be a deeply personal choice. In recent years, there has been an increasing comfortability in talking about Whiteness (DiAngelo, 2018) and being "antiracist" (Kendi, 2019). Texts by these authors, and other texts, are helpful for teachers in framing and exploring issues of race in productive ways that lead to courageous conversations, as we described in Chapter 4. These conversations are not intended to shut down or blame White students or make them feel guilty about the social system they have inherited, but rather to lead them to acknowledge its existence and consequences, and potentially be active in promoting change.

A classroom involving a pedagogy of (dis)comfort means teachers must always maintain balance in considering multiple perspectives. We contend that there are no safe classroom spaces for all students at all times. Some students may shut down, switch off, or compartmentalize to get through a lesson. However, if their thinking is actively and respectfully tapped into, listened to, and acknowledged based on their life experiences to date, all students can participate in the dynamics of generating new knowledge for everyone in the room. To be direct, we don't want classrooms to create students in crisis, purposefully upset to the point of shutting down or not sleeping at night. However, we do want them to be informed, critical thinkers about how historical events impact contemporary times—and topics such as slavery, racial segregation, colonialism, the Holocaust, various genocides, wars, the patriarchy, and so on, have partly shaped who we are today.

Creating Safe Spaces Through Circles

One way to create a classroom environment where both teacher and students feel safe—or brave—to express feelings that may lead to discomfort is through the use of circles. Sometimes used in a "restorative" function after events of conflict, circles also can be used to build community and facilitate the sharing of emotions. This works by having the class sit in a circle and use a talking piece to take turns sharing ideas in response to a series of prompts, typically building from less to more intense (see Figure 5.1). Often a "centerpiece" sits in the middle—a poster with a quote, a grounding word for the circle, or an object of significance. Sometimes students and teachers simply talk in circles, while at other times an opening conversation may give way to writing or creating art. Circles may serve social–emotional purposes, as students discuss topics such as aspects of identity or feeling different. They also may help students process school or larger current events, from a scary fight in a classroom to protests against police brutality.

The circles, as adapted from the Morningside Center (2013), are "grounded in a Native American philosophy and practice that values individuals as they build and maintain supportive relationships and communities. . . . [Circles are meant to] create a safe and non-hierarchical place where each person can speak without interruption. . . . [and where] respectful listening and reflection" are vital components Circles traditionally have been used to peer-educate communities, including the civil rights movement in the United States via organizations such as the Highlander Center (n.d.) and Freire's (2018) development of specific pedagogies to empower the oppressed, which are utilized in contemporary education today (Borovica et al., 2019; Souto-Manning, 2010).

Ideally, in fulfilling this mission for circles, the teacher gives up a degree of control, a loosening that may cause feelings of discomfort. However, as students learn the circle structure, this format can be an optimal way to process and support challenging emotions in the classroom. This type of emotionally grounded discussion can feel corny to some teachers at first, but we often forget that teenagers have a lot of emotions and often are not given space to share them at all, let alone a space dedicated to valuing and listening to these emotions. The circle activities privilege the voices of teen students, allowing them to feel that the classroom is a trusting space as they—and their teachers—navigate topics of discomfort.

Considering Some Cautions

It can be hard for teachers not to react when students say certain things that may be rooted in racism, sexism, homophobia, Islamophobia, or transphobia, what Zembylas (2015) calls "troubled knowledge" (p. 172). Responding to troubled knowledge can become a balancing act that is not always easy. Teachers may have to work against their own initial personal reactions and "strategically empathize" (Lindquist, 2004) to make themselves "strategically skeptic in order to empathize with the troubled knowledge students carry with them, even when this troubled knowledge is disturbing to other students or to the teacher" (Zembylas, 2015, p. 172). Otherwise, dismissing views we don't like or want to hear could have a counter effect of silencing students and shutting them down, rather than promoting engagement. Even with traditionally "unacceptable" emotions, the dialogue should always remain open. Jansen (2009) notes that when teachers "take sides" too early, certain student knowledge appears undervalued. Instead, the need to critically engage with the "troubled knowledge" of students, along with discomfort and emotions, is essential when the goal is to transform knowledge (Zembylas, 2015). When teachers encourage students to examine the sources of their own knowledge and the uncomfortable emotions associated with this process, there exists the possibility of opening up a space to have students reflect upon how their worldviews have been shaped by their lived experiences, cultures, and histories (Boler, 1999). In other words, students may develop an awareness that emotional discomfort is an integral part of learning about the lived experiences of other people.

Another risk identified with the pedagogy of discomfort is the development of passive empathy, meaning gaining a greater level of awareness and

Figure 5.1. Circle Discussion

This circle was done first with staff and then with students after NYC high schools returned to (some) in-person instruction after being remote for the beginning of the 2021 school year. Note that if a school decides to do "schoolwide" circles, it is advisable to have teachers participate in the circle themselves before they engage students in this method.

Circle Activity: The Return to In-Person School

Reminders: Please make sure to put all chairs in a circle with the poster of the poem excerpt in the middle. Teachers should provide a talking piece and remind students of the basic guidelines for a circle: one voice at a time (talk only when you have the talking piece); be present (put cell phones and headphones away); safety and confidentiality (what's said here should stay here, but if teachers are concerned for safety, they may have to ask for support); speak but don't debate (this is not a place to call people out; if you want to respond to something that was said in the room, do not call people out by name).

1. *Opening*
    - Read this excerpt from youth poet laureate Amanda Gorman's poem, "The Hill We Climb" (from Joe Biden's inauguration, edited for educational purposes, also on a larger paper to place as centerpiece). Give each student a copy and ask for volunteers to read it through three times.

And so we lift our gaze, not to what stands between us, but what stands before us . . .

We seek harm to none and harmony for all.

Let the globe, if nothing else, say this is true.

That even as we grieved, we grew.

That even as we hurt, we hoped.

That even as we tired, we tried.

2. *Circle Discussion*
    - **Round One:** Share out one word or phrase—from the poem or that just comes to mind—about how you are feeling on the return to school. *Pass the talking piece around in a circle from person to person. Each person may speak, but a person also may pass and say nothing.*
    - **Round Two:** What are your hopes as we transition back into in-person school? *Pass the talking piece around from person to person. Start in the opposite direction of round one.*
    - **Round Three:** What can you control about your return to school experience? *"Popcorn," a method that passes the talking piece to students who volunteer to speak.*
3. *Closing*
    - What can you not control and may have to "let go"? Write it down on scrap paper. We will then crumble it up and "let go" of it.

Thank students and staff for sharing in the circle.

understanding of inequities but not taking actions to address these inequities. Instead, students may remain silent, fearing being on "the wrong side," resulting in feelings of powerlessness that justify "keeping a safe distance" from the issues at hand. However, for Boler, the evocation of empathy is a crucial first step that needs to be nurtured so students become moved *beyond* their self-imposed comfort zone, toward action. Such changes can be witnessed in classroom interactions (all students are respected, everyone is included in activities), extracurricular activities (starting a LGBTQ+–straight alliance at school), dialogues within families (respectful discussions about diversity-related items in the media), the pursuit of deeper knowledge (choosing a specific major to study in college), volunteering time (to community projects), or writing to political representatives (about issues such as recycling, global warming, and diversifying commemorative statues).

Using the pedagogy of discomfort means teachers must be mindful of ways that discomfort can manifest and how to respond. As Zembylas and McGlynn (2012) note, if the pedagogy of discomfort requires considerable vulnerability, then "the ethical responsibility of the teacher becomes a complex issue" (p. 57). The methodology does evoke emotions, and this gives rise to the ethics of creating activities that lead to discomforting situations. Finally, using discomfort potentially can have the opposite of the desired effect of opening students up. They may respond by closing down, "choosing to reinforce their own identities rather than risk self-transformation," or they may "feel overwhelmed and depressed by the dark side of history and culture, from which they've been sheltered" (Wang, 2005, p. 58). Nothing is surer than that all students will respond in their own way. While some may adopt an openness to embracing diversity and cultivating anti-oppressive attitudes, others may very well resist. However, ultimately it is useful to view conversations that initially may be perceived as difficult or challenging, as being positioned as conversations for healing (Aguilar, 2020).

SELECTED PRACTICES

We approach the selected practices for this topic with a wide net. Much emphasis is placed on teachers as individuals who seek to continue learning, including in areas that may discomfort them. Our suggestions cover areas of increasing self-awareness, a desire to expand pedagogy, and encouraging interactive dialogues with colleagues and students, while also foregrounding some inevitable moral dilemmas that can occur.

Building and Interrogating Comfort

Many of the ways to "build comfort" have been discussed in depth in other chapters of this book (see, for example, Chapters 1, 2, and 4). They are processes of building relationships through ice breakers, SEL approaches, and knowing students' neighborhoods and families, while sharing your own personal stories. They include learning the specificity of students' backgrounds so that the texts in a class can serve as "mirrors and windows" for students, and using culturally responsive and sustaining techniques so that both what and how you teach, engage students' home cultures and learning approaches. Becoming comfortable as a teacher takes time; I (Sarah) vividly remember my first 3 years of teaching being filled with apprehension, on extreme days feeling terror, as I walked up the steps of the school each morning. This, I suspect, is normal and perhaps even expected. I'd go so far to say that, in my experience, teachers who don't feel this terror often have a touch of delusion that belies a job well done. Over time, teachers find their "persona"—who they want to become in front of a room of kids. Teaching is performative, and we present ourselves to those we teach in both conscious and unconscious ways (Berger, 2016). If our teaching persona is true to who we really are, then the comfort of being in our own skin as a teacher grows. Greater self-trust means making decisions intuitively, and this comfort level of being the class leader grows, allowing students to gain trust in their teacher and increasing students' comfort levels too.

Pushing Toward Productive Discomfort Through Journaling

As teachers reflect on their moments of comfort, they may begin to see the need to push toward discomfort. One way to begin exploring "discomfort" is through the practice of journaling and reflection, which many teacher education programs incorporate in their coursework. This can be in traditional written form (Solgot, 2005), through video journaling (Corbin Frazier & Eick, 2015), or by interactive journaling with a mentor (Tillman, 2003). Teachers have always used journals for a variety of reasons, including to help them better understand challenging teaching contexts (Lowe et al., 2013) and in specific areas such as reflecting on race (Milner, 2003). Being able to have a place to record your thinking can be invaluable. Plus, it allows teachers to see their growth over time.

Self-Annotating Lesson Plans

All three of us have—in one way or another—developed systems to think about how our classes went, including reflecting upon the basic components of: What worked as planned? What didn't work as planned? What did I do well? What could I have done better? How might I change it for the next time I teach? If lessons are to be repeated later that day, these thoughts are utilized immediately. However, if lessons are not taught again until the next semester or even next year, we have found that simply writing on the lesson itself (in electronic or hard copy form) helps guide us to improving our practice. Notes can be related to the types of questions asked, the sources we used, student small-group dynamics, the clarity of instruction, and levels of general student motivation and interest. In brief, notes can be about any aspect of the three basic components of a lesson: planning, execution, and assessment of student learning. Another method of keeping tabs on thoughts about teaching a specific course, especially a new one, is to simply use a small notebook to jot down thoughts and ideas at will. This approach of "bulleted points" is very time efficient in comparison to journals. If you wish, your method also can be shared with supervisors when engaging about how you plan and self-evaluate your own practices.

Responding to Supervisor Feedback

No matter how good a teacher is, we advocate that they don't rest on their laurels and are always amenable to feedback, including from supervisors. If your school uses the Danielson Framework (2013) to assess students, examine patterns in your rating or comments and identify areas of interest and potential need for improvement. Maybe "discussion techniques" is an area that is still developing, or "using assessment in instruction" is a place where an administrator questions your practice. It is easy to grumble at the concept of receiving a rating for the often-subjective practice of teaching, but teachers can become so wrapped up in this indignation that they ignore the simple reality that feedback may help them improve. Furthermore, if you don't feel like you are being given specific feedback about areas for improvement you've self-identified and seek to work on, just ask. At your end of the year evaluation conference, inquire about the areas in which your supervisor would like to see growth and development. Then you can ruminate in a relaxed, reflective manner over the summer about how to fine-tune these practices.

Changing Through Constant Awareness

Sometimes during these reflections, we realize that something we have been teaching for years, maybe decades, doesn't have the same meaning, purpose, or effect it once did. For example, I (Fran) read *The Good Earth* (Buck, 2020 edition) in high school and was so distraught over Wang Lung's treatment of O-Lan that a decade later I decided it would be the perfect text to use in 10th-grade World Literature. Yet, a few years in, I couldn't help but question whether Pearl S. Buck was the legitimate voice I wanted to use to represent Asian literature, as she was a British woman who lived in China. I now teach *Wild Ginger* (Min, 2004) to include the Chinese-voiced perspective of the Cultural Revolution. Similarly, *Heart of Darkness* (Conrad, 2021 edition) is part of the standard curriculum for AP Literature at my present school. Yet, I and a colleague felt more uncomfortable every year having the same closing debate and essay analysis on the legitimacy of teaching a racist text. Is this the debate I want to have every year? This year we decided no, we no longer wanted to teach it. Even if its historical merit arguably can be a worthwhile reason to study the text, we thought it best to instead study a more representative "voice" from Africa such as Adichie's *Half of a Yellow Sun* (2006) or Gyasi's *Homegoing* (2017).

Self-Monitoring Complacency

No matter how a teacher reflects, reaching the point where you realize your practices are "too comfortable" is key. Moreover, if you truly have created a classroom that is a comfortable, nurturing environment, making changes, taking risks, and trying new things begin to feel much less daunting. I (Sarah) have taught for 2 decades and try every year—even if I'm teaching the exact same high school English course—to add one new unit over the course of the year and one new lesson in each previously used unit. The new unit may be based on a text I've read recently and loved or a book by an author from an identity never fully represented to date in the curriculum. Particularly brave teachers (with understanding administrators) may attempt a controversial debate or current event topic. Adding new lessons, protocols, or routines can be a place of joy and satisfaction, where you try something that may sound wacky or unconventional but that ultimately can transform your teaching practice. These new elements can include a "snowball fight review" (where questions asked on balled up paper are aimed at specific students by the teacher or other students), writing a song in a "voice" characteristics of a specific poetic movement, final projects for a set text represented on TikTok, discussions via musical chairs, and so on. These new approaches may come from colleagues, students, or your own research via social media, educational journals, or websites. In a more "contentious" school district, new approaches or texts may come in the form of student input; having students connect texts to current events of their choosing gives students the autonomy of choice, lessening any perceived bias parents or school boards might accuse you of having.

Participating in Classroom Visitations

Intervisitations are a particularly effective way for teachers to gain inspiration for new, creative approaches and begin to see how they may be implemented in the classroom. This may happen through a formalized process, such as Japanese lesson study where teachers work together to plan a lesson around one concept or skill, observe it being taught, provide feedback, and plan a subsequent lesson that incorporates this feedback (Rappleye & Komatsu, 2017). Variations on this idea abound. Teachers may all try a new instructional approach, such as using popular music in a lesson, and observe one another. Or, as teachers at my school did, they may identify a problem of practice, in our case students' difficulty in analyzing figurative language in depth. Each lesson was planned around this perceived learning weakness to observe it "live" and provide thoughtful, detailed feedback about it based on our observations. There can be variations on the original Japanese study protocol, such as ours when—in lieu of actually visiting one another's lesson—our English department shared student work to analyze the effectiveness of our new practices.

One of the easier ways to encourage intervisitations is through a "pineapple chart" (see Figure 5.2). In this more informal approach, teachers sign up to invite others into their class (the pineapple being a traditional symbol of welcome), often during a professional period. Schools may have an informal debriefing process such as a follow-up email to the teacher being observed or may have a more formal feedback session during professional learning meetings. Informal peer observations can be very powerful, as they are not evaluative—and are used purely for feedback to improve teaching. Stakes are not as high, but the feedback can be transformative.

Seeking Feedback From Students

In addition to intervisitations, another way to quickly push yourself into discomfort and gather ideas for innovative change is to collect critical feedback from students about your teaching practice (Gehlbach et al., 2018). Students have endless opinions and a wealth of prior experience in classrooms to draw on as they suggest new ideas or evaluate what works and what doesn't work in a classroom. Google Forms and other online systems now make

Figure 5.2. Pineapple Chart for Classroom Intervisitations

Teachers have the option to fill in the chart at the beginning of the week or month or progressively over the course of a month or year. Depending on a school's professional learning goals, teachers may volunteer to open their classrooms when trying a specific practice (such as discussion techniques) or simply whenever they are doing something interesting.

Pineapple Days: Share Your Discussion Techniques!

period	Tuesday	Wednesday	Thursday
2	Mr. Smith—Fishbowl on Civil Rights Movement (rm 552)		Ms. Archer—Fishbowl on Ancient Greece (rm 267)
3		Mr. Bay—Student debate—Mayoral election (rm 443)	Mr. Lopez—Jigsaw—Poetry analysis
4	Ms. Mount—Speed-dating—end of *Invisible Man*		

the designing of surveys and analysis of data much easier than in years past. When creating a survey for students, several factors are key to consider. The first is timing. Some teachers may wish to survey students at the beginning of the year, mining their passions and looking for how they learn best. Others may try a midyear survey, a chance to reflect on past practices and improve them for the second half of the year. Finally, an end-of-year survey allows teachers to process a curriculum in its entirety and plan to revamp in the next year (see Figure 5.3). The second thing to consider is purpose. Consider your "why" for gathering information from students: Did a unit or lesson go poorly? Are you bored with a stale unit? Are you at a loss for engaging, new ideas? The purpose will, of course, affect the questions asked. After reflecting on this purpose, the third consideration is the questions themselves. While it can be gratifying to get survey responses that laud how nice or funny you are as a teacher, this is not useful to push you into new, "uncomfortable" territory. Questions should ask for specifics when possible and, as the goal is to change something, focus on what to change or add, not what works. Teachers simply may ask, "Name three things you do in other classes that you wish you did in this class" or include a fill-in statement like, "If I taught the class for a day, I would add _____." Surveys can even ask students to "choose" between several teaching approaches: "We are studying *The Piano Lesson* (Wilson, 1987) next unit. Would you prefer to show your understanding of the play through (a) a performance; (b) a creative project; (c) teaching a lesson to your peers?" Of course, once you have your survey results, you actually must use them. Make that spreadsheet, break down the data, and put the plan into action. Students also like to see their suggestions go into practice. I have had students debate the best text and worst text of the year and promised them I would keep or cut whichever texts "won" and "lost." This made students feel their opinions actually are valued and affect my curriculum choices.

In his work using popular culture as a model to engage urban students in science classes, Chris Emdin (2007) developed tools to immerse students in learning. We believe it's worth sharing his perspective for ELA teachers, as the "Three-C's" approach he developed is also applicable to the ELA classroom (see Figure 5.4).

Using Established Protocols

In seeking "discomfort," new ideas also may come from online research or social media communities. Humanities teachers in particular often may benefit from looking for new protocols and new ways to read, discuss, and analyze texts. Harvard's Graduate School of Education's Teaching and Learning Lab has a thorough list (https://www.gse.harvard.edu/sites/default/files/Protocols_Handout.pdf), and the School Reform Initiative boasts a website with over 100 protocols to try (https://www.schoolreforminitiative

Figure 5.3. Example of Anonymous Student Course Evaluation

ANONYMOUS 10TH-GRADE ENGLISH COURSE EVALUATION

1. What was your FAVORITE text we read this year? Why was this your favorite?

2. What was your LEAST FAVORITE text we read this year? Why did you not like it?

3. What was your *favorite* activity in English this year [BESIDES watching movies]? Why was this your favorite?

4. What was your *least favorite* activity in English this year? Why did you not like it? What could Ms. Bickens do to improve this activity?

5. In general, what are the *most valuable* skills that you have learned this year? Why?

6. What skills or information do you *wish* you had learned (or learned better) this year but did not?

7. Identify the TWO most important things that Ms. Bickens should change or add next year to improve English class.

8. Identify the TWO most important things that Ms. Bickens did this year that she should continue to do next year.

Anything else?

Figure 5.4. Chris Emdin's Three C's

Emdin (2007) writes that using these three tools combined to form a specific approach to teaching means changing traditional approaches to teaching and being willing to look at the urban science classroom in new ways. It must be seen as more than just a place where students learn science; it must be seen as a field to be studied and understood by both teachers and students while both engage in teaching and learning science. This changed way of thinking requires a redefinition of teacher and student and what their roles are in the science classroom. (p. 773)

We contend that the Three-C's, described below, are also useful tools for the ELA classroom.

1. *Cogenerative Dialogue.* Teachers can develop new connections between students and texts. This is done by creating spaces for open dialogue about the ELA classroom, the canon of literature, curriculum options, the purpose of learning, and relevance of topics to all students in class.
2. *Coteaching With Students.* This approach allows students to learn the content of texts and concepts within literature (such as literary devices) and then teach them, referencing their own backgrounds and cultures, allowing teachers to learn about their students—and use what they learn in future lessons.
3. *Cosmopolitanism.* This concept stresses that, despite differences, all humans share an ethical responsibility for one another. In ELA classes, this means that both teacher and students share the responsibility for teaching one another what they don't know—about the texts being read and analyzed, teaching the texts, and teaching one another.

.org/protocols). Two that have become favorites in my classroom are the "speed-dating protocol" (Figure 5.5) and the "affinity mapping protocol" (Figure 5.6). As with any new approach, the first few tries will be messy and imperfect (hence the value in already having a comfortable classroom culture). But when students begin to learn a protocol, they can take more ownership over their own learning, and, ideally, the process begins to nearly run itself. Perhaps more important, when protocols work and become repeated classroom routines, students learn more. They can focus on the text or processing at hand, rather than a set of complicated activity instructions. Research on trauma-informed pedagogy further validates the benefits of routine protocols (M. S. Thomas et al., 2019). When students, especially those dealing with the uncertainty and erratic nature of trauma, feel they can "predict" the workings of a class, they are comforted by this routine, allowing their brains to focus on learning, rather than protection and survival.

EMBRACING DIVERSITY

As the theme of this book is embracing diversity in ELA classrooms, using the pedagogy of discomfort consciously and strategically allows teachers to

Figure 5.5. Speed-Dating Activity

Similar to the adult version of this exercise, speed dating is a way for students to have many brief conversations with many different partners over the course of a class. This protocol is best used when students have small parts of a text that spark discussion. For example, if the end of a novel has several important quotes, students may respond to a different quote for each round of speed dating.

1. Arrange desks in two circles so an inner circle faces outward to an outer circle.
2. Place a response sheet at each desk. The sheet should stay at each desk as students move for each round. Each sheet should have a quote, open-ended prompt, and space for students to write. For example, the teacher may use the final line of a novel, a question about what this shows regarding final themes, and space to write. (As students become more familiar with this protocol, they may bring their own quotes and questions to class for this activity. Upper-level students also may create their own question for a given quote and then each subsequent round responds to this initial question.)
3. Explain key rules to students: stay loyal to your "date" (no cross-talk); discuss the quote and question first, then write an initial response; keep the paper on the tables.
4. After the first round, move the students (and take time to give very explicit directions about the move). Students move to "their right"—meaning the inner circle moves clockwise and the outer circle moves counterclockwise so that students are paired with a new prompt and a new person in each round.
5. Repeat as many rounds as time allows, allowing about 3–5 minutes per round. Students may continue to respond to the prompts given and also may respond to previous groups' comments.
6. Summarize and close the class by asking students to share out the most important idea or most interesting response on each sheet. If the work connects to a larger assessment (such as a final paper), teachers may archive the classwork by posting photos of it on an online system or making copies for all students.

open up numerous possibilities. For example, teachers can be proactive in teaching the value of human differences and can challenge stereotypical depictions of people that are characterized as damaging, restrictive, pessimistic, and inaccurate (Ford, 2017). They can be mindful of "who is speaking" to inform us about particular issues, ensuring that a variety of perspectives are shared—particularly by people who are minoritized within the traditional mainstream English canon. Educators can unpack pejorative language commonly used, like "retard" and "spaz," to reveal ways in which specific words continue to stigmatize, denigrate, and injure people. Teachers can confront some difficult aspects of history related to ELA texts by utilizing classic and documentary films (Stoddard et al., 2017). They also may (re)interpret (re)presentations, as well as use progressive representations in literature. There are many TED Talks that can serve as a springboard into difficult conversations about gender, race, sexual orientation, disability, and so on. The arts can be used in a variety of ways—from analyzing past and

Figure 5.6. Affinity Mapping

This protocol is adapted from the School Reform Initiative and is most useful when people may have diverse responses to one text. It can be used in a variety of ways: to process a reading, prioritize findings, or create larger rules or norms.

1. The class reads a common reading with a given lens. For example, students may read Zora Neale Hurston's "How It Feels to Be Colored Me" (1928) and focus on Hurston's perception of race and identity. (Students may be given a focus theme or idea, or a question of focus, or simply may record anything that they view as significant.)
2. Each student is given 3–5 Post-its. Students write different ideas about what they see around race and identity on each Post-it.
3. After reading, students convene around a poster paper, either as a class or in smaller groups of 5–10. If working as a whole class, students may use multiple pieces of poster paper.
4. Students put all of their Post-its on the paper silently.
5. Then, remaining silent, students read one another's Post-its and try to group ideas into "natural" categories. Students may move Post-its around; remind them to not be offended if their Post-it is moved.
6. Once students settle on groupings, then they may talk. Students discuss why they made the groupings they did and create names for their categories. Then, they neatly place their Post-its under each category.
7. The class debriefs and discusses larger themes, ideas, and priorities that came from their categories and how they relate to the initial question of focus.

present political cartoons to using visual expression in tandem (or instead of) written expression. "Talking back" to dominant discourses can be done in creative, moving ways. See, for example, "My Name Is Jay," in which a Black graduate student responded to a White teacher portrayed in one of his set texts with poetry and a montage of images in a video (Baglieri & Moses, 2010). Teachers can link all civil rights movements together—those of Black citizens, women, the LGBTQ+ community, the disabled, and trans people—so commonalities can be seen in demands for equal rights ensured by law.

REFLECTING ON MORALITY

While we have encouraged teachers to push their own thinking and that of their students around challenging and sometimes contentious topics, we also feel obligated to add a caveat. What happens, say, when an issue arises that completely goes against our own beliefs, something that causes physical, psychological, and/or emotional harm to other people? In other words, what if we—as teachers, as individuals—consider certain actions immoral?

Recent examples include points of view that accept that police brutality is necessary to keep cities safe, immigrants without documents should be separated from their infants and children as a deterrent/punishment, and conversion therapy is the answer to change gay people into straight ones. In exploring aspects of arguments around these and other issues, teachers can frame discussions with a warning about "false equivalency," namely, that both sides of a position hold equal weight, and can note that there are always moral dimensions to our thinking. Of course, what constitutes moral and immoral will always be food for debate among people, even when what appears undeniable to one person is not viewed the same way by another. However, our thinking on this topic of (im)morality is similar to the Hippocratic Oath *Do No Harm*. If actions of one human to another have caused physical, psychological, or emotional harm—or in extreme cases, death—then morality must always inform the lens through which we see. To further this idea of "do no harm," teachers also may frame one of the community agreements of the classroom as recognizing that we have diverse backgrounds, families, and experiences, and that these backgrounds are not always apparent on the surface. In embracing diversity, we also want to point out the danger of assuming sameness. Young people often do this, making comments about illegal immigration or homosexuality, not thinking that their peers, whom they often see as just like themselves (even if to adults the differences are more obvious), may lack citizenship documentation, have a gay parent, or be LGBTQ+. Students can be encouraged to think about whether a possibly controversial stance would make a classmate feel personally attacked or endangered.

Take, for instance, Senator Scott Baldwin's comments on cowriting and proposing Senate Bill 167 about banning "concepts that divide," in which he stated teachers should be unprejudiced when teaching lessons about Nazism and fascism. "I believe we've gone too far when we take a position," he said. "We need to be impartial." He continued, saying that teachers should "just provide the facts," and he was "not sure it's right for us to determine how that child should think" (Yang, 2022).

To any teacher, this rationale is deeply disturbing, as well as impossible. There are times that we cannot be impartial or neutral, for that would make us complicit in injustices that exist. Furthermore, not exploring moral dimensions of issues would lead us to shape students to think along amoral lines, becoming indifferent to human suffering, devoid of empathy. We actually think that there are some issues that evoke a moral responsibility in us to take a side and to be role models for students in doing so. This does not mean that we wish to impose our views or ideologies onto students, but rather that we want them to contemplate the needless harms that humans can inflict upon one another using all kinds of rationales.

Although Baldwin walked back some of his words, largely as a result of a backlash of public opinion, he still stood by the bill, which

> prohibits kindergarten through 12th grade schools from teaching students that "any sex, race, ethnicity, religion, color, national origin, or political affiliation"

> is inherently superior, inferior, racist, sexist, oppressive. Teachers would also be prohibited from making individuals feel "discomfort, guilt, anguish, responsibility or any other form of psychological distress" when it comes to meritocracy and the notion that it was created by one group to oppress another. (Yang, 2022)

This bill symbolizes the backlash against progressive teaching that does not seek to sanitize history, but instead acknowledges the past and present harms of racism, genocide, extremism, sexism, and so on—along with resistance, resilience, and contributions to society by all people, so we can learn from everyone. As ELA teachers, we know that these lightning rod issues are inextricably embedded in the texts we teach so readers will understand the realities of diverse people and grow as critical thinkers.

In closing, we have dedicated time to discussing (dis)comfort zones, as we truly believe they are an integral part of teaching. Many of us have taken calculated risks in discussing topics that may be difficult for a variety of reasons. They may not always result in entirely predictable lessons, but they do touch students in ways that make them wish to respond and engage. If the lesson becomes too heated, there are ways to lower the temperature, so to speak. Students can be redirected to journal about why they feel so passionate, asked to share their thoughts and feelings in a homework assignment, or requested to jot down bulleted points that can be discussed in a protocol of pairs. Sometimes, the topic may need to be shifted by a skillful teacher with words of encouragement, such as, "This has been an excellent discussion. I'm pleased to know you all have opinions that will be channeled into your writing," "Let's keep the option open of taking this up again tomorrow after we've had more time to reflect on the issues," or, "I'm impressed by your knowledge and abilities to present your points. And we'll incorporate your thoughts as we explore the next related topic." There are many respectful ways to facilitate shifts in classroom conversations and activities that allow teachers to maintain an ambience conducive to discussions and explorations, without negating or dismissing student knowledge and perspectives (Kibler et al., 2022).

SUMMARY

While nearly all teachers long for the cozy, comfortable classroom that feels like a family, and a job free of anxiety and doubt, in fact, the fear and discomfort can play a major role in helping teachers' growth. Striving to confront practices and topics that make you uncomfortable is what moves a good teacher to become a great teacher. Self-reflection and student surveys can help teachers pinpoint areas of complacency or simply areas in need of a "refresh," and intervisitations or trying a new protocol can provide concrete examples of how to make these changes work in a real classroom environment.

QUESTIONS FOR FURTHER REFLECTION

1. What teaching strategies do you use all the time? Why? Do they work? How could they be done differently?
2. What practices do you do that are the same as when you were a student? To what degree are these approaches effective? How do you know?
3. What are a variety of ways that you can seek out feedback? Which are you most comfortable with? Why? Which are you less comfortable with? Why?
4. Ask a colleague to watch you teach a lesson you've taught many times but in which you're now including new information and activities designed to push your own comfort zone and/or that of your students. What are areas of strength and areas to develop in your practice?
5. Ask a fellow teacher whether you can observe them teaching something that you're less comfortable or confident about. How did they approach challenging or controversial content?
6. Using the Three-C's approach by Chris Emdin, consult with students before starting a new unit to determine the activities and assessments that will be the most rigorous and engaging.

CHAPTER 6

Adapting to Different Educational Contexts

I (Fran) am not a crier, but on my last day of work at the New York City Title I public high school where I had spent the past 11 years teaching, I wept buckets. Carrying my last crate of belongings out the door, I stopped to sob in the arms of our safety officer, whose son I had taught a few years before. She hugged me and told me they would miss me. She looked ready to cry too. Having invested every ounce of my being into my first teaching job, I still couldn't believe I actually was leaving, as I'd wanted to remain there until retirement. I loved the students whom I taught, my coworkers were some of my best friends, and I'd met my husband there. How could I possibly be leaving? To this day, there are times when I still wonder whether I made the right decision. It's difficult, if not impossible, to know where your choices eventually will take you.

Flashback: Eleven years earlier I had sat in the principal's office for yet another interview. I had already taught a demonstration lesson, and this was now the third round of questions. I was just finishing graduate school, and all my education professors had told us we probably wouldn't get a job until August and might even have to serve as substitutes to get our foot in the door. Yet, it was June, and I was trying to say whatever I could to convince this man that he should hire me. I realized he kept circling back to ask the same question, "What will you do if a student disrespects you?" He looked skeptically at my 5'1" frame, clearly doubting that I had the ability to keep a class in order. However, I must have come across as a fairly confident person. Less than 2 months later, I was setting up my first classroom.

WHY ADAPTING TO EDUCATIONAL CONTEXTS MATTERS

Most teachers will experience several moves in their career (Goodson, 2003), motivating us to include a chapter on this topic as we hadn't come across any in the professional literature before. Because each school has its own unique culture, and likely has different notions of what constitutes diversity, along with the degree of commitment to it, we thought it would be worthwhile to first consider why teachers change schools, then how teachers adapt to a new school culture, and finally discuss the implications for maintaining a commitment to embracing diversity as an integral part of their careers.

Let us begin by contemplating some factors that push teachers to leave their jobs to work in another school.

Family-based reasons:

- To accommodate their spouse/partner's new job in another part of the state, region, or country.
- To be closer to their own children's school or aging parents in need of support.

Professional reasons:

- To cultivate professional growth through a different certification area. For example, some teachers may switch from special education to ELA, or vice versa—and move to where positions are available.
- To take on a leadership role in the education system by becoming administrators.
- To deepen their interest in pedagogy by becoming professional development specialists and teacher coaches.
- To feel more supported by school administration.

Practical reasons:

- To earn more money in higher-paying districts.
- To shift after a position has been eliminated.
- To lessen a commute by being nearer to home.

Personal reasons:

- To be more philosophically compatible with school administration.
- To seek a different school culture more in tune with their interests and disposition or in a community where they are more familiar and comfortable with the culture and language.

We share these examples to show a variety of understandable reasons why teachers may seek to change schools. Often, it's a combination of several reasons—and something that all of us have done.

The Excitement and Challenge of Changing Schools

In changing schools and/or roles, there's a level of excitement felt about embracing something new. At the same time, we all know that while change offers growth, some aspects of it also can be difficult. For example, moving to a new school means restarting in many different ways. To some educators, the shift may feel almost like the breakup of a relationship, with the need to begin over, still unsure of exactly what's expected in the next relationship—even while wondering if you shouldn't have left the first one. I say this because I (Fran) was in love with my first school. I felt proud to be a NYC public school teacher, and I couldn't imagine not being that person. However, when my own children's public school was rezoned due to overcrowding and our apartment felt increasingly smaller with two growing children, we began to look beyond the city to schools in Connecticut, where my in-laws lived, and where I soon was made a job offer. Then, 3 years later, I decided to move again to teach in the district where I live. The salary was higher and the district's schedule synchronized with my children's vacation breaks. As a working mom, practicality became the priority for me.

In reflecting on my career to date, I have enjoyed teaching in all three schools, and I am thankful to have worked in these different environments. I've also learned that things are not always done the same way in all schools, nor do they need to be. Interestingly, changing schools has alerted me to some possible downsides to working in only one school for the duration of a career. For example, it is easy to become accustomed to practices, ways, and beliefs that are taken for granted within a specific school culture and not discussed, challenged, or changed, inadvertently causing what may be termed "educational tunnel vision." Teachers without access to knowledge about other schools and a wide range of practices may think what they have experienced is *the one and only way* of education. Likewise, when David worked as a professional development (PD) specialist in a district office, he realized that one of the most effective forms of PD for teachers and administrators was to visit other schools with a specific lens through which to study them. For example, when assistant principals and teachers were asked to participate in redesigning special and general education models at their school to create inclusive classrooms, he facilitated visits to schools that already had successful models. During these visits, participants had "aha" moments—usually commenting along the lines of "I didn't think of doing it that way," or "I didn't know we could do that"—involving things such as creative ways of programming classes, scheduling teachers, providing direct and indirect instruction, and expanding the use of paraprofessionals. In another example, when Sarah moved from one high school to another, she changed from a highly structured environment to a more creative one with a broader view of assessment, requiring her to adapt many of her practices and see the value of different pedagogical options. Ultimately, our point here is that we've always found coming to know other schools and positions as beneficial for the "big picture" of our own educational experiences.

SELECTED PRACTICES

In the remainder of the chapter, we focus on different considerations when changing jobs and acclimating to a new school culture, including adapting to administrators and school rules; connecting to coworkers; teaching curriculum; adjusting to expectations and social norms for students; collaborating with parents; and preparing for tenure again, if it's offered. After each of these areas has been addressed, we also discuss implications for teachers who support embracing diversity, as they become integrated into a different school culture.

Adapting to Administration and School Rules

New York City is so large that its million-plus students are educated in schools divided into 32 geographic districts that are overseen by 46 superintendents, some tied directly to these 32 districts, others to school grade levels, and others to alternative and segregated settings for students with disabilities. Within this organization, each of its 17,000 schools becomes a unique entity, in which the principal is more influential than the superintendent. I (Fran) can't remember a single superintendent in the 11 years I taught there. However, no one could possibly forget my principal. He was the epicenter of the organization, championing the school's motto of the 3Rs—"Reason, Respect, and Responsibility."

On the first day of each semester, all faculty were required to teach a lesson instilling these values. One year on the first day of spring semester, I instead decided to begin a new curriculum, thinking my students had heard enough of the 3Rs. To his surprise and my chagrin, the principal entered the room, witnessed my lesson, and called me into the hallway, accusing me of "insubordination." When I returned to the classroom, he stayed for the entire period to watch me deliver a spontaneous new lesson, content that it met his standards. My risk had not paid off. Since starting there, I'd learned that the principal had a clear vision that included the 3Rs and was unwavering in his efforts to achieve it—that of having students being college-ready, confident that they could be accepted into, and thrive in, higher education. If I wanted to keep my job, I knew I had to adhere to this vision.

All of his decisions supported this vision. For example, the principal required all entering students to attend a Summer Bridge program before 9th grade to prepare them for the rigors of high school. In addition, he created Saturday school for the 2 months leading up to the end of year when students would take the state's mandated Regent exams. Here, teachers led students in study sessions followed by sitting down to eat pizza together. As attending college was an expectation, teachers took entire classes of students on day tours and overnight trips to visit colleges, and all sophomores were required to take a SAT-prep class. Unsurprisingly, the school was very successful and highly sought after by parents. It won multiple awards from the city for being an exemplar of how to prepare students—most entering with "below-expected" grade-level skills—for the rigors of college. While we may have had disagreements on occasion, such as how much to teach the 3Rs, I understood that the culture of the school emanated largely from a demanding principal.

In contrast, when I applied to a suburban school 11 years later, the interview procedures and questions I was asked were much different than my city experience. This time the head of the English department interviewed me, asking about developing curriculum and the various levels of classes I'd taught. In a telling shift of focus, before introducing me to the vice principal, he asked me how I'd deal with a difficult parent and never inquired how I'd handle a difficult student. On being called in for a second interview, this time with the principal, I discovered it was a formality before she directed me to visit the superintendent to sign my contract.

As it turned out, the principal had taught at the same school for decades before moving into an administrative position. Thankfully, she never forgot her classroom experiences and possessed a deep compassion for teachers in their daily practice. Possessing this disposition made her very approachable, and teachers often came to her with ideas or problems that they might not broach with another administrator. When I resigned, she hugged me and told me if I wasn't happy at my new school, she'd always welcome me back. In reflecting upon these experiences, I'm reminded that institutional memory, a sense of identity, and genuine community, among other things, are so important in maintaining a supportive school culture.

Interestingly, in some suburbs the superintendent holds a lot more direct power than in larger city districts. Many districts face a high rate of superintendent turnover, as so many leave after 1 or 2 years, frustrated by what can be complex local politics, often influenced by parents they deem difficult and demanding (Grissom & Andersen, 2012). One superintendent in Greenwich quit after less than a year, citing that she had received 40,000 emails between the start of the academic year and Thanksgiving. It's important to remember that Board of Education members are usually interested citizens elected to the position and can come to hold immense power in making decisions about local school policies, curricula, hiring practices, tenure consideration, and rules for behavior. School board meetings also have become the battlegrounds of community members of all political stripes who have become increasingly hostile, spawning conspiracy theories, threatening those who support masks, and igniting fears of critical race theory, making the meetings "weird—and scary" events (Cottle, 2021). These meetings can run for over 4 hours, suggesting that attendees have time on their hands—are largely retired or unemployed, or can afford child care services.

We share this information to inform teachers that, when entering a new district, it may be important to know the role of the principal, superintendent, and school board members, among other key players. These figures can have a huge impact on the teacher's position within a school. While the principal mostly affects a teacher's day-to-day life and job status, the superintendent often sets the tone for the whole district. In our present intensely political world, the people elected to the Board of Education also can have a tremendous influence on what is taught and what is not. It is also worthwhile to be mindful of shifts in power (actual or potential). For example, when your principal resigns or a new superintendent is hired, a shift in vision can significantly affect the culture of schools and daily classroom lessons.

Connecting to New Coworkers

On my first day of teaching in the city, I met my two coauthors and my husband, all of whom were strangers until that moment. I was 23 years old, never had a "real" job before, and was eager to make friends and figure out exactly what I was supposed to be teaching in 9th grade. Within the 9th-grade faculty of five teachers, three of us were new. The "veteran" teachers were not overly friendly, and no other English teacher offered to help plan any curriculum. I even ate lunch alone in my classroom the first few months, because I felt overwhelmed by how planning and grading left me no free moments. The phrase "forged by fire" became all too true. Admittedly, the first year of teaching isn't easy for anyone. Since then, because of my own experiences, when I come across a first-year teacher, I offer to share any of my curricula, advice, or anything that can make that year more manageable.

Eventually I started eating lunch in the teachers' room and, as peer relations developed, began going out for drinks on Fridays after school with my colleagues. Retrospectively, it is clear to me how important it was to push myself out of my comfort zone and make those connections. While colleagues can be invaluable for feedback in planning units and preparing to teach new courses, celebrating the end of the week with them, including sharing triumphs and struggles, is equally important. By my second year of teaching, I was dating my future husband, and my coworkers had become an essential support system that helped me navigate going forward in my school and career. It became clear to me that working together in solidarity makes teachers' jobs easier in many ways, contributing to overall job satisfaction and general happiness, which, in turn, positively impacts a faculty's dedication to supporting students.

When I started at my second high school, the ELA department was much larger. Instead of five teachers, each with our own room, we had 19 who shared classrooms and one giant office. I wasn't exactly sure what to expect from my coworkers. Unlike in Manhattan, there wasn't a nearby local bar to walk to on Fridays after work. Many people, myself included, had children they had to rush home to, and others drove an hour commute each way to get back and forth from work. Everyone seemed pleasant and dedicated, and, luckily, there was another new English teacher, Jenn, who was exactly my age, also with two children. Everything seemed perfect, until we realized that no one was talking to us. Jenn and I would sit together with the rest of the teachers in the lunchroom and chat with each other, but no one initiated conversations with us. At the department and faculty meetings, again, no one sat nearby or talked to us. Jenn began to try harder to get the English teachers to like her, bringing desserts to each department meeting and coordinating a collective pose for an end-of-the-year photo. I admit it all felt weird.

Then the strangest thing happened. When Jenn and I started our second year, *everyone* talked to us. Many people asked how I'd spent my summer and about how my children were. Others wanted to plan units together. People even pulled up a seat and talked to us at lunch. What can be made of this phenomenon? We've come to believe that probably at any job, coworkers watch new additions to the organization during their first year, wondering whether they'll come back the next year and therefore will be worth investing time in. What I learned was to give any new position time—at least a year. In retrospect, I'd taken a lot of my social and professional "capital" for granted, without realizing people at my new school didn't know whether I was competent. I therefore had to prove myself all over again simply by doing a good job. Everything feels better once you've adjusted to what you're doing and established faculty come to know who you are. Once you understand the ways of our profession, you also can seek to change some of them for the better. For example, when a new teacher began that second year, Jenn and I made every effort to include her in our lunch conversations and to tell her all the things we wish we'd known the year before. It's important for teachers to be cognizant of what it's like as a first-year teacher. Not only is the job demanding, but all dynamics take place in a social environment sometimes composed of long friendships (and occasional rivalries). When individual teachers reach out to new hires, and groups foster community, staff are more content in their jobs and likelier to stay there longer.

When I switched 3 years later to another high school, I remembered what I learned from my first two transitions and was not in any rush to force my way in. At this school, every English teacher is paired up with a social studies teacher so that the 9th- and 10th-grade classes are grounded in a humanities approach to their studies. On the first day of work, I was surprised to find that my new teaching partner did not talk to me. His desk was next to mine, but he wouldn't even make eye contact. At first, I was insulted, then mildly amused. I'd heard he had been very close to his last partner and was sad when she moved out of state, experiencing a sense of loss. I figured it likely would take him a while to warm up to me, so I accepted his behavior until he was ready to approach me. At lunchtime on my first day, I sat at my desk and ate my peanut butter and jelly sandwich (a teacher's go to, if ever there was one). I hadn't wanted to bring anything more substantial, as I didn't know whether there was a refrigerator to store my food in or a microwave to heat it up in. As I was finishing, another English teacher came and laughed, telling me I'd got the lunchtime wrong and that the whole department ate together at the communal table—a bit later. I wish she'd told me that before lunchtime! Unfortunately, I didn't get to go to my department's holiday party that year, because I had no one to watch my children. Nor did I go to the end-of-the-year department party because I wasn't sure I'd have enough people to talk to. Yet, time and patience worked their magic. My partner and I now plan all our units together and two of my best friends are my coworkers. Also, the 12 people in my office are some of the kindest and funniest people I know. I can't imagine my days without these people. Almost 40 months of lunchtime discussions, faculty and department meetings, and shared free periods all work in unison to help bond people in meaningful ways. The humor my colleagues bring to the mundane, the support they offer on stressful days, and the camaraderie they bring to each time we "break bread" at lunchtime make every day qualitatively better.

Teaching a Different Curriculum

I have friends in the business world who spend days or even weeks planning the perfect pitch to a client for an hour-long meeting. They make sure they have the best research to back up their claims and state of the art visuals to engage their audience, and meticulously rehearse their delivery. Additionally, they anticipate what clients might ask and what reticence they may have to the "buy-in." And then there are teachers who do this every day, often presenting different information and using varied materials each hour.

The number of classes a teacher has to prepare for each day greatly impacts the quality of those lessons. When I started out, I taught the entire 9th grade at my first school. I had five classes every day, but each class was the same lesson. While it was a lot of grading (I had more than 130 students), there was not a lot of planning to do. It was also strange to me to self-reflect as the day progressed. My first lesson would be a little shaky, as I discovered parts that took longer than I expected or areas where students encountered unanticipated difficulties. The second and third lessons were usually very strong, with familiar jokes and anecdotes, and the timing nailed down. However, by the fourth and fifth lessons, I noticed I inadvertently could become a bit rote, losing some of the spontaneity and excitement that existed earlier in the day.

Nowadays, I have four different classes to prepare for. Not all of them meet daily, as we have a rotating schedule, but on some days I have five classes with four different lessons full of content. This is a lot, and I often feel like I may be risking a disservice to some classes if I spend too much time planning one specific lesson. In addition, by their very nature, some classes take more time to prepare for than others. For example, an AP Literature class has so much reading and complex material to teach that I always have to spend more time planning those lessons than my 9th-grade English classes, where texts are shorter and I've taught the material many times before. One way to combat this demand on planning time is to use similar structures across classes. For example, when I have a specific type of discussion in my 11th-grade class, such as a structured debate or use of the Socratic method, I use that same format in my 12th-grade class (see Figure 6.1). Likewise, teachers can integrate the same method into other teaching activities, such as vocabulary routines (e.g., mix and match words and definitions, or combining two words in one sentence), but using different words.

In addition, planning and sharing curricula varies significantly from school to school and from department to department. The way the social studies department in my school plans and shares lessons is vastly different from how the English department works. For example, the social studies teachers have collections of lessons for each unit that they all share, along with assessments that students are mandated to complete for each course. On one hand, it is wonderful to be given these resources and not to start from scratch for each new course. On the other hand, some schools expect teachers to adhere to scripted lessons, almost verbatim. While this ensures that all students are getting some standardized material and it can be helpful in supporting brand-new teachers, a highly scripted approach to instruction also can stifle a teacher's creativity and inhibit the incorporation of new resources, innovative materials, and improvisation, which are integral to professional growth (Philip, 2019). In addition, it makes differentiation for students' interests and needs difficult to implement.

An important "to do" for new teachers (and we'd argue when teachers are new to a school) is to observe other people's classes, particularly educators who have reputations for excellence (see Figure 5.2). In my first position in NYC, the principal required all teachers to visit another teacher each semester for a full class and do an official write-up of the lesson. In addition, each weekly grade-level meeting featured a protocol in which one teacher shared an assignment they'd developed, with student work samples as a result of that assignment, to get feedback from their peers (McDonald et al., 2013). At the time I thought this process to be excessive, but having taught at schools that don't require these protocols, I now realize how valuable it was. Seeing how other teachers approach topics and content, and ways in which they interact with students, including how they give feedback, is so valuable, pushing all educators—but especially novice teachers—to reflect

Figure 6.1. Using the Same Discussion Format Across Classes

Classroom Activity (also applicable to activities in other chapters).	9th/10th-Grade Book Adaptation	12th-Grade/AP-Level Book Adaptation
Speed Dating. Students face each other in concentric circles with a piece of paper/prompt between them. Students discuss and then record ideas. Each circle rotates in a different direction (one clockwise, the other counterclockwise), leaving papers behind so the next pair will build on their ideas. (See Figure 5.5.)	Students are given quotes from the final chapters of *The Color Purple* (Walker, 2019 edition) describing characters' final decisions. For each quote, students debate whether the character made the "right" decision. Each rotation can agree or disagree with the group(s) before them.	As a homework assignment, students bring in their own quotes and thematic questions from the end of *There, There* (Orange, 2019). Students write quotes and questions on the top of a piece of looseleaf paper, thus making their own speed-dating prompts that can be used in class to analyze the end of the book. (This is recommended after students have participated in a speed-dating activity several times.)
Hexagonal Thinking. In groups of 3–6, students organize hexagons with character names, events, themes, symbols, and conflicts related to a book. There are no "right answers" in this activity; rather, the value is in students debating what goes where, creating a poster of their "hexagons," and presenting them to the class. The hexagonal shape allows students to indicate relationships between concepts. For example, if a theme is "morality," more-moral characters may be close to that hexagon, while more-immoral characters may be further away.	Students may be provided with prefilled hexagons and instructed to organize characters and events around 3–5 themes. For example, if reading *When I Was Puerto Rican* (Santiago, 2006), students may be given character and event names and themes such as identity, culture, confusion, and love. Then they debate in their groups which characters and events are most closely linked to each overall theme.	For advanced levels, students may create their own hexagons for a book. For example, for *The Woman Warrior* (Kingston, 1976), groups may fill their own set of 15–20 hexagons with characters, events, quotes, themes, conflicts, and symbols. At this higher level, students may be given free rein to create their own organizational systems, e.g., ideas in opposition, progression of events, evolution of a character, or others.

Dueling Discussions. The class is divided into two groups to have a student-led discussion of a reading. Students pick roles such as leader, timekeeper, and secretary. The secretary tracks who speaks and how many times they speak, allowing the teacher to "bounce" between two groups and support student discussion.	Students in the lower grades may be given structured discussion questions for homework the night before, coming to class with ideas and quotes preorganized. Both groups may discuss the same question, allowing the teacher to provide more guidance about where to find evidence to support answers. For example, in reading *Persepolis* (Satrapi, 2004), students may discuss their ideas about how living under an oppressive government affects its citizens.	In reading a book such as *Love in the Time of Cholera* (García Márquez, 2014 edition), older students may create their own questions around a broad theme (love, suffering, mortality) or each group may discuss a slightly different lens, coming together to synthesize their findings at the end of the class. For example, one group may discuss the significance of Florentina and Fermina's reunion at the end of the book, while the other analyzes the meaning of their ship being sentenced to exile.
Newspaper Analysis. Lens In groups of 3–4, students analyze a significant event from the book as if composing a newspaper. A type of jig-sawed groupwork, this activity asks students to analyze the event through a specific lens depending on their role. Students may be the editor, cartoonist, analyzer, or "straight news" reporter. Students discuss which details to include in each role and then present their finished "papers" to the class at the end.	In reading *I Know Why the Caged Bird Sings* (Angelou, 2009), students may report on Maya becoming the first Black, female streetcar conductor in San Francisco. Students may pick roles, or the teacher may assign them as students report on this historic event.	In reading *Americanah* (Adichie, 2014), students may report on Ifemelu's blog about Black identity in America. Students may be challenged by taking on various overall biases, for example, a newspaper writer from an African American perspective and one from the perspective of a recent African immigrant.

on their own work more consistently. Informal observations benefit us in other ways too. For example, we also can learn about a different "micro-culture" that may exist in another teacher's class or deepen our existing knowledge, while seeing how students engage with other teachers. If we stay in our own realms all of the time, we don't realize what other, and often better, ways exist to contemplate our curricula and refine our pedagogy (Pressick-Kilborn & te Riele, 2008).

Adjusting to Expectations and Behavioral Norms for Students

On a warm August day as I was setting up for my 12th year of teaching and my first year at my new school, the head of the English department asked if I needed anything laminated. So, I printed out some bright blue bathroom passes and asked him to have those done. He looked at me and laughed before explaining that teachers don't use passes, they just let students go to the bathroom—but I was welcome to use them if I wanted. As was my custom, I started with the bathroom pass, but within a few days it became clear that students did not want to carry them back and forth. Unlike my previous school, there were no safety officers walking the halls to ensure that students were not cutting classes. As I threw the passes into the garbage, it dawned on me that these were not the most hygienic things to make students use. I also began to realize the vast discrepancies between the level of freedom students in suburban and wealthier schools are given over urban students, who frequently are scanned and monitored much more (Young, 2017).

A few years later, walking through the cafeteria after students left after their lunch, I was shocked to see tables littered with food containers and floors covered in dirty napkins and empty water bottles. I watched as janitors pushed the trash off the tables onto the floors and created giant mounds that they'd eventually shovel into trash cans. I asked a colleague walking by, "Why is this allowed? Why aren't the students made to clean up their mess?" She replied, "It's like this every single day. It's just the culture of the school." I remembered seeing my first principal march students into the cafeteria and demand they pick up every scrap of trash. I also know that Japanese schoolchildren often are tasked with cleaning their entire schools, including the bathrooms, in efforts to minimize costs and maximize student self-sufficiency (Phillips, 2015). I couldn't help but think the culture of the school I'd moved to needed to shift. Interestingly, my current school is trying to address the issue by a committee called "reimagining the cafeteria," composed of both teachers and students, with the goal of promoting more community-minded, responsible behaviors in the lunchroom.

These shared examples of student expectations within schools are linked to the level of autonomy or "freedom" they're given and vary greatly from school to school. In cities, depending on the neighborhood, students often are allowed to go out for lunch. Some suburban schools permit students to walk or drive off campus or leave early if they have a free period at the end of the day. In addition, degrees of permissible clothing can vary significantly between schools. I've worked at schools that require students to put on baggy T-shirts that say "I love school" if they arrive wearing inappropriate attire, and at schools where both teachers and administrators are afraid to comment on improper outfits (such as curse words on T-shirts, or shorts revealing buttocks) in case parents become upset. Sarah's school culture, for example, is very opposed to the idea of a dress code as clothing is seen as a form of self-expression, an extension both of her school's performing arts focus and of its commitment to supporting a range of gender identities and expressions.

Another potentially problematic issue is the varying cell phone policies. Many schools and teachers have strict rules delineating in what circumstances cell phones are allowed and not allowed. For example, while a middle school might require students to leave their phones in their lockers or have a phone storage collection in the front of the classroom, some high schools allow students free access, including in class. At one school, I asked a student who kept using his cell phone in class to turn it over to me. He promptly stuffed it down his pants to prevent me from taking it. Flabbergasted, I wished the school had a clearer policy.

On (re)entering any school to work, it's important to find out what the rules and regulations are about these, and other, issues as they can greatly affect a teacher's everyday interactions in the classroom and around the school. Many teachers tend to choose foregrounding some rules more than others, and you'll likely have to ask yourself: Do all school rules carry the same weight? Or, are there ones that are important to you that should be emphasized, while others are less so? Equally important is to understand how your school handles behavioral challenges (Milner et al., 2018). For example, at one school, I could escort a student with excessively disruptive behavior to the principal's office any time of day. At another, there was daily detention proctored by a teacher. And at still another, there was no formal system, with teachers expected to handle almost all disciplinary issues themselves.

Collaborating With Parents

I (Fran) had just finished grading my 10th-grade essays on *Catcher in the Rye* (Salinger, 2001). As I was entering the scores into my high school's online grading system, my desk phone rang. Before I picked up, I knew who the caller would be. That year I had a polite young man whose mom had set the school's online grading system to alert her any time a grade below 90 was entered for her child. Years ago, when we switched over to an open digital gradebook, I decided to enter scores only *after* I'd returned the assignments to students. This was because I never want a student to wonder why they received a low score or have parents know grades before a student does. Picking up the phone, I explained to the concerned mother that her son had his essay with him, we'd gone over the returned assignments in class, and I'd be happy to discuss his areas of strengths and weaknesses as documented on the rubric. She started yelling, demanding that her son receive an A, telling me I had to let him rewrite his essay and that if I didn't, she would go to the principal. As she continued to shout, I used every ounce of my patience to stay calm. My colleague at the adjacent desk could overhear everything and said, "Hang up! She can't speak to you like that." It was only my second year at this school, and while I hated the idea of a parent complaining about me to the principal, I calmly asked her not to yell and told her I'd be happy to work more with her son, but that the grading had been fair, and that she was welcome to go to the principal about it. The next day when I spoke to her son again about his essay, he said he deserved the grade he'd received and apologized for his mother's behavior, commenting, "She's kind of intense."

There are forceful parents everywhere. As a mother myself, I can empathize. High school grades "count," and often it's difficult for a parent to not worry that every poor grade, missing assignment, or conceptual struggle is going to somehow impact college acceptances. Yet, the important thing to remember as a teacher is: *You can only control your own actions and reactions.* Making sure directions are clear, rubrics are explained, and extra help is offered, usually calms even the most anxious of parents. Also, the longer teachers teach, the more confident they grow in planning, assessing, and grading for when similar scenarios present themselves. For example, recently I had a parent of a student in my AP class email me that he had a colleague read his daughter's paper, in which she earned a grade of B+, and the colleague thought the paper should have gotten an A. Similarly, I calmly responded by talking about the grading rationale and offered to meet with his daughter to ensure she understood how to improve for the following assessment. The issue ended there, and his daughter earned an A on the next assignment. This vignette also illustrates the need to politely and firmly stand your ground if you are confident that your assessment is fair. Parents with greater resources possess "cultural capital" (Bourdieu, 1999) that they sometimes choose to invoke, meaning they understand how systems of power work and leverage them to get exactly what they want. As teachers, it's useful to recognize power moves without yielding to them—as that actually would be a disservice to the students in these examples, who'd think they'd achieved a higher standard than they'd actually accomplished.

On the other side, there are parents who, for many good reasons, may be hard to get in contact with or have come to visit the school. Just like teaching, parenting has its difficulties. For example, there are many single-parent homes with adults whose jobs leave them very little time to help their children academically or meet with their children's teachers. There are also parents who don't speak English and may be too inhibited to visit school, even feeling embarrassed at what they perceive as their own shortcomings. There are parents who, for whatever reasons, have strained relationships with their children that can impact school performance. I recently had one father who was at a total loss about what to do with his son, a smart young man, always engaged in class, but who would complete no work outside of school. At our meetings, my student's father would ask me what he should do about his son, who spent his time talking on his phone and playing video games instead of doing homework. Neither teachers nor parents are always prepared for the obstacles that arise before them, and both groups carry within them their own unique experiences as students and adolescents.

Ultimately, as we both have the interest of their child at heart, teachers should view parents as collaborators, asking ourselves: How can we work together to ensure that students are learning and growing academically, socially, and emotionally? There are moments in both teaching and parenting when, without tangible results to show for our efforts, the role can feel unsatisfactory. However, we know this is for the short term and, even in times of uncertainty, strive to build strong foundations that hopefully will support long-term success, even if we're not always there to witness it. In *Families With Power,* Cowhey (2022) suggests establishing help sessions for caregivers in multiple languages to assist them in understanding how to read report cards, get help for their child, assist with homework, understand standardized test scores, and schedule a teacher conference. Aiding all caregivers in getting and understanding pertinent information can help level the playing field for all students. Promoting open communication with parents, through initiating and maintaining the process, is crucial in cultivating them as partners. Once a relationship is established, communication in different venues (open school night, IEP meetings, community events) and via different means (emails, phone calls, check-ins with guidance counselors, and even talking to other teachers who share students) can be very beneficial in making sure the whole surrounding community seeks to help that student flourish.

Preparing for Tenure (Again!)

Teacher tenure exists in most states, despite historical and contemporary efforts to undermine or abolish it (Hess & Maranto, 2000). Achieving the status of tenure is usually an integral desire for most educators, serving to motivate us. Originating in universities, tenure is a time-honored tradition for educators that has been passed down over centuries. Providing job security for life, tenure allows teachers to have a very privileged position in society. Most states grant tenure to teachers who have served satisfactorily for a specified number of years. As pressure to hold teachers to higher standards has mounted over the past few decades, what once may have been a period of 3 years can now be 5 or more. Some districts, such as New York City, have begun to transition away from solely time-based tenure toward being more inclusive of merit-based criteria, combining both administrative observations and student performance. The reasoning behind this change is that teachers should be rewarded not only for persistence, but for creativity, pedagogical skills, and commitment to their profession. Overall, the tenure process is much more rigorous than it once was, with teachers now required to prepare for a minimum 5-year period, take additional classes in education, submit a portfolio, have a superintendent visit the classroom, and receive frequent official classroom observations from the principal.

Debates about the pros and cons of tenure remain ongoing. On one hand, teachers claim it protects them from arbitrary dismissal by an administrator with whom they may clash over professional issues, such as the curriculum's content, the most effective teaching methodologies to use, or personal reasons—such as having a different religious affiliation or sexual orientation. For example, there has been a history of LGBTQ+ teachers "outed" and fired (Graves, 2009), and it was only in 2020 that the Supreme Court ruled this practice was no longer legal (Higgins, 2020). Most recently, the Florida law named "Parental Rights in Education," better known in colloquial terms as "Don't Say Gay," includes the statement:

> Classroom instruction by school personnel or third parties on sexual orientation or gender identity may not occur in kindergarten through grade 3 or in a manner that is not age appropriate or developmentally appropriate for students in accordance with state standards. (lines 97–101)

In brief, while subject to interpretation, there is latitude here to omit any acknowledgment of sexual orientation throughout the entire curriculum, as to include it could result in disciplinary proceedings, including being fired. To state the obvious, tenured teachers do feel a greater sense of security and less anxiety about job loss (something that we recognize most of the workforce has to manage). They also feel they can advocate for students, ideas, and curricula that may not always be in line with principals and school boards. Given the rewarding yet challenging nature of our profession, many people believe the opportunity of tenure is an attraction for potential teachers in a field that already struggles with a 50% retention rate (Carver-Thomas & Darling-Hammond, 2017). On the other hand, teacher tenure often is linked to a growth in complacency, underperformance, unquestioned prioritization of seniority, and the expense of legal procedures when a tenured teacher is dismissed for valid reasons.

We have included the issue of tenure as, when we change districts or states, we "lose" the tenure we've earned and begin again in establishing ourselves and our reputation as being deserving of it. For example, when I moved from New York City, I lost my tenure, which felt very scary as it meant no longer being assured of job security. However, I also understood the district was taking a chance on me and I had to prove I was a good choice before they would grant me the privilege of tenure there. Luckily, some educational certifications do "travel" and are acceptable in other states. For example, as New York is considered to have one of the highest standards for teacher certification, mine transferred—even though tenure did not. In sum, it's important for teachers seeking to change states to find out whether state reciprocity of certification exists.

Tenure in the suburbs is different than it is in NYC and differs again among neighboring districts. For example, in my first suburban district, the tenure process took 4 years, requiring a few classroom observations and one visit by the assistant superintendent. In contrast, in a neighboring district, teachers have to effectively teach an entire unit of study to get tenure. That means the head of the department visits every day to observe for the duration of the unit. Then, every 4 years, teachers are observed teaching another unit to evaluate whether they've maintained or enhanced their own standard. Although an intense process, teachers are provided with the opportunity to reflect deeply on their practice, and the district has maintained high standards expected from committed educators. That said, we are mindful that in less diverse schools, educators have to push for more diversity in texts and content, as not everyone sees what is missing in the curriculum. There's also a benefit to be had in acclimating to students' cultures and languages—including the histories of students' culture, as well as ways in which teachers can center students and their families within the overall school culture. Recently, for example, the state of Connecticut introduced a required high school course in Black and Latino studies (Léon, 2021).

CONSIDERATIONS AND IMPLICATIONS FOR EMBRACING DIVERSITY IN YOUR NEW POSITION

This chapter is somewhat different from others in the book, as we have focused upon newly hired experienced educators gaining an awareness of individual school cultures, and how to understand and adapt to them, with the goal of being comfortable in a work environment that allows them to teach to the best of their ability. At the same time, as this book's primary interest is to support teachers in embracing diversity, it is important to consider some implications for everyday practices when changing schools. As we've mentioned, making the transition to a new school is exciting, as teachers have accrued experience, built confidence, and made the choice to move. At the same time, starting over also can make a teacher feel vulnerable in many ways, including how their commitment to diversity may be perceived and received at their new school. In this section, we discuss some considerations in relation to the areas previously addressed in this chapter.

In terms of adapting to administrators, it is always preferable that teachers new to the school do their homework by researching as much as they can about the school before they even visit—via official means such as the school's webpage, mission statement, and report card, as well as less formal means if possible, such as talking to teachers in the school about the general environment and specific aspects of their work. The interview process itself is usually layered, offering opportunities for the teacher who is applying for a job to share curricula they've developed and lessons they've planned, discuss an interest in actively supporting diversity, as well as have questions prepared. It is useful to see the interview as an interchange in which teaching philosophies, experiences, and goals can be discussed. This interchange allows the administrator and colleagues to gauge whether the school will be a good fit for the potentially future teacher and, conversely, for the teacher to judge whether they'll be a good fit for the school. Asking about the curriculum, what texts usually are used, and the degree of flexibility in incorporating others, can yield valuable insight into how much potential "say" a teacher may have in decisions about what they teach.

Customarily, at least one potential colleague is part of the application process, and similar questions can be asked by the teacher candidate about the existing curriculum and classroom practices, such as typical types of pedagogies and assessment methods used. The more a teacher candidate can discover about the school culture, departmental expectations, and future colleagues, the better prepared they are to make an informed decision as they strive for a "win-win" situation. To state the obvious, another indicator of a school's commitment to diversity is the degree to which diversity is reflected in its own faculty.

Once at the school, the newly hired teacher usually is focused on teaching, getting into—and through—the rhythm of the year. In a very practical sense, a newly hired teacher's primary goal is to "find their footing" by simply doing a good job, letting the work speak for itself, and becoming integrated into the school culture. As that gradually happens over the cycle of the first school year, the teacher gains a strong sense of the existing curriculum and likely feels more comfortable to make suggestions for changes, if needed, and to take calculated risks in incorporating multiple voices and juxtaposing perspectives. We have found that relationships with colleagues are somewhat organic—grown from conversations across time in department conferences, over lunch, at grade-level or content meetings, during extracurricular school activities, and in other social spaces. Newly hired teachers can ascertain which colleagues already support diversity-themed issues and who would be likely to support potentially proposed changes in the curriculum, commit to some changes in texts, be open to focusing on methods centering diversity and to discussing issues such as culturally responsive pedagogy. Depending upon the structure of the school, with time (and arguably, tenure), recently hired teachers can elect to be on curriculum committees or to be grade-level team leaders, where they can support colleagues in healthy, respectful conversations about what is taught, why it's taught, and how it's taught in ELA and interdisciplinary classes.

If disagreements arise among school board members, parents, or students about what texts are used and topics taught, well-informed teachers supportive of centering diversity can engage in conversations with individuals or groups at parent/teacher association meetings and school board gatherings, as well as in classes, culling from a large body of research that supports proactively teaching diversity and the benefits it brings to all groups (Banks, 2018; Cuauhtin et al., 2019; Gay, 2018; Nieto & Bode, 2017; Sleeter, 2020).

Finally, we know that untenured teachers are potentially vulnerable and we recognize that this vulnerability can influence many decisions, including when and how to address issues of diversity in schools, classrooms, and curricula. Many untenured teachers find themselves forced to bite their tongue, "choosing their battles" and eschewing risks. Others feel an obligation to speak up in the moment, to illustrate examples of inequity and advocate for immediate change. All three authors having been in those situations, it is not for us to judge but rather to acknowledge the right of individuals to respond in the moment as they see fit. On one hand, there is the analogy of instructions by flight attendants, telling adults that in the event of an emergency to put on their own oxygen mask before tending to their children. Tenure can be seen as that oxygen mask, once secured, providing the opportunity to take care of others in need. If it's not secured, then the job—and potential years helping others—could be lost. However, we also see the immediacy, even urgency, to speak up in preventing unfair practices, systems, and structures from prevailing. And if speaking up is done respectfully, purposefully, and persuasively, the process itself is educational, and practices can be critiqued with a view to improving them.

Finally, and on a positive note, there are many things that can be done to prepare for going up for tenure in a new environment. These include knowing specific requirements of state certification for permanent licensing and documenting proficiency in instruction via formal observations required over a period of time. Additionally, there are informal things a teacher can do, such as having an "open door" policy during their untenured time and inviting colleagues into their classes to see students make presentations, share creative work, or hold a compelling debate, along with evidence in the form of student artifacts. Of course, the ideal situation is that a teacher is a good "fit" for the school, and the school is also a good "fit" for the teacher.

SUMMARY

There are almost 100,000 elementary and secondary schools in the United States (Bouchrica, 2020), and each one is run in a different manner. During the course of their careers, teachers change schools and must adapt to different school cultures. Such a big change is both exciting and challenging, as newly hired teachers must negotiate their place in an unfamiliar professional/community network of administrators, other teachers, parents, and students. Coming to know a new school environment also provides opportunities to continue and deepen a commitment to embracing diversity. At the same time, an adjustment to the new school's ways, norms, and expectations must be made too, including evaluating the important role that tenure plays in building confidence to support a diversity-centric curriculum.

QUESTIONS FOR FURTHER REFLECTION

1. In moving to a new class/school/district/state/country, we recommend teachers ask themselves: (a) What assumptions do I have about this school? How are these assumptions forged from my own schooling experiences and/or my previous teaching experiences? (b) How do I need to change to be successful here? (c) What do I already know and feel confident in that I can use here? (d) Who are my best resources to guide my development? (e) How can I plan ahead and stay on top of my work to ensure I don't become overwhelmed by these changes?
2. When searching for a new school, what are some additional sources you can research in addition to our suggestions? For example, how can the school's mission statement or news articles inform you?
3. In evaluating a potentially new school where you could teach (realistically or hypothetically), assess by multiple means how it compares with your current site in terms of generally centering and supporting diversity. Is it better, about the same, or undeveloped? How can you tell, using evidence? In what ways might such a comparison influence your decision about where to move?

CHAPTER 7

Considering What the Pandemic Has Taught Us About Teaching

Several years ago, when I (David) was chairperson of the Special Education Department at Hunter College, a male graduate student with a learning disability came to my office at the end of a long day, panic-stricken. He'd just had his first class of the semester.

"Why are you so upset?" I asked.

"I dated the professor," he replied. "I met her on Irishsingles.com."

"Wow," I replied. "I've never had to deal with a situation like that before." I was truly unsure of what to do. "It'll probably be fine. Let me get back to you tomorrow; I need some time to think." (I realize my initial few words were wrong. My only excuse was that our exchange happened after 9 P.M. when I was frazzled and trying to leave the office.)

Overnight, the situation didn't leave my mind. By morning I'd pondered "worst-case scenarios," including coercion, blackmail, disagreements about grades, or potentially embarrassing disclosures in either direction. I figured the easiest thing would be to change the student to another section. On opening my emails early the next morning, I received a message from the instructor saying, "I'm not comfortable with this situation. He can't be in my class. Please don't let him know that I wrote to you." This verified my plan of action. However, soon after I called the student in and explained to him that it was better for everyone if he simply changed sections, I received an email from him, copied to the College president, provost, and dean, about being treated poorly. What I recall the most about the exchange was that all of the other sections of that class were online. He wrote (I'm paraphrasing here), "With my learning disability, I cannot handle all of the technological demands. It makes me anxious. I don't learn well that way." This did elicit my sympathy, and I wished he'd told me about it before copying everyone in the higher echelons of our institution. I now had no other option than to ask the chairperson from another department, who oversaw that course, to change the instructor. This request did not go over well. It led to an experienced adjunct being immediately let go, while scrambling for a new instructor (as it turned out, less qualified and less popular, resulting in many student complaints). However, despite these repercussions, I knew I had to defend the student's rights. I share this tangled little tale to highlight that there are many anxious learners who are not comfortable, confident, or skilled in technology, and fear that learning via an online format won't allow them to fully demonstrate their knowledge and skills.

In another example, this time considering the teacher's point of view, I had a colleague who'd had a sterling career of over 40 years as a teacher, principal, and professor in teacher education. But when the COVID-19 pandemic hit that spring semester, and all classes abruptly shifted to online, he was lost. My colleague struggled with setting up his classes on Blackboard, and coordinating and operating Zoom, and—resigned to failure in setting up virtual class dynamics—his frustration got the better of him. The professor ended up simply posting assignments and readings for students to complete, without any live interaction. Student evaluations of the course reflected dissatisfaction with their disjointed, solitary experiences. He quit, saying he could see that online learning was the foreseeable future and it wasn't for him.

We've included these perspectives to recognize that there are both teachers and students who may have reservations about—and may even resist—teaching and learning online. Interestingly, K–12 online learning in the United States is not new; it has been around for over 30 years (Barbour, 2021). However, what the COVID-19 pandemic did was to abruptly foreground online learning in the national dialogue about education in ways it had never been before. In efforts to avoid transmitting the virus in brick-and-mortar schools, a range of tech industry associations, vendor corporations, venture capitalists, and philanthropists, all with a history of promoting virtual education for years, became prominent players in this brave new world. Undoubtedly, many of the new technologies did help teachers to remain connected to their students (Selwyn, 2020). That said, as Molnar and Boninger (2021) write, "the nation's experience with virtual technologies during the pandemic also revealed fundamental limitations of these new approaches and spotted serious problems with the rosy vision of a bright new virtual future" (p. 3). For example, district Internet connections were disrupted by hackers, classes were Zoom-bombed by malicious strangers, students' data were held for ransom, and general struggles occurred for all parties—students, teachers, and parents—to adapt to technologies required for virtual education. The digital divide of who had access to technology, and who did not, became very apparent.

WHY CONSIDERING WHAT THE PANDEMIC HAS TAUGHT US ABOUT TEACHING MATTERS

Interestingly, full-time virtual schools have been around since the 1990s (Greenway & Vanourek, 2022). Historically, they have yielded poor outcomes.

For example, in comparison to national statistics of 85% graduation rates for traditional schools, virtual schools graduate 54.6% of their population, with blended schools doing better at 64.3% (Molnar & Boninger, 2021). Alarmingly, there was little research on successful K–12 virtual school practices to guide policymakers when faced with how best to respond to the COVID-19 pandemic, and, arguably, evidence to date did not justify their expansion (Molnar, 2021). In sum, online learning—despite the paucity of knowledge about it—has grown so exponentially that it has outpaced the research about it. Where, then, does that leave us in trying to figure out the best ways to teach—including balancing in-person, hybrid, and fully online instruction, during this period of time?

From our current perspective, it strikes us that in a post-pandemic world, teaching likely will never be quite the same again. In this chapter, we share what we have experienced, observed, and learned about teaching online, offering thoughts and suggestions about effective ways to engage students within diversity-centered approaches to education. We illustrate what we perceive as some potential benefits of online teaching and caution about some of its drawbacks. Ultimately, we are guided by seeking ways that ensure students in all classes are heard, connected to their peers, and provided opportunities to engage with a rich array of texts to share their thoughts in multiple formats.

Experiencing the Abrupt Shift

In Fran's case, she had never used any form of online teaching until the spring of 2020. She'd taken some online graduate-level courses and recalled being dissatisfied with the lack of student interaction as a result of the instructors' didactic and unimaginative style. While proficient in Google Classroom and other online platforms for posting assignments and collecting work, she'd had no experience teaching live online classes herself. When her high school went virtual in Spring 2020, it came with a directive that teachers were not allowed to teach live classes. During the subsequent year, a hybrid program was developed, with 45% of her daily schedule teaching at school and the balance at home. In other words, half of the students came to school Mondays and Tuesdays, and the other half Thursdays and Fridays, with a fully remote day of instruction on Wednesdays. Depending on various factors, some students had the option of being fully remote all year, and chose to be. School administration required teachers to interact with the students both at home and in the classroom, and have students interact with one another.

On Sarah's part, she had done a unit with an online message board discussion with students and used Google Classroom intermittently, but had never taught or taken a class fully online. Of course, the lack of interaction and inability to touch base with students in person was a struggle, not to mention the general stress and fear that came with the initial wave of the pandemic. However, as a teacher who loves the unit-planning, worksheet-making, discussion-prompt-creating aspects of the profession, Sarah found this shift to a text-based medium in some ways an invigorating challenge. After many years doing many variations on the same activities in class, she had to rethink how to engage students. The task was not easy, but it did inspire a new infusion of creativity and innovation that Sarah had not had to turn to in years.

David historically had resisted teaching graduate courses online for years, preferring the energy generated within dynamic in-person classrooms. There is something stimulating about the spontaneous aspects of teaching, reading student body language and processing students' comments as they engage with the material. His university had always encouraged faculty to teach online as it saves much-needed space and provides different formatting options for students and instructors. However, a couple of years before formally retiring, David purposefully experimented with teaching (a) in hybrid format (every other week), and (b) an online class with an in-person meeting at the start and end of the semester. Surprised at how much he enjoyed teaching in this novel manner, he was pleased that an online option would allow him to continue teaching in retirement—from any part of the world. So, when the COVID-19 pandemic began, unlike many colleagues teaching in higher education, he'd had a head start. Self-described as "low intermediate level in technology," David recognizes he can do what's needed but isn't inclined to take many risks as technology can feel like an additional layer of things to plan for, check, and manage. He discovered that most students are usually fine, often likely to have more technological skills than their instructor, reminding us of how technology has outpaced educational change.

By fall semester in the first year of the pandemic, reactions across the country varied enormously as to what were the best ways to respond, influenced by national, state, and local politics; school board governance; and shifts in scientific-based recommendations. Fran was given almost 2 weeks to prepare for all students to come back into the building. Along with her colleagues, she was very nervous and didn't think teaching live would last through Halloween, with COVID-19 transmissions a major fear. She spent the first week in her office trying to figure out the complicated camera and microphone system that the district had purchased over the summer. After many tests, Fran and her colleagues realized that students at home could hear the teachers, students in class could hear their peers at home, but students at home could not hear their counterparts in the classroom. Eventually, teachers discovered and purchased, out of pocket, $50-a-piece "snowball mics" to replace the expensive ones the district had purchased, allowing conversations between students at home and students in the classroom.

Sarah's experiences were different from Fran's, largely because the New York City teachers' union fought, with mixed results, for teachers to avoid a simultaneous in-person and online teaching scenario. While spared from what she describes as "the impossible task" of teaching both modes simultaneously, the necessity for balancing remote cohorts and smaller class sizes, to ensure social distancing, created a complicated hybrid schedule. Students attended either an in person or remote class twice a week and then completed asynchronous assignments the other 3 days. This, of course, resulted in less actual teaching and fewer units "covered" over the course of the year. Plus, the situation meant Sarah had to prioritize the skills and assessments that *really* mattered for students to be college-ready, cutting any "filler" from the curriculum. She figured out what work students could navigate independently, and for what work they needed direct instruction or coaching. Moreover, her seniors got to experience a schedule that was more like college—taking classes a few days a week, self-managing time to complete self-paced assignments, and working on summative tasks.

As can be seen, developments in virtual instruction for teachers occurred abruptly, with very limited time to plan. Much of finding out "what works" in practice has occurred via trial and error, with teachers both following the lead of their institutions and also figuring out some options themselves to best manage their classes in new ways. For example, Fran notes that she tried a variety of modes for holding debates and for students to do group-work or interact with one another until she found some that worked best (i.e., breakout rooms vs. shared documents vs. Jamboard vs. avatars). She also found this time to be a wonderful opportunity for sharing among colleagues, with bonds created among teachers who constantly were sharing new tech hacks they came up with. While most of the teaching force is now back in the classroom, we acknowledge that various systems to support online learning are now in place, should another national crisis occur. In the next section, we examine some of the benefits we've found that online teaching offers, as well as noting some of the cautions for teachers to consider.

SOME BENEFITS OF ONLINE TEACHING

While we have recognized the limited research base on online learning and the emergency situation that triggered its widespread use, we also realize that online learning is likely here to stay, and ELA teachers have continued to integrate technology into their in-person classes. Having all taught online courses, we also know that this pedagogical format, when crafted well, can have a positive impact on teachers and students. Here, we share some of our observations and thoughts about what it potentially can offer.

Shifting Priorities in Practices

The pandemic made us think, as teachers, about what is really important within our practices. One of the things we have all experienced is our becoming more flexible in general. This includes changing deadlines along with moving, modifying, or cutting assignments. Identifying priorities also can mean reverting to practices that are "tried and true." For Sarah, this includes utilizing the framework of Understanding by Design (Wiggins & McTighe, 2005) to create a big assessment, such as a research paper or culminating presentation, that reveals the degree of mastery students have accomplished. Using backward planning, she determines what knowledge students will come to have and what skills they will possess. Instead of the day in, day out idea of work, she now recognizes that if the two big projects of the semester are done well and mastery of X, Y, and Z is demonstrated, then students will pass the class. This approach once would have bothered her, causing an ethical dilemma: What should be done about a student who didn't do all of their homework but would pass a final assessment? However, Sarah now sees the value in the overall processes around completing the larger task and subsequently designs more, smaller assignments that are essential to finish the overall assignment. In other words, she asks herself: What will be more of an authentic assessment and how can I reduce anything resembling "busy work"?

Increasing Opportunities for Working One-on-One

Something David noticed immediately when teaching online classes is that they hold possibilities of equalizing student voice. In traditional in-person classes, there's a pattern that often goes like this: Three to five students dominate whole-class discussions, with the remaining students divided equally among those who participate periodically and those who rarely participate or don't participate at all. However, when responses are required in print, all students participate in similar ways. Whether it's in the format of a public discussion board or a private journal entry, all students have equal access to the instructor, and all instructors have equal access to all students. This means that teachers can form and maintain personal connections with all students, gaining a better understanding of who they are, what they know, what they think, and what they may need. A solid teacher–student relationship can make all the difference in a student's educational success (Bernstein-Yamashiro & Noam, 2013). Conferencing with individuals via Zoom for a variety of reasons, from simply a teacher's request to "check in" about a student's well-being to a student's request for discussing instructions for an assignment in depth, lets students know that teachers are supportive and care about them. In addition, the ability to share a document—such as an essay analyzing literature or creative writing—and work on it together "live" helps focus students on important tasks and assignments.

Self-Managing Skills for Students

The availability of remote teaching may forever end snow days or injured or sick students from having to miss classes. In other words, students arguably have an increased amount of self-accountability when learning takes place at home. One aspect of the pandemic is that, in contrast to the graduate student in the opening vignette, we have seen students thrive with online learning. They adapt quickly to utilizing technology, managing time, and mapping out their work weeks. In many ways, these executive functioning skills serve as a preview to college life, as a significant number of students struggle during their first year of transitioning into being independent learners (Clark, 2005).

Increasing Proficiency With Technology

Admittedly, some teachers' technological skills were underdeveloped prior to the pandemic, with the need for remote instruction driving them to become more adept. Those newly acquired skills have now been further developed, with teachers feeling more confident in making informed decisions about when, how, and why to utilize technology. What comes as a revelation to many in-person teachers when they transition into using technology is that everything that is done in a traditional classroom has a technical equivalent in an online and a hybrid environment, from individuals raising their hands to working in groups, from making presentations to the whole class to submitting homework and papers (Nilson, 2021; Pass, 2021). However, as we mention elsewhere, teaching often can feel more two-dimensional than three-dimensional, and new logistical challenges are posed such as "reading the room" and managing often-unseen students whose engagement may be partial at best.

Bringing Diverse Speakers Into Virtual Classrooms

Teachers had been inviting guests to classes via platforms such Skype for a while before the rise of Zoom and the popularity of Google Hangout helped transform virtual appearances into a new norm. In brief, during the pandemic, being a guest in another person's classroom became more commonplace. Schools began to use speakers from afar. For example, Fran's high school invited James McBride to speak to students about his texts such as *The Color of Water: A Black Man's Tribute to His White Mother* (1995) and *Deacon King Kong* (2021), taking advantage of how the new norm of virtual connections makes many authors more accessible. At the college level, David was invited to present on intersectional issues of race and disability in teacher education and doctoral programs at New York University and the University of Miami, illustrating how peers potentially can be used to present in colleagues' classes, including at the high school level. From elementary schools through high school and beyond, multiple authors and speakers have shared information remotely. If it were not for the technology that facilitates hearing different voices and perspectives, many of these visits would never occur due to distance and related costs.

Organizing the Practice of Teaching

Teaching sometimes can feel sprawling, messy, boundless—hence the need for lesson plans, materials, assessments, and so on. In theory, teaching can be "tidier" when using technology, as everything is in one place. Moreover, a class webpage or Google Classroom serves as a hub for all information needed by students, can be updated when necessary, and remains a permanent record for the duration of the semester. Virtual classes also are not restricted to the 8:00 A.M.–3:00 P.M. of traditional schooling, with class websites allowing students access 24/7, compatible with various bio-rhythms, schedules, and miscellaneous other obligations. Moreover, homework that is submitted electronically can be located in a specific place, with a time stamp, and can be returned the same way—keeping track automatically.

Likewise, teachers have the ability to view the progress of almost any student work on an assignment. For example, teacher and student can open an essay in progress and conference over a video meeting, making edits and additions in real time. If students have to revise a paper, teachers can see on the final draft the revisions made. Or, if a student says they're "almost done" with a paper, teachers can check their actual progress, as well as have tools to scan for plagiarism (unfortunately, a reality in both high school and university settings). When it comes to planning, teachers have the opportunity to set up their classes in advance. And while we know the meticulous planning that is necessary can sometimes feel like a treadmill, it also demands of us a level of organization that is good to model.

Saving One of the Most Precious of Commodities—Time

For every teacher we know, there's never enough time to always get everything "right," and we all wish we had more of it! From a practical standpoint, teaching online *can* save time. If we cut out round-trip travel for every teacher and all of their students, those hours and minutes can amount to time self-reassigned for planning, assessing, researching, and locating materials. Sarah, for example, found that she finally was able to spend the professional time needed with her collaborative teacher to ensure that all students with disabilities were fully supported in their class. With a lighter live-teaching schedule due to hybrid learning, she had time to meet individually with students, using Google Meet and Docs to look at writing in progress and conference with students in a genuine way she had never been able to do while hastily looking over a shoulder at a notebook in class. All that said, we are mindful that for some teachers, using unfamiliar or nonintuitive technology also can *add* time.

SOME CAUTIONS ABOUT ONLINE TEACHING

In many ways, while online teaching opens new doors for teaching and possibilities for learning, there are some aspects of it that make us cautious, and we must recognize the valuable common-sense approach of not putting "all of our eggs in one basket." In this section, we consider a few cautions that we believe teachers who are required to develop online or hybrid classes should bear in mind as they move forward, and, where possible, we suggest what can be done.

Acknowledging an Over-Digitalized World

The term "over-digitalized world" is admittedly a subjective assessment. As ELA teachers and based on their own experiences growing up, Fran and Sarah love to read from actual books versus digital counterparts. Studies have shown mixed results about whether digital reading allows the same level of retention as reading a physical book (A. K. Taylor, 2011; Yienger, 2016). However, having contact with an actual paper text and using a pencil to mark it up—making connections, asking questions, noting what to look up, and having the ability to turn back, reread, look for notes—all help create a form of physical relationship with the book. While electronic equivalents exist to highlight and insert notes, we argue that it's not quite the same for book lovers and encourage at least giving students the options of using a physical or digital text. After all, the physical format is the one that most books were originally published in and most writers envisioned their work as.

We also have observed that many teachers make not only texts, but *everything*—activities, worksheets, and assignments—digital. We suggest a compromise in which paper copies are not abandoned altogether. It's always good to give students a choice of format, as some may process and retain information in one way better than another, especially students who have various learning challenges (Bains, 2008). As most readers will know, when it comes to planning a large project or revising a lot of information for an exam, it's useful to have physical notes (sometimes transferred to sticky notes) that can be manipulated for different reasons, for example, to prioritize concepts studied, to make connections, to cluster ideas, and so on (Lagares & Connor, 2009). When everything is digital, we also may inadvertently run the risk of slipping into a mechanistic form of teaching in which even the best of assignments may seem like a list of tasks with subcomponents to be "checked off." We recall that some of the first student responses to working at home in the pandemic, self-posted on YouTube, were very painful to watch. Teenagers who were already stressed by the unprecedented mass deaths and shutting down of the world as they knew it, were then besieged by excessive amounts of work requested by their teachers.

On their part, educators were well-intended, thinking their actions were responsible and well-purposed. However, colleagues had neglected to coordinate among themselves as to the type and amount of work being requested of students. This oversight resulted in students who were already upset and scared, now feeling overwhelmed and depressed, pedaling as fast as they could to plow through a deluge of work, many with little feedback or support. Several students appeared to be at a breaking point, pleading with teachers to understand their position, coordinate better, and give them manageable workloads. Since then, these feelings have been documented by research that discusses both the individual and collective trauma experienced by students (Margolius et al., 2020). Thankfully, in the push-and-pull of getting it right, teachers began to better understand students' realities and concerns, and adapted their work accordingly—while still feeling pressure from their own local education authorities to maintain rigorous standards, prepare for mandated examinations, and maintain school rankings. With the passage of time, many of these initial issues have been ironed out, but with so many things to do and largely self-managing the tasks, students can still become either overwhelmed or obsessed in clearing their "to do" lists. We therefore need to be cautious that schools don't appear to students to be primarily about compliance rather than authentic engagement.

In many ways it can be argued that the pandemic heightened our already tech-obsessed world. Every morning, Fran notes, she comes into a classroom full of students using their cell phones. This situation reflects the norm of what we usually see entering a bus or subway car, bar or restaurant. And while it is now the norm, nonetheless it strikes us as strange that everyone together in a space is electing to be in their own world. Multitasking via technology is also part of these norms. Once class is underway, it's Fran's practice to walk behind students so she can see their laptop screens. When doing so, she's always aware of a few students who have 10 plus tabs open, skilled in their ability to quickly flip to the "correct" one as she passes by. While we're compelled to mention this issue, as we are concerned about the impact of multitasking on a learner's focus, we realize it merits more attention than we can give it here.

Being Mindful of Inequities in Technology

One of the things the pandemic has highlighted is the technological divide, which has existed since the inception of technology. The gaps in earning in the United States mean that it is one of the most economically stratified nations in the developed world (Jacobs & Dirlam, 2016). Economic inequities impact districts, teachers, students, and their families. For example, some districts may operate under the assumption that all students have their own personal computer equipment (or at least can use their parents' or household's), have access to Wi-Fi and a stable Internet connection, and can be provided a designated place to study and complete their work. When we say schools are based on largely middle-class, White norms, these are examples. Yet, for working-class, poor, and homeless children, these assumed basics for participating in instruction are not "givens." There may be homes without a secure Internet connection, equipment to borrow, or a private space. Incidentally, the same must be said at the college level. For example, when learning shifted online, the City University of New York had to develop a program that allowed students to borrow a laptop for the long term, as—despite being in college—many of them could not afford their own.

Online etiquette was another area that developed, influenced by the fast-paced rollout that yielded surprises. For example, appropriate clothing became an issue, as students showed up in pajamas or shirtless. In some cases, punctuality wasn't as good as it was during in-person classes, even though students didn't have to travel! Learning spaces weren't always private, sometimes with parents passing behind, photo-bombing the class. Moreover, seeing inside every student's home often revealed discrepancies in habitats that might cause some students embarrassment and others criticism or ridicule. All in all, it appeared as if the teaching and learning weren't being respected or understood with quite the same gravitas as they would be in physical space, a trope that has existed for a while (Shah, 2016). Shifts occurred across districts in managing online learning that solved some of these immediate problems, while seeming to create others. For example, in some districts students were no longer required to turn on their camera, ensuring a self-selected right to privacy, leaving teachers in a surreal situation teaching to a screen without seeing actual students. In others, students had to be on camera to receive a grade for attendance.

All three authors noticed how, in online classes, students often were trying to focus and engage in class but sometimes were distracted by younger siblings seeking attention or, in the case of graduate students, their own children. Pets frequently made surprise appearances. For instructors, there was an acceptance of a new form of flexibility, recognizing that students were equally challenged and frustrated at times, juggling many obligations, and struggling to stay positive in a frightening world. At the same time, we knew that for some students, particularly those who struggled with self-management, focus, and/or executive functioning skills, this learning situation might feel like an uphill obstacle course.

In addition to limited access to technology and designated instructional spaces in some homes, school districts vary enormously in budgets they are assigned and the expenditures that they're willing to make on technology. Teachers sometimes can feel the pressure of working with technology that is limited or not sufficiently up-to-date. In order for technology to enable us to do many teaching-related tasks well and efficiently, it also needs to be installed, checked, maintained, cared for, fixed, updated, and replaced. We all know that sinking feeling when we're about to teach or present and our technology falters. This has led us to always keep a form of backup records, including both digital and pencil-and-paper options.

Missing Physical Proximity to Students

As noted in this chapter, despite some initial reservations and anxieties, we have all adapted successfully to teaching online and truly can see the value in it. At the same time, we also know that "live" teaching in-person is what energizes us as teachers. While the convenience of staying at home admittedly has multiple attractions, we also must be mindful of the social and emotional realms of learning that appear to have been significantly impacted for many students (Osofsky et al., 2020). The sharing of physical spaces in which to engage in in-person dynamics is missed by most students, who need to physically be with people to become intellectually stimulated, to learn better, to feel connected, and to have a sense of belonging. In contrast, some students have thrived in an online environment, particularly those with anxiety and, we suspect, those who endured bullying in school. The issues of isolation and alienation that had been acknowledged by our culture before the pandemic (London & Ingram, 2018) have now been exacerbated in ways we are yet to fully discover. Writing in *Education Week*, Sparks (2021) discusses a survey distributed to high school students about their mental health, noting how certain disparities were highlighted:

> A wide majority of all students reported they are experiencing more problems now than they did in January 2020, before the pandemic began, but 77 percent of Black and Latinx students reported more struggles, at least 9 percentage points higher than the percentage of white or Asian students who said the same. Low-income and LGBTQ students were also significantly more likely to report experiencing more problems in the wake of the pandemic. (para. 9)

Even at the college level, David's students craved to be back in physical classes rather than taking classes online, believing their graduate experience during the pandemic has been isolating and two-dimensional. In a vote put to the class, over two-thirds of students elected to come to college. Of course, this raises the dilemma of preferred formats. In some cases, teachers were asked to teach both online and in-person classes, creating more work and longer days, until fairer practices became established, often at the instigation of the teachers' union (Gerber, 2020).

Finally, there's something to be said about "proximity control," meaning the closer a teacher is physically to their students, the more likely students are to respond to requests, follow directions, and engage with the work at hand (Weaver et al., 2020). There's definitely something to be said for having an in-person connection, mutual recognition, and respect. Looking out over a classroom full of students, teachers develop exceptional skills in reading and interpreting body language, which helps them understand students and plan their responses accordingly. There's a "live" element of teaching that can't be underestimated, part teacher-performer, part student-audience, forging a tangible connection that is very much "in the moment." Those tangible connections are special and unique. They transition into sustained teacher–student relationships that are integral to the teaching–learning process. Such interchanges sometimes feel tempered in online forums by a technological barrier between teacher and students, rather than the openness of an actual classroom environment. Fran noticed that with a hybrid format, students physically in the room participated more, and it was easier to troubleshoot with them. The technological barrier, Sarah also has found, makes it easier for some students to drift away, and even withdraw. Understandably, when students don't come to class, don't do any work, and don't respond to emails and calls, it leads to feelings of frustration. At times like this, having a student physically present means Sarah can sit down and talk with them face to face, with a much greater likelihood of achieving a needed intervention.

SELECTED PRACTICES

In this section, we describe several practices we've found that worked. We offer these as examples of how to think, or what to do, in terms of approaching online learning. We're also mindful that each teacher will develop their own ways of connecting with, engaging, and assessing students online. That said, these suggestions can be a springboard for more extensive conversations around this topic.

Ensuring Joy, Care, and Love

We begin by focusing upon three areas that we hold crucial to maintaining a healthy classroom—joy, care, and love. Overwhelmingly, we have found that educational literature at the high school level is dedicated largely to curricula, standards, skill sets, desired outcomes, examination preparation, and college readiness. Educational practices have always been tied to social efficiency, with schools designed on a factory model in which the "raw material" of the populace becomes transformed into the product of desirable citizens (Mondale, 2002). This model also means that a number of students who drop out—or are pushed out—don't receive the quality stamp of completion in the form of a high school diploma (Bridgeland et al., 2006). Unless teachers are critical and reflective, they inadvertently can become a bureaucratic cog in the wheels of production, spinning like a hamster in a wheel to "cover the curriculum," often duplicating restrictive knowledge that preserves the status quo. They also can lose sight of the importance of factoring in the creation of opportunities to experience *joy* within classrooms. A classroom filled with happiness, while not possible at all times, is worth striving for, as it cultivates connections with students who receive pleasure in learning.

Both Sonia Nieto (2013) and Gholdy Muhammad (2020) include the core concept of joy in their teaching and writing—including centering culturally responsive and socially just practices, and helping youth to see the joy in themselves and others. The pandemic made Sarah think a lot about how to consciously remember to teach in ways that acknowledge, and make room for, joy. She is therefore more mindful of ways in which to balance joy in class with the "realness" of the world, especially for students of color, realizing that false optimism can deflect social and historical realities. This stance of "keeping it real" is rooted in a sense of caring. Nel Noddings's (2013a, 2013b) work also speaks to the central grounding principle of caring in the work of professionals. When applied to education, it can be seen in the form of having an authentic connection with students over a period of time, a willingness to change and adapt to their needs, and supporting them toward their goals. Noddings's (2005) work acknowledged the emotional connection between teachers and students as being a powerful force in learning, rather than an impairment of professional discourse of detachment. Finally, perhaps no other educational writer spoke more clearly, passionately, and powerfully about how to authentically connect with students than bell hooks. In addition to seeing teaching as a form of transgression (2014), she never equivocated in claiming that love was at the center of her work as a teacher and writer (2001). The elements of joy, care, and love can be seen as a philosophy that informs a teacher's disposition to know the children they teach (Love, 2019). In practical terms, such a disposition can see the brilliance in students, rejects deficit-based understandings of individuals, seeks authentic connections, and enjoys being with students. In sum, these very elements that strengthen student–teacher connections, while ideally needed all of the time, have been particularly pertinent to teaching online during the pandemic.

Including Social Issues

Whereas we consciously have focused on centering diversity in all previous chapters, this one has been dedicated specifically to the "whys" and "hows" of teaching in a pandemic, while considering the benefits and challenges of teaching online in general. But regardless of its format, teaching is never context free, and we do wish to incorporate some of our experiences and learnings in regard to the civil unrest experienced in the United States, triggered by George Floyd's murder by police in plain sight of witnesses and recorded on video. The subsequent media coverage, protests, and foregrounding of the Black Lives Matter movement impacted everyone.

Sarah noted a watershed moment at her school, soon after George Floyd's murder, when a group of senior Black students wrote an email to the faculty about not being heard, about not being "okay" and feeling offended at the "business as usual" approach of instruction in the face of what occurred and the subsequent mass protests across the country and world. She interpreted this message as students wanting their reality acknowledged, and a space in class to process what had occurred and what was happening as a result. Sarah was glad to help create this space, and the experience made her cognizant of continuing to provide other opportunities during times since then. As a White teacher whose students are mostly youth of color, she also faced a dilemma of what is the right amount of time and space to allot to something as deeply painful and egregious as institutionalized racism. She noticed that some students became "talked out" and shut down, realizing that if every class is a talk about police brutality, it easily could become overwhelming and demoralizing for students. To gauge the situation, she'd ask the class, "Would you like to talk about this?" Admittedly, she knows that with so much racial injustice manifest in this country, it can be hard to find a balance between when to address current issues and when to teach with a view to giving students a sense of routine and normalcy.

In Fran's case, she too knew it was imperative to address what was going on in the outside world, as incidents, trends, and societal practices were affecting students and the school's climate. One project she developed with her social studies partner was on COVID-19, tackling it from a range of angles, from its individual impact on their families to different countries' responses to the virus. In another project, they studied the Black Lives Matter movement, including its origins, growth, and present goals. Her collaborative partner was able to teach students research skills by addressing topics of police brutality, structural inequality, and historical racism, which had been a major part of their recent discussions. As the topics were "real" and touched their lives directly, students were highly engaged and able to understand the complexity of the world at that particular moment in time. Additionally, making cross-connections among movements and allowing students to pursue areas of interest also deepened their engagement. For example, when Fran teaches feminist writers at the turn of the 20th century, she has students connect the suffragette movement to a contemporary protest movement in order to analyze similarities and differences.

Revising Content for Diversity

One thing to consider when revising a course—whether online, in-person, or hybrid—is to be proactive in analyzing for diversity and taking the opportunity to make changes. In David's case, he elected to revamp a longstanding course called The Study of Learning Disabilities a few years ago (Connor, 2022). He did this to consciously: (1) provide multiple perspectives of disability and differences; (2) include voices of people with LD and/or ADHD, equally balanced with research/expert texts; and (3) diversify examples of knowledge sources in terms of race, ethnicity, and gender, as so many of the materials, examples, and research within in the field of special education are White and middle class (Blanchett, 2010). In addition to "traditional" texts, he used TED Talks by powerful speakers with various forms of LD and/or ADHD, documentaries about dyslexia, and autobiographies of people who have always struggled with reading, writing, mathematics, organization, attention, or any combination of those. He also purposefully sought to teach the concept of LD as diversity rather than pathology, as it traditionally has been taught within the field of special education (Kauffman et al., 2017). Using an intersectional lens throughout the course, he illustrated ways in which LD impacts—and is impacted by—other markers of identity in unique ways (Connor, 2008). David also broadened major assignments, including offering students a traditional option to research an aspect of LD and effective ways to teach students, but also an option to look at social, cultural, and historical aspects of disability, such as overrepresentation of students of color, discrepancies in discipline practices, the school-to-prison pipeline, the neurodiversity movement, experiencing LD with another form of disability/difference, culturally responsive pedagogy and LD, and so on. These latter choices allowed students to examine historical practices, systemic patterns, and cultural shifts in society. In sum, the entire curriculum is always a work in progress, but by revising it to keep it up-to-date, we also can ensure that the content, concepts, sources, examples, and choices consciously encompass and reflect the general population and their experiences.

Incorporating Different Instructional Formats

One of the fears some teachers initially have with online learning is whether they'll have the same options of *how* to teach. Admittedly, looking at your computer screen and seeing rows of faces (or thumbnail pictures) resembling a sheet of postage stamps doesn't feel quite the same as scanning the landscape of an in-person classroom. However, we've come to see that virtual classrooms have most, if not all, of the same features, and have additional options and considerations. For example, teachers have the ability to mute all students except for the one who speaks. Students have the icon of a raised hand to let the teacher know that they wish to contribute. A parallel conversation can be had at the side of the screen, allowing all students to comment, insert resources, ask questions in writing, and so on.

As educators who are comfortable incorporating groupwork in classes, whether in dyads, triads, quads, or more, it is easy to place students in groups that are either random or assigned. Fran continued to do a lot of breakout groups so that students could have some relatively "normal" interactions. For the first time in her teaching career, she admits she didn't care if students goofed off a bit, as she wanted to facilitate some informal peer interactions, allowing space for students to reconnect and talk about things they chose to. There are also basic mechanisms in platforms such as Zoom and Meet that allow teachers to enter and exit any group whenever they wish, facilitating overseeing group conversations—in a similar way to how they'd circulate around an actual room.

Sarah loves student-led class discussions, yet also pushed herself to figure out multiple ways to engage students that went beyond the traditional formats. For example, she did a lot of collaborative document work, permitting students to analyze and mark up texts and artifacts together. She also facilitated virtual jigsaws, namely, having each group prepare for a role in which they'd be responsible for sharing "expert" information with the whole class. The use of Jamboard, a digital whiteboard used for collaboration in a shared space, or Padlet allowed students to digitally brainstorm as a starting point for discussion. Flipgrid provided the opportunity for students to "discuss" or present asynchronously, posting brief videos and then watching and replying to the videos of peers. (For more information, see Figure 7.1.)

As David developed courses during the pandemic, he saw the value in asynchronous work, as it allowed students to complete it anytime during a specified time frame. Weekly student journal entries, following a course-related writing prompt, meant he could get to know all students on a personal level, read what they were thinking, and respond in ways that further engaged students via questions and comments. Student drawings and other artifacts were posted to create a virtual Gallery Walk, and Discussion Boards were set up requiring a contribution from all students about challenging topics. Traditional formats for assignments were still used too, such as the uploading of book reviews, film critiques, and research papers. One of the initially most challenging things David did was to have students make virtual presentations, realizing that online formatting might have some advantages over in-person. For example, he found that when students uploaded their presentations of 15 PowerPoint slides narrated over 15 minutes, a "bank" was created from which students could be assigned a certain number to listen to, watch, and respond to—when it was convenient for them. It also allayed students' nerves, as many suffer from "stage fright" in front of peers, but self-recording meant they could do as many takes as they needed to achieve a product they were satisfied with.

Taking Advantage of Smaller Class Sizes, Where and When Possible

The various policies developed by school boards, parental decision-making about sending or keeping their children out of school, and the fluctuation in the number of sick students all contributed to what can be seen as an unexpected phenomenon—smaller class sizes. We all agree that smaller class sizes are better in terms of getting to know, and supporting, students. When

Figure 7.1. Selected Technology Platforms

Sarah's Choices:

Padlet

Padlet is an online tool that allows students to post comments, respond to text, and respond to one another. It works similarly to Jamboard (the free Google platform), but is much easier for students to use, especially on a cell phone (on which Jamboard can be challenging). It also has many premade templates for different types of discussion, as well as fun colors and designs and the ability to post gifs (which Jamboard does not yet have). These last two pieces are, of course, not essential, but when fighting to keep students engaged, any aesthetic perks that draw them in can't hurt. Finally, it can be set up for students to "like" other posts, up or down vote posts, and reply to one another in a visually "clear" way. When first using Padlet, I tended to think of using it as I would use a big poster paper. I thought of activities where groups might make a poster or put a bunch of Post-its on a larger paper to see everyone's thoughts. In this vein, I used it to "open" the year and had students post ideas for class norms around technology use. Later, I had students post and reflect on English class goals. Students even brainstormed research paper topics on a Padlet and suggested subtopics to one another on it. As I started to expand my thinking around using Padlet, I saw how it could be used as a class "jigsaw" might be used. So, to start a unit on *The Brief, Wondrous Life of Oscar Wao* (Diaz, 2008), I assigned students several categories of background research: Dominican immigration, science fiction, Rafael Trujillo, and others. Students posted definitions and quotes from their research and then had to reply to two other posts with connections to their own research focus. As I became more confident using Padlet, I expanded into using it as I might use a speed-dating or "human bingo" game. For a poetry analysis task, students first read the poem and posted main ideas. Then, they posted the most important quote. Finally, they posted literary device analysis connected to a theme. After each round, my online class would stop and discuss responses, which were most thorough, and which could be combined. One great element of Padlet (and many other online platforms) is that it creates an online, collaborative resource that students can reference outside of class. So, for this poetry activity, students could use the class analysis to pull ideas from when they wrote their own poetry analysis essay. Padlet can be used asynchronously, as with a homework assignment, and also can be used in class. As described above, with a Padlet, where more basic opening ideas build to more complex conclusions, teachers may pause after each round of student responses and have students view and discuss responses.

Flipgrid

Flipgrid is an online platform that allows students to post videos and then view and respond to one another's videos. The site has some nice templates for videos and allows students to add some special effects and text. Students also may use various effects (smileys, hearts, etc.) to reply to one another. During online teaching, I thought of Flipgrid as serving the purpose that short student

(continued)

Figure 7.1. Selected Technology Platforms (*continued*)

presentations might serve. For example, I often have students spend several classes dissecting poems from a literary movement (such as Harlem Renaissance). Each student (or pair) focuses on one poem and, after traditional analysis, creates a way to present it creatively to the class. This may include dance, tableaux, choral reading, addition of music, or acting the poem out. When in the classroom, students simply would present their poem in person to the class; online, they could use Flipgrid. Students would post their video of the poetry reading. Then, their assignment included having to view three other presentations and identify two ways their own poem was similar and one way it differed. This asynchronous work then led to a larger online classroom discussion about major themes (and diversions from said themes) in the poetry of the Harlem Renaissance.

Sarah had classes that were "blended," that is, a combination of in-person students with others online, the six to 10 students who were physically present could be worked with one-on-one. Such individualized conferencing allowed her to sit and read parts of an essay or discuss sections of a book, as well as having an informal general check-in. Fran had a similar goal during a year of teaching in a hybrid format—to hear from everyone. Like Sarah, with 10 to 12 students in class, Fran felt like she got to know them better, and enjoyed the smaller group interactions. As for the students at home, Fran found some to be consistently good participants, but others would never speak or seemed very disengaged, clearly doing something else. Subsequently, she began to try different activities and formats that forced everyone to talk at least once during a class. Using the chat function and Jamboard also helped her elicit responses from all students and have students be able to see one another's responses.

Gathering More Information

One of the things we noticed with the increased use of technology for all aspects of teaching—planning, executing, and assessing—was the increase in the number of data sources available for all students. For example, Sarah realized that when she was looking at logs submitted electronically, instead of, say, walking around the room and visually checking that a vocabulary log was done, she noticed things she hadn't before, such as that some kids were still struggling with parts of speech. David, too, realized that every submission made via a centralized system of Class Blackboard meant records were now automatic, with documentation as to who submitted what and when—making it easy to double check scores and tabulate grades. Fran also has used this feature, in part to ensure that students are leading balanced lives. For example, she reaches out and chats with students who are submitting their work at 3 A.M., making sure they are not depriving themselves of sleep.

THINGS WE WONDER ABOUT

Right now, as we write this chapter at the beginning of 2022, the pandemic has left many people, including educators, feeling less safe and secure in the world. It's true that teachers largely have done an outstanding job in difficult circumstances, supporting students who have responded to the COVID-19 crisis in various ways. We have attempted to frame this topic in a constructive manner, sharing what we perceived as benefits and cautions. We also are left with some unanswered questions ourselves and know others will have similar thoughts. In this last section, we share some of the things that the pandemic has left us still wondering about.

Sarah now sees the value of smaller class sizes and hopes policymakers will note the difference in the quality of education when the teacher-to-student ratio is reduced. In terms of sustaining strong, supportive relations with students, she sees the plus side of "looping" groups of students, moving with them as they progress through grade levels. Having some 11th-graders from last year who are now in her 12th-grade class, she knows existing relationships can continue if classes go remote—providing stability in an inconsistent time. She also wonders how to bring what was learned during online learning into physical classroom spaces. This raises the issue of ways that online and in-person instruction can mutually inform each other, allowing best practices to emerge.

It seems to us that online learning enables some students to fly, go forth, become more independent, self-directed, and self-managed. But we also know it can have the opposite effect, and everything in between. There are concerns from teachers, parents, and policymakers about online learning's unfettered growth, which has outstripped regulation and research. There are also fears of "lost learning time" (Engzell et al., 2021), particularly for more vulnerable students in terms of disability, economic status, and/or acquiring another language, a phenomenon experienced around the world about which we have yet to know the full repercussions. Our colleagues and friends share cautious tales about students who have "fallen behind" in acquiring skills expected within specific grades. We do not wish to be alarmist, but knowing the breadth of situations across the country, many people hold concerns that some students may have missed—at least to some degree—the establishment of foundational knowledge in reading, math, and even social skills. To date, these areas have yet to be responded to in educational policy.

Finally, as teaching and learning online have had an unprecedented growth spurt, it is unlikely that everything in the workplace and educational environment will "return to normal." Online teaching will remain an integral part of education at all levels. If there are more pandemics in the future, as many predict, how will we handle them differently based on what we've come to know? How will we know whether our schools should be kept open or be closed for longer periods? Is distance learning a feasible option for the future, should it be minimized, or is there a healthy balance in educational formats?

SUMMARY

In this chapter, we reflected upon the sudden shift to teaching online during the COVID-19 pandemic and ways in which teachers adjusted to the increased use of technology. We explored some of the many benefits of online teaching and alerted readers to some cautions. Additionally, we shared some practical approaches to creating and sustaining virtual classrooms, grounded in a strong ethic of care. We ended with some lingering thoughts and unanswered questions about online teaching during the COVID-19 pandemic.

QUESTIONS FOR FURTHER REFLECTION

1. What do you think and how do you feel about the increased use of technology in education becoming the expected norm?
2. Reflecting on your own experience in middle and high school, undergraduate and graduate school, what have been some beneficial experiences of using technology as a learner? What were some areas you may have struggled with?
3. Generally speaking, how has the COVID-19 pandemic influenced your perceptions of teaching and learning?
4. In reviewing the suggested practices in this chapter, which ones seem within your reach right now? Which ones may require some practice?
5. In addition to the examples mentioned, what are some ways of including a focus on diversity when teaching online?
6. Explore an online platform or educational tool you've never used before. Some ideas include Mentimeter, Parlay, Flipgrid, Mote . . . How do you think this platform or tool would benefit students?
7. Plan a virtual unit early in the semester using Understanding by Design (Wiggins & McTighe, 2005). What are ways you can familiarize students with different technological tools? How might these tools and skills be useful for both you and your students if classes shift to being fully online?

CHAPTER 8

Reflecting Upon What Teaching Has Taught Us

A note of the format of this chapter. From the time we conceptualized this book, we agreed to have a final chapter in which we'd have a dialogue. This format, we thought, would help braid together the main elements of the text, since we'd be writing personally about how our chosen profession has impacted our own existence—making us constantly reflect about what it means to be human, to engage with others, to open doors that encourage people to explore thinking in different ways. We wish to reconnect with an idea we shared in the Introduction, namely, that the realms of personal, professional, and political experiences are impossible to disentangle. Bearing this thought in mind, and fresh from a Zoom conversation in which we managed to weave a constellation of issues—including the ongoing importance of critically reflecting on Whiteness, the prohibition of critical race theory, banning books, cancel culture, deciding when to stand up for a cause, and how COVID-19 has made us reevaluate ourselves as educators and individual people—we've used that conversation as a springboard into the final chapter. Our method was to simply shift the live conversation from synchronous online to an asynchronous interchange via email that allowed us more time to think and compose our thoughts. The result is a broad conversation between we three, as follows.

Sarah: I love the Desmond Tutu quote, "A person becomes a person through other persons." Coming up on 20 years of teaching, I think about all the people I've encountered—students, coworkers, families—and how they have helped me evolve into the person I am today. Sometimes I like to do the math—150 students a year, times 19 years—you get the idea. The power of sometimes seemingly banal interactions and the sheer volume of these interactions you have as a teacher are staggering. Of course, it's not a straight upward trajectory. I don't think that when I hit a teaching milestone, I'll unlock some superpower and become a saint, perfect in both my personal and professional lives. It's more a respect for the often-messy growth we've tried to honor in this book, the mistakes made, incorrect assumptions acted on, certainties challenged. As David said, we are lifelong learners. While this holds true as professionals in the classroom, we value it in our personal lives and use it to inform our political perceptions.

Reflecting on the personal, professional, and political makes me reflect on some of the more universal truths that I've come to realize inform all three of these spheres. Most of these are ideas I've held in some form since childhood and, as such, are nothing revelatory, but they point to the ideas of growth and learning we champion throughout.

Second (and third, and fourth) chances are essential. Students make mistakes, my own children make mistakes, I make mistakes. This seems simple, but it can be easy to forget in the fog of frustration that accompanies forgotten homework, a mean comment, or a poorly taught lesson. My students (who generally predate my own children) have shown me this so many times: the 9th-grader who yelled at me became the senior who confided in me; the English student who refused to open the novel, morphing into a group discussion leader. It's so easy to forget people can change and to not allow them the space to do this. So, when I realize I'm being hard on myself about confusing groupwork instructions or I yell at my daughter for again leaving clothes on the bathroom floor, I come back to this idea my students have taught me so many times.

Dig deep for kindness and empathy (and this may not be easy). I often do this around political opinions, testing the limits of my empathy as I try to put myself in the shoes of someone arguing for a passionate idea I do not support. To be honest, it works maybe half the time, but the attempt is, in my opinion, what matters. I am not a naturally empathetic person. (Something about the narcissism of a childhood in the 1980s? Or maybe I took *The Fountainhead* [Rand, 2005 edition] too seriously in high school?) When I became a parent, I realized I had to break from my self-centeredness, and—not surprisingly—it made me a better teacher. I began to truly see my students as other people's children (and began to really know what that meant) and, instead of being burnt out on kindness and patience from wrestling with my own kids, I found more of these qualities.

Find joy and gratitude every day. This may be the most touchy-feely of my principles, but it touches the personal and professional. Looking for the joy certainly can be a bridge to kindness. It can provide a starting point for second chances. And, if you have joy—even a teeny, tiny bit—you can be motivated to keep going, keep reflecting, keep learning.

Fran: I like your Desmond Tutu quote. Did you know he was one of the speakers when I graduated from Teachers College? And Pete Seeger and a minister from a church in the Bronx. The minister was the best (-; The personal and professional have become one. I have a "teacher voice" that comes out when my son's hockey team becomes too rowdy in the locker room or when random children I have never met are picking on a child at the playground. When I check my own daughter's grades on the online portal for her middle school, I immediately ask her where the rubric is if I don't like one of her grades. I'm sure there are other professions where you can't separate the two. My older sister and her husband are both doctors. They constantly have family members and friends calling them or texting them photos to see whether they should go to a doctor or ask their opinions about vaccines and masks. I imagine a priest or nun would have similar separation issues. Sometimes you are what you do. My friends laugh because I send out discussion questions before our book club meetings, but I do find it helps us have better discussions, or at least actually discuss the book. I worry sometimes about retiring, because I can't imagine what I would do.

The longer I teach, the more I realize how socioeconomic factors and one's parents and caregivers are two such huge indicators in how we see the world and where we end up in life. My parents both went to college and have graduate degrees. My sisters and I all went to college and have graduate degrees. My mother loved to read and started her own book group in every state she has lived in. My parents let me and my sisters choose what colleges we wanted to attend and what careers we wanted to pursue (although my dad is still disappointed that I didn't become a lawyer like him). I grew up in a household where I didn't have to worry about any financial concerns and where I was encouraged to think freely and question authority. We discussed the news at the dinner table every night. I grew up not having a lot of concerns about my future. What a luxury. Had I been born in a family that valued sports, maybe I would be more athletic and wouldn't have read all those books. Had I been born in a family that hadn't pursued higher education themselves, maybe I wouldn't have gone to college. Had I been born in a family that couldn't help me pay for college, maybe I would have pursued a much more lucrative career path. Had my family held very strict religious or political views about the world, I imagine my perspective on many topics would be vastly different. The point is that we are all products of where we come from.

The interesting thing about being a teacher is that every year I have this collection of students with such different background experiences and views of the world all put into one place. Adolescence is all about, to some extent, pushing back from where we came from and what we have been taught. So, what happens when these varied, questioning minds come to us? It would seem irresponsible and insincere not to encourage them to embrace their curiosities and question who they are and what they want to become. As a parent, I am so thankful for my children's teachers and not just their schoolteachers but all the people who help them see the world differently or develop skills they are just uncovering. When they come home and share some new information they learned in class, often something that I myself did not know, I am thrilled. When my son comes and tells me about the new shot he learned from his hockey coach or the reason why an octopus has three hearts, I am thankful that he is moving beyond the small realm of knowledge that I can convey. I want my own children and my students to question my authority and everyone's authority. I want them to find knowledge and use it in ways we haven't even thought of yet. All throughout life we have teachers; we just don't always call them that.

David: I think you've both touched on many important topics. I agree with Sarah that there has to be an open-endedness (not sure that's the best description) in teaching, and an acceptance of our own mistakes and current limitations, and those of others. Particularly with students with whom we "started off on the wrong foot," "misread," "didn't like the things they said," "didn't like how they behaved," and so on. Every day is a chance for a new start, and there should always be opportunities in place for students to adapt to the teacher and get back on track. I know I came to learn not to take student anger and occasional outbursts personally. Many of those students were stressed by challenging home situations such as a seriously ill parent, living in a group home, being in a tumultuous relationship, or the general grind of a 90-minute journey to school. If I was calm, consistent, and didn't engage in battle-like dynamics, situations deescalated and students usually apologized. I also learned about displacement, when anger is channeled elsewhere instead of the source that ferments it. This learning was a big shift for me, to not rise to the bait of feeling disrespected, but rather accept that the student was in a momentary crisis and I was in the line of fire. Helping the student in this situation by acknowledging their feelings ("I know you're very angry now; I can see how upset you are"), talking them down, giving them space, was a great lesson for me. Like Sarah, some of the students I initially battled with in one way or another became my favorites as mutual respect grew and we understood each other better. Many students initially may not buy into the idea that we're both on the same side. There is an element of proving ourselves to students. Just because they're a captive audience, since the laws of the land require them to be there, doesn't mean they're going to eat out of our hand. (I smile because this is exactly the same situation as when presenters meet a room of teachers during professional development.) And yet, by making informed decisions about how to connect with students (or teachers in PD), engaging with their interests, giving them the opportunity to share their existing knowledge, introducing them to new concepts by making connections, and so on, we do have ways to nurture teacher–learner relationships.

The other thing I wanted to comment upon was Sarah's comment about "other people's children." When I read Lisa Delpit's (2006) book of the same name, it changed my world. From the beginning, I'd always tried to carry the sentiments of "imagine if your students were your family members, sons and daughters, or nephews and nieces." I wasn't perfect by a long shot, and I recognized my failings, but thought this was a good code to live by. I wanted to be loving (without being taken advantage of), caring (without it being perceived as a weakness), fair (as all students want a fair deal), firm (consistent, so necessary boundaries are drawn), and determined when need be (we have to take a stand sometimes).

Fast-forward several decades, and what wasn't addressed sufficiently in my teacher education program or inservice professional development—the relationship between historical and cultural inequalities being reproduced within educational structures—is far more present nowadays. As someone in teacher education, I've witnessed some embracing of, and some resistance toward, educators reflecting upon and understanding "Whiteness" as it relates to themselves. It seems to me that teachers who are interested in and willing to embrace centering diversity must at least have a healthy knowledge of what Whiteness is and their own relationship to it. It's not always easy, but I do think it's necessary.

Sarah: Yes, we can't ignore this idea of Whiteness, something, like David says, I had the privilege of ignoring for most of my life as a White person. On one level, as Franny said, being a parent has bridged this gap. A student may be from a different racial, socioeconomic, religious, or family background than me, but (hopefully) someone at home is worrying about them just like I'm worrying about my daughters in school. Being a parent has already reminded me of all the "tenderness" of being a young person that I forget as I age, of trying on three outfits before you head to school or worrying your classmate will see your bad math score and tease you. This definitely builds my (sometimes lacking) empathy muscles and makes me a better teacher.

The other, more challenging piece of this is the self-reflection we've championed throughout this book. This is one of the key places where the personal and professional and political intersect. While parts of my undergrad and grad school educations touched on issues of race, it wasn't until fairly recently that I've spent more extended time reading about Whiteness, power structures, and identity. I've been able to more deeply interrogate my own privilege and biases I bring to the classroom and to my beliefs in general. I've tried to read authors of color and reflect on perspectives I may not have considered previously. In checking my assumptions and biases, I have been able to deepen relationships with more students. I've been able to see more of the brilliance students bring to my classroom that I previously may have been unaware of, especially if this brilliance fell outside of the strict parameters of stereotypical "good student" behavior. And then, I've tried to change. I've tried to find ways to make space for these aforementioned students to shine in ways schools don't always value. I've changed the books I teach and the way I teach these texts to respond to my students, rather than meeting some internal idea of good literature or teaching that is an antiquated relic from my own childhood. In some ways this connects to the idea about second and third chances, but for me too.

David: Regarding Whiteness, Sarah said, "This is one of the key places where the personal and professional and political intersect." Agreed. One of the reasons I attempted to address race and disability within university special education department meetings was that a graduate student sometimes would come to me upset, stating one of the kids they were teaching had called them "racist," or another White graduate student had been asked by a Black student she was teaching, "Why can police kill unarmed Black men and get away with it?" This was before George Floyd's murder. In such instances, I had to calm the student down, ask about the context of their dialogue, and their relationship with students, how they responded, and so on. It concerned me that our department did little to prepare graduate students for working with a diverse student body in terms of race, ethnicity, socioeconomic status, emergent bilingualism, and so on. I was shocked when half of the department in New York City, which was 90% White and without any Black faculty, tried to close down even talking about race. One professor told me I was "shoving it down their throats." This was after engaging in in-house professional development for three once-a-month 1-hour sessions to discuss documentaries such as *13th* (DuVernay, 2016). That was an example of White privilege right there, not having to think about race and when asked to do so, them trying to shut it down without talking about it. My goal had been to open the door to how students in the public school systems often have different realities than their teachers, most of whom do not live in their students' neighborhoods. To not even acknowledge this, was being complicit. I could provide numerous additional examples that only proved to me the importance of discussing Whiteness—not to make people feel guilty or bad (although this may be an initial reaction), but to acknowledge the existing historical inequities in society, many of which are perpetuated through an uncritical look at education and our teacher education programs.

The "up" side of having those initial difficult conversations is that half the faculty thought it was necessary that we look at issues of race in (special) education. The resistance by traditional special educators also pushed me and my colleagues to engage the academic discipline of special education as a whole—as it attempts to be "innocent" when so many of its practices actually reveal the structures of our society (Cavendish et al., 2020; Connor, 2017, 2019; Connor et al., 2019; Ferri & Connor, 2005, 2014). Think, for a moment, about who gets the gifted label and enters exclusive programs, and who then gets the behavior disordered, emotionally disturbed, and intellectually disabled labels that fill the school-to-prison pipeline (Heitzeg, 2016).

I get concerned when books such as Pulitzer Prize–winning *Maus* (Spiegelman, 1986) or *The Bluest Eye* (Morrison, 2007 edition) are being banned for fear they bring up the Holocaust or race. I taught these over 30 years ago and students loved them. When Fran says "back to basics," it's more like back to times when issues of race and ethnicity weren't discussed. How can we not discuss race when teaching incredible writers such as James Baldwin and Toni Morrison who foregrounded Black experiences in the United States? Undergirding all of the banning rhetoric is a desire to *not* engage with taboo issues that are there in plain sight, hence the Black Lives Matter movement. If half of the professors in my department want to leave things alone, to pretend things are alright, and be race evasive, that's many things—including self-absolving from any responsibility.

Fran: Shifting the focus a little, although we critically reflected on Whiteness in our Introduction, other aspects of our identity also shape who we are in personal, professional, and political ways. Most obviously, my gender has a huge impact on how I teach. I constantly am analyzing curricula and wondering why so few women authors are taught. I make a concerted effort to push more female authors and to make sure male and female students' voices are being heard in the classroom. I would like to think my male coworkers do the same, but I am not sure they have the same drive as I do. Sometimes other personal traits also have unforeseen impacts. I attended Catholic school from 3rd through 12th grades. Frequently I ask students questions about symbols or characters' choices in a novel that are biblical references. Often only a handful of students have any idea what I am even asking. My parents both have graduate degrees. When I was growing up, they discussed the news at dinner. They used large vocabulary words, which now are part of my repertoire. I have an auditory learning disability and really struggle to just listen. I need to see. If students are presenting speeches, I ask to have a copy in front of me. If groups are presenting projects, I make sure they have a visual element as part of the presentation. I am 5'1" on a good day. Many of my students physically look down on me. I have to exude strength of personality and mentality to engage my students, as my deep voice and commanding presence isn't going to cut it. The point is that who we are, how we see the world, and how we learn greatly affect who we become as teachers. It should be impossible to ignore one's biases. We need to address who we are coming into a situation so that we can see more clearly what we aren't seeing.

Sarah: I would second Franny's point about not ignoring one's biases. I do think, though, that often—at least for me—I don't always perceive from the start these biases that stem from different parts of my identity outside of race. So much of our identity has been baked into us from a young age that we often assume our values as the norm or stop seeing differences about ourselves that may be obvious to others. I've mentioned earlier in this book not really having thought about my solidly middle-class upbringing until I encountered my Ivy League classmates with their prep school educations and vacation homes. It's interesting that Franny mentioned her religious schooling as I have had quite the opposite experience.

I was raised in the Unitarian Universalist church, a religion that very much resists dogma and many of the traditional beliefs of Christianity. As an adult I've grown to become agnostic and often assume most younger people around me feel the same. But my students, many from strong religious communities, often have deeply felt religious beliefs, and I sometimes have to check my own biases when it comes to issues of faith or devotion in literature.

Finally, like Franny, being a woman informs a large part of my identity and my choices in the classroom. I try to emphasize women's voices in my choices of literature and, as a formerly introverted and nerdy high school girl, look to build confidence in young women that remind me of my former high school self. And while of course I have to check myself in favoring students who remind me of myself back then, I do find that students I take under my wing cut across various racial, cultural, and socioeconomic categories, a fact that for me shows that even diversity of "personality" comes into play in the classroom.

David: I agree that many aspects of identity, in addition to race, can profoundly influence how we teach—and of course there are always intersectional experiences for everyone. Two areas in addition to Whiteness for me are being from a working-class background and being a gay man. The UK has always been very class conscious and snobbish, with many subtle and explicit messages circulating throughout our culture that *position* people "in their place." Like the microaggressions experienced by people of color, women, the LGBTQ+ community, and other groups, these messages are often internalized—making people feel inferior, unworthy, and out of place in many situations, including universities for first-generation attendees. At university, I learned that my own assumptions about middle- and upper-class people had to be challenged too. They were not necessarily more intelligent (or automatic snobs), but they undoubtedly had more confidence attending university, as they'd been prepared by cultural and social norms and expectations. In turn, I learned their assumptions about working-class people's intelligence could be challenged simply by engaging in all kinds of discussions with them. It may seem strange to an American audience, but on attending university for my undergraduate degree in the UK, I'd be told things like, "You're the first working-class friend I've had," "I love your accent," or "Say [insert word] again." While appreciative of my newfound friends, it made me feel like an object of curiosity, and although it was not their intention, my friends' words were patronizing. That said, I benefitted from leaving my comfort zone, coming to know people from other social classes, and learned how to work against feelings of inferiority. I bring this point up as I think educators have to be mindful of social class when working with students and parents, to accept people for where they are, and not see social differences through a deficit lens. It can be tricky to navigate one's different social class background and the cultural capital that brings (including "school readiness" and expectations of college), the curriculum, and the strengths and resources of local communities, and provide culturally sustaining pedagogy, all without acritically inscribing middle-class values and norms—but that's the reality for many teachers. One thing I've always tried to do is encourage students to not feel confined by social class, but see it as a strength from which to build who they are and pursue what they want to do. Being raised working class also influenced *where* I taught—which consciously has always been in public education systems.

The other aspect of my identity that I'll touch upon merits more space than I'll offer it here. Being gay in education has implications. There have long been all kinds of stereotypical anxieties projected onto LGBTQ+ people, including movements to prohibit being in the teaching profession and featuring anything LGBTQ+-related in the curriculum—a phenomenon that, unfortunately, is still with us in many parts of the United States today. In the 1980s, when I started teaching, even in a progressive city such as New York, teachers were rarely "out." Being gay was an open secret, that is, people knew but no one talked about it. I had come out as a teenager, angry about the misinformation about, hostility toward, and almost nonexistent representations of happy, healthy, well-adjusted gay people in literature and media. I was a community activist, and the youngest member of a nationwide grassroots network that provided peer counseling and support. I marched in demonstrations, wrote letters to representative politicians asking to change discriminatory laws, was interviewed on the radio, and created several informational exhibitions designed to educate. And yet, when I went into teaching, I felt the need to be very cautious about being open in the classroom. At the time, besides the usual stereotypical fears, there was a hostile national environment due to AIDS. At times, it caused me great ambivalence to be out to my colleagues but not to my high school students. On the other hand, I would not allow homophobic slurs in class, was vigilant toward bullying, and felt protective toward LGBTQ+ kids. Based upon my own experiences, I do think if a person experiences what it's like to be minoritized, misunderstood, and discriminated against, it can allow them to become empathetic toward other minoritized groups. Of course, discrimination isn't interchangeable, and we can't make assumptions about experiences we haven't had ourselves. However, I know that my sexual orientation influenced my advocacy of inclusive classrooms, which at first emphasized including students with disabilities, but naturally grew to also encompass different types of diversity so students can feel represented and have a sense of belonging.

Sarah: To Fran's point, celebrating the beautiful, complicated, multifaceted aspects of everyone's identity, teacher included, can be a way to bring joy to the classroom. So often teachers associate a focus on diversity with a focus on oppression, when, of course, joy also must be a part of our pedagogy. This makes me think of a lesson I taught recently that really emphasized the essential nature of joy in the classroom. In my AP English lit class we just finished *Their Eyes Were Watching God* (Hurston, 2006 edition) and were reading Hurston's essay, "How It Feels to Be Colored Me" (1928). In this piece Hurston argues—in part—that she doesn't want to think about slavery or racism as she is "too busy sharpening her oyster knife" to seize the pearl of life, to live life to its fullest. In this essay she centers the joy of being Black, of Black brilliance and culture. When we analyze this in class, I pair it with an excerpt of Richard Wright's critique of Hurston's novel as being too emotional, too worried about feelings, implying she is avoiding a more uncomfortable discussion of racism to appease a White audience. This leads to a really interesting discussion about the burdens of representation—in TV and film, and in classroom reading lists. Some students were adamant about centering racism when discussing Black identity: "We have to talk about race and oppression or people will pretend it never happened." Others expressed a fatigue with what one Black student called "trauma porn"—"I'm tired of just seeing Black people deal with slavery, fight racism, be abused, die. We're so much more than that. What about the positive stuff?"

Of course, we didn't reach a solution (not that I remotely expected us to), but it raised the question of balance—one I think we try to address in this book. Teachers certainly have a responsibility to expose injustice, to shed light on dark parts of our past and analyze how this darkness informs (and still exists in) our present. But there also has to be space for joy, for celebration. This is true when selecting books and readings. We have to look at the breadth of diverse groups' place in America. But it's also true in our personal and professional lives. You can't yell at your kids (students or family) so much of the time that you forget to make some silly jokes. You can't be so singularly focused on test prep that you refuse to pause and listen to a student talk about her awesome skateboard trick. Teaching is a marathon, not a sprint for sure, and if you lose this balance, forget the joy, you'll never make it to the finish line (whatever that is, haha). . . .

Fran: My students constantly ask me whether we ever read any happy books. They are few and far between. It's not that books we read don't have happy parts or maybe a happy ending, but why would anyone write a story without struggle? This is true with the older texts: *Antigone* (Sophocles, 2005 edition), *Of Mice and Men* (Steinbeck, 1937), *The Odyssey* (Homer, 1997 edition). It is also true with the newer texts: *The Bluest Eye* (Morrison, 2007 edition), *Middlesex* (Eugenides, 2007), and *The Nickel Boys* (Whitehead, 2020). I think the world is very angry and unhappy at present (and maybe rightly so), and I think there is even more of a backlash against unhappy portrayals or painful stories. I have heard so many people lately tell me they can't read dystopian literature right now, as it is too close to home.

I'd like to discuss the question: Have you ever put yourself out on a limb?

David: I'll respond to Sarah's point first. I like that we're touching upon the notion of joy in classrooms, as we do refer to it a few times in chapters. I see "joy" in a couple of ways. Teaching can be a joyful experience, make us feel happy in what we do in life (so important!). Classrooms can be places filled with laughter, as students like teachers who are not afraid to be funny (especially at their own expense), and that makes for an environment that has a certain ease to it, that they enjoy being in. There's also potential "joy" in the content of what's being taught—whether it's contemporary rap lyrics juxtaposed with classical poetry, introducing students to new authors in both traditional and Young Adult fiction, or doing a dramatic reading of a play. I agree that the notion of "balance" is important in so much of what we do. I agree that the past few pandemic years have made it difficult to teach certain texts as they would have been taught before—as we have experienced forms of dystopia that negatively impact students. Teaching a dystopian novel can create further imbalance. At the same time, the very premise of literature is storytelling in one way or another, and all stories tend to have conflict and struggles, for that's what engages us. That said, if we're balancing content, the endings of the stories taught, can impact students. At the end of the day, as educators, we always want to be (should be?) on the side of hopefulness.

Let me turn to Fran's question. (Have you ever put yourself out on a limb and challenged something at your school or the status quo? Was your protest worth it? Effective?) I felt I always had to be cautious, figure out how things worked within a school, who was listened to and respected, who was dismissed and not respected. Then choose my battles. Bottom line was I always wanted to keep my job. I'm practical, and needed to pay rent. There were some times where I bit my tongue, and there were other times where I spoke up. Again, it was about balance. I'll share a couple of examples with mixed outcomes (a bit of a metaphor for life if ever there was one).

The first was my asking to be on the high school's HIV Awareness Committee around 1990. The NYC Department of Ed required one in every high school. While I knew one existed in my high school, it had no presence or discernible impact. Once I joined, I realized the committee was not being taken seriously by the majority of people assigned to be on it. So I volunteered to make it more formal, and less lip service, by taking minutes, requesting items to be addressed, and suggesting we use the school's professional development day to address issues that HIV raised. Why? I was witnessing firsthand the ravages of the AIDS epidemic and the complacency of a society in which the majority thought that HIV didn't apply to them, only to the undesirable and therefore expendable people—gays, drug users, prostitutes, disabled people (hemophiliacs), Haitians (often darkest-skinned people, and associated with being immigrants from the poorest country in the "Western world"). I knew many of my students were sexually active, and therefore at risk while thinking they weren't—and this bothered me, as I wanted them to develop a greater self-awareness. Based on our school's total population of over 2,000 students, a science teacher used statistics to calculate the numbers of who would likely get HIV. That was a sobering conversation. The HIV Awareness Committee *did* increase its profile in the school, and we helped teachers teach mandated lessons on HIV prevention. We also managed to get half a day for schoolwide PD. But it didn't quite go as desired. We contracted a community-based awareness organization that presented on safe-sex practices to classrooms of teachers, many of whom had no desire to talk about the topic. This resulted in a role reversal of a learning situation, where the majority of teachers-now-students giggled about dental dams or how to safely apply a condom, and didn't engage seriously. It was disappointing, but also educational for me. In the future I knew I'd plan better; I knew what to expect; I knew I wanted to keep HIV awareness on the radar. So I wrote a letter to every teacher in the school asking for a donation and completed the annual AIDS walk in NYC. I was happily surprised with the funds raised from my colleagues. I also agreed to do professional development for the Superintendent's Office, where ELA teachers in Manhattan high schools were asked to integrate HIV awareness into their curriculum. These were my baby steps into becoming interested in professional development. I'll never forget facing an audience of teachers who'd been sent for this mandated training. Some were genuinely intrigued, a few were on board, but many were angry, stating that their lessons would be unnecessarily contaminated with this nonsense. I took a deep breath and pushed forward, exploring examples of how we could talk about sexual mores within literature and differences in contemporary times, using Stanley and Blanche from *A Streetcar Named Desire* (Williams, 2004 edition). Some bought it, some didn't, but I knew I had to at least try.

The other area I always supported was increased access for students with disabilities. Once I recognized how the educational system marginalized them, and saw how unfair it was, I became a strong advocate for inclusive practices and learned to engage about the topic with all kinds of audiences in education—general and special educators, administrators, paraprofessionals, parents, psychologists, educational evaluators, counselors, and so on. Audiences ranged from supportive, to curious, to hostile. What kept me going was my experiences as a teacher, and a conviction—based in civil rights discourse—that separate was not equal. This grounding has remained with me throughout my career, influencing what and how I taught in various teacher education programs, and in my writing that has attempted to always connect theory, research, practice, and policy around inclusive approaches to education.

Sarah: Franny's question got me thinking; I'm such a rule follower that I pretty much always at least try to *appear* like I'm following the rules, but there have been a lot of times that I've bent them to my desires or goals. For sure I've let some school policies I thought were unfair or inequitable slide if I thought it was better for the kids. An overly strict uniform policy comes to mind for this, as does banning eating in class. (I'd rather have you in my class with a bagel than outside missing class to scarf down breakfast or, worse, trying to focus when you're hungry.) As I become more confident in my teaching "persona," I also let rules slide that I see as obstacles to building authentic relationships with kids. I've been known to laugh at cursing rather than chastise, or to gently tease kids I've known for several years. I've also pushed the limits with the books I teach, hoping admin doesn't actually read whatever it is. For example, when I taught *The Brief, Wondrous Life of Oscar Wao* (Diaz, 2008), my Dominican American principal was reticent for us to teach books with discussions of sex. I ordered and taught it anyway, hoping that he wouldn't actually read it, but figuring if he did, that my students' high engagement with the text would be my best defense. Fitting with some of the themes of this book, I've also definitely pushed other (usually older) teachers to teach more diverse books through some "curious questioning" and humble bragging about how kids loved a more modern and representative book.

I'm going to respond to Franny's question with a related question. What do you do when something crosses a "moral line" for you—either in the school at large or in your classroom? Our (dis)comfort chapter got me thinking about this. I feel like our society today is such a strange mix of jumping to cancel culture and then, on the flip side, treating all opinions or perspectives as equally valid. I still bristle if a student says something I find immoral or offensive in a class discussion, but struggle with how to approach it. Typically, I make a sort of broad statement like, "Well, we can't generalize for all people," but then feel bad that I didn't have a stronger moral backbone. Sometimes I even find myself mentally prepping before a contentious debate about, say, immigration, thinking about what my line will be. Do I allow a student to say they think all undocumented immigrants should be sent back to their home countries? Do I allow that (even though I strongly disagree) but draw the line at saying the same thing, except for "dreamers"? I don't have an answer for this—it's such a complicated push and pull between encouraging dialogue and "good faith" debate, and making sure all students feel safe and supported (and not attacked, even unknowingly) in your class. It is also another really common and powerful way the personal, professional, and political intersect.

Fran: David, it's interesting you say that teaching should sway "on the side of hopefulness." I assume you mean for humanity. I think overall, yes, but in some instances it seems impossible. When we've seen our former president using derogatory terms for so many groups and supporting an insurrection and then claiming if he was reelected he'd pardon those criminals who were involved in the attack, it's difficult to be hopeful. I think sometimes, especially in a social studies class studying horrible events in history, or when connecting literature to certain horrible modern events, it's kind of important to be hopeless (just a tiny bit) to look at how dire some aspects of life/humanity are (the environment—hard to be too hopeful?!).

Sarah, I like your idea of bending the rules. I definitely find myself doing that, but I think it's sad that I have to sometimes "sneak in" valuable and engaging resources. It belittles our professionalism. I have found myself digging in my heels more often than I ever thought I would in this profession.

As for the moral line, that is a tough one. My coworker last year was doing an argumentative writing unit. Students could pick their own topics. One of her students picked sexual assault crimes (or laws, I forgot the exact wording). Students were supposed to do a counterclaim and talk about the other side in their presentations. The student came to my friend and said that she refused to defend rapists and blame victims. I was impressed with this 9th-grader, and I couldn't help but think she is right. There are not always two sides. My two tactics are (1) ask for evidence (when a student tells me vaccines don't work), and (2) turn to the rest of the class and ask if anyone agrees or disagrees with that point. (I have never had an entire room of brainwashed students yet, but sometimes I do worry that some schools in the country might!) New question: What do you worry about for the future of education in America?

David: Two issues you've raised that I'd like to respond to: the complexities of morality and the notion of hope. As we're winding down creating this book, I think it's apt to comment upon hope. Fran, I understand the challenging of it in certain circumstances, and the harsh realities of how humans have treated one another—and continue to do so. I certainly don't want to sound naive or Pollyanna-ish! And yes, it's hard to see, for example, a world that is not as serious as it should be about climate change and anger shown to those who want to prioritize it. I've just read *Brief Answers to the Big Questions* by Stephen Hawking (2018) and, based upon evidence to date, he's not overly optimistic about human survival in the long run unless, it seems, we head into space. Maybe the notion of hope is a bit idealistic, it's true—but what is the world without its share of dreamers, of those who want to go against the grain?

I'll share a personal story. I will keep it as short as I can. I happened to meet Sonia Nieto when she was a visiting scholar at Hunter for a year. I was at an all-time low for me (very uncharacteristic). On the personal front, my marriage of 27 years had ended, and I was deeply sad and trying to pull myself out of depression. On the professional front, I was worn down with all kinds of thankless and noneducational bureaucratic responsibilities as a university department chairperson. After 3 decades, I'd hoped to see far more changes in education for the better than I had. The country was in a political crisis, there's no other word for it. Everything seemed inescapably heavy. I was also part of my School of Education's Equity and Advocacy Committee, a group interested in social justice issues and centering diversity. One night, after a community-based presentation by Sonia at Roosevelt House, the committee took her and her poet sister, Lydia Cortes, to dinner. On leaving the venue to walk to a nearby restaurant, Sonia happened to take my arm, linking us, and began to chat as we walked along a cold East 65th Street together. I didn't really know her personally, although I'd admired her work for years, so found the gesture to be a pleasant surprise. In light of her presentation titled "Advocacy in Action," I found myself telling her my dilemma. Of essentially being a positive thinker, a "can do" creative person who liked to make things happen but who was—for the first time—experiencing destabilizing doubts about the possibilities in life, including in education, and for social change. Her response was simple: "Hope." It wasn't a new thought, or dare I say it, an original one, but it was the word that I needed to hear at that very moment. It made me reflect on many things, helped me stay grounded and move forward. I think, even in the most atrocious of human experiences (and I am in no way comparing my then-temporary depression to them), hope has always had to exist. What else is there? I'm not religious, so I can't invoke a higher being. My experience did get me thinking about how people reaffirm hope in humanity, and I'd like to think that all of us have that potential and can help others when they struggle. Of course, I also thought of Emily Dickinson's (2019 edition) poem.

> "Hope" is the thing with feathers—
> That perches in the soul—
> And sings the tune without the words—
> And never stops—at all—
>
> And sweetest—in the Gale—is heard—
> And sore must be the storm—
> That could abash the little Bird
> That kept so many warm—
>
> I've heard it in the chillest land—
> And on the strangest Sea—
> Yet—never—in Extremity,
> It asked a crumb—of me. (p. 94)

I like how hope is portrayed as omnipresent and intangible. I have to admit, in rereading, that there's almost a religious feel to the poem and, if I switch gears, Sarah's point about drawing moral lines in classrooms is a good issue to raise, even though it also can be quite nebulous. I don't want to sound trite, but morality—like beauty and ugliness—is often in the eye of the beholder. By that I mean it can be contentious, as there may be as many versions of it as there are humans. Yet, we all have some moral compass embedded in our thinking, some code of rules by which we live. And, of course, there is a collective sense of morality about some of the issues we raised in Chapter 5 in addressing the potential value of (dis)comfort zones. In sum, I think there will always be some perspectives that cannot be morally justified that may enter a classroom discourse, and teachers must address them as they see fit. I am wary of the power of even recognizing some, because naming them provides some form of legitimacy of existence.

I cringe when thinking of it, but the Tennessee school board banning *Maus* and *The Bluest Eye*—both of which I taught and students loved—is immorality masquerading as morality.

Sarah: I actually have been mulling the "what's the future of education" question around in my head for a while in this COVID era. As with many aspects of our society, COVID exposed cracks and flaws that had long existed, like a stress test for society. In education we saw the potential for and limits of digital technology in the (virtual) classroom. We saw the inequities of race and social class in access to tech and learning pods and which schools opened and which didn't. There was a period of time in 2021 that I was hopeful. I really hoped that in showing how the system was broken COVID would allow us a "pause" to tear the old system down and build a new one. We talked in my meetings with my administrative team at school about not falling back into old habits and routines that didn't work. In my classes, I thought about how to restructure my curriculum to be even more responsive to student needs, to use technology to be more differentiated for each child's unique experience of the pandemic. I read all these think pieces that looked at COVID as a chance to hit the reset button and have the ______ (schools, relationships, neighborhoods, social safety nets, etc.) that we always should have had to begin with.

And then, of course, the pandemic continued and continued, way past the point we thought it would last. And we got (or at least I got), so tired, like I was treading water or running uphill. I just didn't have the energy—physical or emotional—to tear anything down and start from scratch when I was just struggling to survive myself. The NYC Department of Ed in general seemed to feel the same way (although this wasn't said outright); there was no shifting of paradigms or revolutionary practices; if anything, it was finding comfort in returning to old routines. Even if I wanted to teach in an entirely new way, I really wouldn't have been able to within the confines of the system that had always existed. So, I did what I said I wouldn't—I fell back into the old patterns and habits and lessons I'd done for years. This year marks the longest I've ever taught one grade and the longest I've ever taught nearly identical slates of books in both of my courses. True to plan, this makes it easier to teach while also managing the mental health of 130 young people, not to mention the emotional health of my own kids and myself. However, it also makes me feel like I'm stuck (and sort of bored), so I'm not sure this choice to change little in my classes has been worth it ultimately.

On my end, I know I have to teach new books and maybe ask to teach a new grade. But this is a long-winded way to getting to what I'm worried about in the future of education. Really it is what I described above. That education will just "plod on" in the same way it always has, with a focus on compliance from children and "good enough" tasks that seem mostly intellectually lazy, with a widening separation between how we educate wealthier, mostly White children versus how we educate poorer, mostly students of color. This is really what has happened. My children's education—technology not withstanding—doesn't look that much different than my own education 30 plus years ago. In truth, I don't know what my ideal form of modern education would look like. Definitely more authentic, definitely more responsive and engaging. But I know it would be different from what is happening in most schools today. I don't really have a positive ending for this thought. If an unprecedented global pandemic hasn't really changed how we teach and learn, what will?

Fran: David, I like your thoughts on hope. My closest friend from when I taught at Darien High School lost her 11-year old son over Christmas break. He died unexpectedly, and it really made me reassess all the things I complain about and all the things I don't value on a daily basis. I will say the reason I teach literature (new or old) is to try to help students think differently (both analysis and empathizing). In addition, I get to interact with/see these young adults right as they are being permanently formed. And, usually once per day (at least) I get a glimpse of the beauty of kindness (and the potential for humanity to be good). On Friday during flex time (a glorified 30-minute study hall at the end of the day), eight girls were playing cards together. One girl, Nicole (who happens to be the only Black student in this class), was sitting on her phone near the girls by herself. After one round of cards, I heard Sofia (a girl who just moved from Stamford to Greenwich) ask Nicole if she wanted to play. Nicole said she didn't know how to play that game, and Sofia said she would teach her. Nicole joined in happily. I was so impressed that as a 9th-grader Sofia noticed who wasn't included and made two efforts to include Nicole. I walked away from the end of the day feeling good about humanity and hopeful that the world can get better, so those little moments are so important to keep me going.

As for Sarah's thoughts on change post-COVID, I 100% agree. It's funny. When Barack Obama was elected, I felt so good about where the United

States was. I really felt like we had overcome this hurdle and now had this intelligent leader at the forefront as we would wander into the sunset as a nation. I now look back and think I must have been delusional. I had no idea there was such racism and anger going on at the time. I was flabbergasted when Trump came forward and heartbroken when he won, and then the awfulness just continued and then COVID and then the insurrection. It does seem like we are (as a nation and a national school system) just a mess. But, I do see changes. I, for one, stopped teaching *Heart of Darkness* (Conrad, 2021 edition) this year. I just couldn't do it again. I also got to teach *The Nickel Boys* (Whitehead, 2020) last year. I also have merged some of my old teaching techniques with new technology that I haven't used in the past. I even finally learned how to find and use more interesting Slides templates (-;. I also see my daughter using all these new technological programs. Things we did not have growing up. Her math class has these online assignments that tell you if you have the correct answer right away and give you a second chance to attempt the problem. I see her working on a project with group mates at home on a shared document and am impressed with the ease of "doing your part," so I do see some positive changes, just not as many in curriculum as I would have hoped for by now.

On that front, do you think today's education in the United States is giving students what they need to be successful in the future (which is always changing so rapidly)? If not, what are we not doing that should be instituted to better the foundations that we are helping students build?

Sarah: Franny, you're right, always pulling me out of my doom and gloom. There are always moments of hope, and we do have to not let that get lost in the stress of everything else (didn't I say a few responses back to always find the joy?!?). I like your comments on your daughter's use of technology and more subtle differences in how kids learn today. I do think COVID was/has been so extreme, that I was hoping—unrealistically of course—that we would just scrap the whole educational system and start anew in some kind of Finlandian utopia. But if I'm being honest with myself, I do see changes in my own kids' education. For one, I know people complain about too high, stressful expectations for young kids, but the level of math my kids do today—in fairly typical classes, nothing exceptional—is head and shoulders above what I did in school. My 3rd-grader was calculating the areas of unusual shapes (something that isn't really that hard), and I remembered that I didn't do that until 9th-grade geometry as a kid.

The second is the online collaboration aspect, which I also see with my kids and gives me hope for the potential technology has for communication and teamwork. I really think that online collaboration is "the future" of education, as it is, even now, at the heart of how almost all professions function. Almost any job, at least those that require a college degree, already relies heavily on collaboration and working together digitally. This includes teaching. I often work on teams at school and feel just as I did when assigned a middle school group project—frustrated that people weren't pulling their weight, but determined to figure out how to get the thing done. The negotiation and decision-making that come with that (Do you have a talk with the team? Do it all yourself? Passively-aggressively assign things to people on Google Docs?) make up a large part of many jobs. And, of course, technology will come with that too, so knowing different platforms, online etiquette will be key.

That said, there is an old-school part of me that is concerned for the basics and wants to ensure that this isn't lost in the shine and sparkle of high-tech things. My now 9-year-old's classes went virtual for COVID in 1st grade, when she was age 6. After a semester of spelling words and weekly tests, the teacher made the call to stop this routine during online school. As a result, she is now a 3rd-grader who really, really struggles to spell. I think a combination of not getting this early practice and not seeing spelling emphasized as important in her early grades led to this. While computers can handle bad spelling, seeing her misspell "birthday" as she fills out a card for a friend makes me sad for the foundational things she lost. So, I love the rigor of the math kids seem to be doing in elementary school, and do think some of that old-school foundational stuff is important—memorizing words and multiplication facts, editing an essay and rewriting until it's almost perfect. Really some of this is teaching kids the lesson that achievement takes hard, focused, sometimes boring work. That you have to persevere and stick to it. While I love that social–emotional learning, creativity, and technology are getting greater influence, at the risk of sounding like a grumpy old lady, I want to champion the basics too.

David: I think we're touching on some of the historic tensions of schooling. What's included in the curriculum, and what's excluded? How do we balance solid, basic knowledge skills with creativity and critical thinking that lead to originality of thought, greater motivation and higher interest, and individual growth? You've both mentioned a lot of interrelated topics, and I'm going to try to distill a few. Much of it boils down to what are schools for? We could spend the rest of our lives debating whether it's ideally to educate a population that will have knowledge, skills, and competitive drive required by society's employers (capitalism); have a body of historical knowledge that all citizens should possess (nationalism); or allow everyone the opportunity to pursue their dreams and become who they want to be (idealism and individualism), or a combination of these and potentially other ideas. My guess is it will depend upon whom you ask. Schools also have been viewed as conservative institutions, meaning they hold onto traditional knowledge and ways of doing things, and serve as instruments of social reproduction in the form of our class structures. This leads me to share a not quite original thought: *some things change, some things stay the same* (and what arguably is a variation of it, *the more things change, the more things stay the same*).

The use of technology has rapidly revolutionized almost everything we did within our lifetimes. Schools have tried to keep up, and while you've both shared good examples of student engagement and acquisition of skills, you're also aware that there are also many bad examples. One of my doctoral students recently defended his dissertation in which he described studying a Cape Verdian American high school student with autism in a segregated setting that had *one* computer between 12 students. The teenager in the study was highly literate, technologically savvy, but was in effect denied access to learning via a computer—what is a norm for many students. There was also minimum direct instruction time in school and lots of "work experience" of picking up community garbage and washing windows. I bring this up to highlight great discrepancies that exist across the country in who is provided a quality education and who isn't. Technology is an integral means to being educated. Of course, it's the means by which we now mostly learn, and not the end per se. But it does involve skills that include researching, analyzing, synthesizing, evaluating, problem solving, and so on. In our lifetime, the shift from a manufacturing economy to an information-based economy (in the "developed world") has meant jobs now need skill sets that former generations didn't require. "Back in the day," as the saying goes—which is not that long ago—people often had the same job or profession for life. Periodically, I come across articles that say contemporary high school students will have numerous jobs and professional positions throughout their lives. We might not even know the jobs that will be needed in 5 or 10 years. Success is closely related to abilities such as flexibility, creativity, criticality, collaboration, ease with technology, multilingualism, and so on. My personal take is that public education is quite behind in responding to the shifts in society. I'd argue that in many ways, teacher education is too.

Fran asked, what should we be doing? I wasn't sure whether she meant "we" as a nation, or "we" as teachers, so I'll briefly respond to both. As a nation, there should be far more investment in public education to provide equal access to resources, including quality, well-supported teachers who stay in their chosen field. As teachers, I do think educators hold a lot of power in who they teach and can provide all of the things we've described in terms of being supportive of students while engaging them in a critical understanding of society, including its diverse peoples and cultures. I could say a lot more, but hope we have shown, in part, in this book that literature is the door into other worlds, perspectives, histories, and forms of understanding that can broaden an individual's knowledge about what it means to be human.

Fran: I think you are spot-on about future skills required for success, and the importance of online etiquette. I frequently have discussed with students how their tone in an email easily can be misconstrued, or the importance of editing online communication. I also have noticed poor spelling by my 9th-graders, and I think a lot of that is due to the last 2 years of online learning.

I do think schools are everything that David lists, but, and I am sure you two will cringe when I say this, I also think they partly need to function as glorified day care. Little kids can't be at home by themselves, and older students can't be trusted to be unsupervised. While we do hope to develop all of these skills in our students, part of our job is to just keep them safe while their parents work because there isn't room in the work world for them yet. I do agree that we don't often know where we will be sending the kids in the future, so adaptability and communication are probably the most important skills we can help foster in our students.

One of my big concerns for the future is the cost of college. I worry that it has become so expensive that it will separate the haves and have-nots so completely that eventually only a specific segment of the country will go to college and then their kids, and so on. It's like we are going backward on that front. I also think in the past 2 years specifically and the past decade overall, we have gone too technological, and I like to have some classes each week where students don't touch a device. Then I don't have to worry about them having a million tabs open or being distracted. Good old-fashioned paper books and pencils are more valuable than I realized.

David: You had me at "glorified day care." Yes, I cringed at the phrase. :) (It reminded me of when folks say special educators have become "glorified paraprofessionals" in inclusive classrooms.) But there's truth in your accompanying statements about how our society is arranged. If we shift the concept from "child care" as noneducational time, schools *are* child care. If we subscribe to the social contract, society is supposed to care for its citizens, and that includes schools and teachers caring for children and youth, and that, in turn, encompasses what they're taught. You're right in that parents are freed up to do other things, but they also are supposed to trust the schooling system—and that their children are being provided a decent education.

In shifting to the topic of college, which is the next step after high school for a large percentage of students, I think it's already quite divided. As we've discussed in places throughout the book, middle-class people—even if feeling strain—usually can muster the resources to visit, apply to, and attend the college of their choice. Working-class and poor people don't have the same social and financial capital, so their options are far reduced. I know many universities have scholarships dedicated to diversifying their population, and that's great, but it's only the financial aspect. There's social, emotional, and cultural aspects, too, that "disadvantaged" students have. Plus, there's all kinds of old-boy practices such as making large donations guaranteeing entrance, and family members of alumni being given preference—so colleges are part of reproduction, too, in this sense.

This is the world that high school students who aspire to college must enter. If you're the first in your family to go, you have no familial knowledge or ties to benefit from. It takes a fair bit of courage to transition to college, and a strong drive to finish. The playing fields are still not level. But a good overall high school education, including expanded knowledge of the world through ELA classes, does provide a solid grounding. For many of us, attending college introduced us to a far more diverse social circle than we had in high school.

Sarah: In the spirit of hope I'll push back a bit on the glorified day care idea. If anything, having parents have to teach their kids at home has, I think, shown many that schools are so much more than this. Parents have seen that, yes, schools are important in freeing them to work, but also that teaching takes more skill than they may have thought. Moreover, the role of school in socialization and building independence for kids is also essential (and teachers are often the guides for this too).

It's funny you mention the divide in college readiness and access, David, as my own experience in college with this divide is what inspired me to be a teacher. As I talk about early in this book, I was shocked when I arrived at Brown at the level of privilege—we're talking private planes, boarding schools, famous parents, and third-generation legacies. I had so many privileges I was aware of even then—White, middle-class, college-educated parents, a decent suburban public school education—but I really felt my lack of what can only be called cultural capital and this made me doubt myself and feel generally like an outsider at times. On top of these more nebulous social class advantages, my peers had incredible academic advantages over me. Now I can see that some of this was my own imposter syndrome, but there were many times when I struggled in a class or with a paper, and the gaps in knowledge and skills between me and the rich kids who had had 13 years of prep school rigor were all too clear. When I entered public schools in Providence as a college tutor, I had my first experiences with the even larger gap between the resources and rigor of many urban public school educations and suburban ones. It was maddening, frustrating, and sad that the students I met in these city public schools—nearly all students of color, poor, often immigrants—were much less well prepared than I, rendering the fancy college in their own backyard essentially inaccessible to them.

Oddly perhaps, this story, the "why" of me deciding to become a public school teacher, is my kernel of optimism that I always return to on hard days. I started teaching in urban public schools in a small attempt to right what I saw as a systemic injustice in how we educate some kids versus others. It can be frustrating on days when I realize I can't desegregate my students' neighborhoods or provide documentation for their parents, but I do feel that if I can give them a challenging, rigorous, creative education and better prepare them for that college experience, then I am doing my small part in the uphill battle to make education a more just endeavor.

Fran: When I see the cost of college tuition climbing, I worry as a middle-class family that my own children will not be able to attend the college of their choice. I worry if I am having this fear then families who make less than I do won't be able to send their kids at all. In addition, I think Sarah makes a great point about the foundations students of wealth have and how that possibly sets them up for more success than other groups. More than 50% of my 6th-grade daughter's friends have tutors so that they can stay at the class levels they are in. I have always championed the idea that students should be at a class level they can succeed in without tutors, but in a wealthy environment parents have the means to push their children to levels that other families don't have. The long-term results of these options perpetuate inequalities in who goes to college and which colleges they get to attend.

I do teach a class that fosters skill development and helps with the college process for first-generation students. In that respect, I feel like I am helping a handful of students get to college prepared for the rigorous environment they will face.

Last year I had lunch with a former colleague, now in her 20th year of teaching (I am in my 20th). We were talking about the various stresses at our different schools over the past few years. She said, "I don't know if I have another 20 years in me." We talked about what she could possibly do instead. It's funny. Sarah's and my principal at our first school always encouraged us to go into administration. He thought we should "go bigger." After 19 years in the classroom, I can't think of anywhere I would rather be. I feel like I have my niche. On some days I wish I could have tried other professions. I love to argue and imagine I could have been a feisty litigator. I love to bake and dreamed of owning my own bakery. I love to read and wish I could be the great American author of the 21st century. Yet, 95% of the time my classroom feels like home, and there is no place I'd rather be.

David: While you two are significantly into the middle of your careers, I am winding down mine. After 35 years of teaching children, youth, and adults, I figured it was okay to stop this year. As I started teaching ELA to high school classes of students in segregated special education classes, I did have the urge to come full circle and write a book about teaching literature and embracing diversity. It's my hope that in sharing our thoughts, experiences, and recommendations, our text also has shown the interconnected personal, professional, and political realms of three educators' lives. Along with our successes, readers have been made aware of some of our challenges and doubts. It all goes with the turf. And for every point we made in this book, there was so much more that could be said that couldn't be included due to page length limitations. Nonetheless, I hope that in some small way, we've helped other teachers—aspiring, new, seasoned, and veteran—to think about ways in which they teach diversity within high school ELA classes.

Notes

Introduction

1. While we can't speak for the country as a whole, based on our own experiences, we did notice that work in Whiteness and racial awareness is being done in city schools more than in suburban and rural schools, where it is likely much more needed. Another point of note is that the patience of teachers of color in schools may, understandably, become worn thin—as they have been confronting these issues, which may shock White teachers, all of their lives.

2. In fact, all three of us have had similar experiences and therefore assume other White teachers have too. Initial responses have included laughing (comfortably or uncomfortably), feeling flattered, and feeling sad. However, these moments deserve further probing not only about what we *think* students may mean but about what they actually mean.

Chapter 1

1. In their book *Letting Go of Literary Whiteness*, Borsheim-Black and Sarigianides (2019) have a whole chapter on teaching *Huckleberry Finn*, the n-word, and the importance of teaching satire purposefully in order to teach it effectively.

2. I use the terms *Latino/a* here as they were used during the time period I am describing. In contemporary terminology, the preferred term is *Latinx* to reflect nonbinary gender.

Chapter 2

1. Maslow's "classic" theory of human motivation, which still intrigues and influences disciplines to this day, claims that there is a hierarchy of needs that impact human development. If one "level" of needs is not met, this can inhibit or prevent attaining the next level in a satisfactory manner. First, the basic universal level is physiological needs (including clothing, food, to ensure the body feels well). The second level is ensuring safety. The third is feeling love and growing a sense of belonging. The fourth relates to esteem and awareness of one's capabilities. The extended hierarchy of needs includes cognitive, aesthetic, self-actualization, and transcendence needs. Of note is that levels in the hierarchy of needs occur simultaneously. Maslow's theory has implications for teaching and learning in classrooms and schools. For example, if a child's basic needs are not met and they are hungry and/or in distress, then learning can be severely impacted.

References

Achebe, C. (1994). *Things fall apart.* Penguin.

Adichie, C. N. (2006). *Half of a yellow sun.* Anchor.

Adichie, C. N. (2014). *Americanah.* Anchor.

Aguilar, E. (2020). *Coaching for equity: Conversations that change practice.* Jossey-Bass.

Allen, R. L. (2004) Whiteness and critical pedagogy. *Educational Philosophy and Theory, 36*(2), 121–136.

Allison, D. (1992). *Bastard out of Carolina.* Penguin.

Allred, J. B., & Cena, M. E. (2020). Reading motivation in high school: Instructional shifts in student choice and class time. *Journal of Adult & Adolescent Literacy, 64*(1), 27–35.

Alsup, J., & Miller, S. J. (2014). Reclaiming English education: Rooting social justice in dispositions. *English Education, 46*(3), 195–215.

Alvarez, J. (2010). *How the Garcia girls lost their accents.* Algonquin.

Anderman, E. M. (2002). School effects on psychological outcomes during adolescence. *Journal of Educational Psychology, 94*(4), 795–809.

Anderson, M., & Hill Collins, P. (2022). *Race, class, and gender: Intersections and inequalities.* Cengage Learning.

Angelou, M. (2009). *I know why the caged bird sings.* Ballantine.

Aronson, B. A., (2017). The white savior industrial complex: A cultural studies analysis of a teacher educator, savior film, and future teachers, *Journal of Critical Thought and Praxis 6*(3).

Atwood, M. (1998). *The handmaid's tale.* Knopf.

Baecher, L. (2019). *Video in teacher learning: Through their own eyes.* Corwin.

Backus, F., & Salvanto, A. (2022, February). Big majorities reject book bans: CBS News Poll. https://www.cbsnews.com/news/book-bans-opinion-poll-2022-02-22

Baglieri, S., & Moses, A. (2010). "My name is Jay": On teachers' roles in the overrepresentation of minorities in special education and what teacher education can do. *Disability Studies Quarterly, 30*(2). https://dsq-sds.org/article/view/1243/1287

Bains, L. (2008). *A teacher's guide to multisensory learning: Improving literacy by engaging with the senses.* Association for Supervision and Curriculum Development.

Baird, R. P. (2021, April 20). The invention of Whiteness: The long history of a dangerous idea. *The Guardian.* https://www.theguardian.com/news/2021/apr/20/the-invention-of-whiteness-long-history-dangerous-idea

Baldwin, J. (1992). *The fire next time.* Vintage Books.

Baldwin, J. (2013). *Giovanni's room.* Vintage Books.

Banks, J. A. (1993). Multicultural education: Historical development, dimensions, and practice. *Review of Research in Education, 19*, 3–49.

Banks, J. A. (2018). *An introduction to multicultural education* (6th ed.). Pearson.

Barbour, M. K. (2021). Research into virtual and blended schools: The lasting legacy of little impact. In A. Molnar (Ed.), *Virtual schools in the U.S. 2021* (pp. 43–66). National Education Policy Center.

Beers, K. (2002). *When kids can't read, what teachers can do: A guide for teachers 6–12*. Heinemann.

Berger, A. (2016). *The postmodern pedagogue: Teaching as a performance art*. Createspace.

Bernstein-Yamashiro, B., & Noam, G. G. (2013). Teacher–student relationships: A growing field of study. *New Directions for Youth Development, 137*, 15–26.

Bheekie, A., & van Huyssteen, M. (2015). Be mindful of your discomfort: An approach to contextualized learning. *International Journal of Research on Service-Learning and Community Engagement, 3*(1). https://ijrslce.scholasticahq.com/article/21560-be-mindful-of-your-discomfort-an-approach-to-contextualized-learning

Bickens, S., Bittman, F., & Connor, D. J. (2013). Developing academic skills through multigenre autobiography. *Journal of English, 102*(5), 43–50.

Blanchett, W. (2010). Disproportionate representation of African American students in special education: Acknowledging the role of White privilege and racism. *Educational Researcher, 35*(6), 24–28.

Boler, M. (1999). *Feeling power: Emotions and education*. Routledge.

Bondy, E., & Ross, D. D. (2008). The teacher as a warm demander. *Educational Leadership, 66*(1), 54–58.

Borovica, T., Humphries, A., & Baird, R. (2019). Using Freire's cultural circles to engage young people. *Researching Young Lives: Methodologies, Methods, Practices and Perspectives in Youth Studies, 4*, 8–10.

Borsheim-Black, C., & Sarigianides, S. T. (2019). *Letting go of literary Whiteness: Anti-racist literature instruction for White students*. Teachers College Press.

Bouchrica, I. (2020, June 10). 101 American school statistics: 20/21 data, trends, & predictions. https://research.com/education/american-school-statistics

Bourdieu, P. (1999). *Language and symbolic power*. Harvard University Press.

Breyer, S. (2022). *Breaking the promise of* Brown: *The resegregation of America's schools*. Brookings Institution Press.

Brookfield, S., & Hess, M. E. (2021). *Becoming a white antiracist: A practical guide for educators, leaders, and activists*. Stylus.

Bridgeland, J. M., DiIulio, J. J., & Burke Morrison, K. (2006). *The silent epidemic: Perspectives of high school dropouts* [Report]. Civic Enterprises. https://files.eric.ed.gov/fulltext/ED513444.pdf

Brontë, C. (1983). *Jane Eyre*. Bantam Classic.

Brontë, E. (2002). *Wuthering Heights*. Penguin.

Brooks, G. (2005). *The essential Gwendolyn Brooks*. Library of America.

Brown v. Board of Education, 347 U.S. 483 (1954).

Brown, C. (2014). *My left foot*. Minerva.

Brunzell, T., Stokes, H., & Waters, L. (2019). Shifting teacher practice in trauma-affected classrooms: Practice pedagogy strategies within a trauma-informed positive education model. *School Mental Health, 11*(3), 600–614.

Buchanan, K. (2006). *Upstate: A novel.* St. Martin's Griffins.

Buck, P. S. (2020). *The good earth.* Washington Square Press.

Bukowczyk, J. J. (2017). *History of the Polish Americans.* Routledge.

Butler, O. (2004). *Kindred.* Beacon Press.

Cannella, S. G., & Reiff, J. C. (1994). Teacher preparation for diversity. *Equity & Excellence in Education, 27*(3), 28–33.

Carlile, A., & Paechter, C. (2022). *LGBTQI parented families and schools: Visibility, representation, and pride.* Routledge.

Carlson, T. (2021, June 25). *Tucker: It's not critical race theory, it's racism.* Tucker Carlson Show [Transcript]. https://www.foxnews.com/transcript/tucker-its-not-critical-race-theory-its-racism

Carver-Thomas, D., & Darling-Hammond, L. (2017, August 16). *Teacher turnover: Why it matters and what we can do about it.* Learning Policy Institute. https://learningpolicyinstitute.org/product/teacher-turnover-report

Cavendish, W., Connor, D., Gonzalez, T., & Jean-Pierre, P. (2020). Troubling "the problem" of racial overrepresentation in special education: A commentary to call to rethink research. *Educational Review, 72*(5), 567–582.

Chang, L. S. (2009). *Hunger: A novella and stories.* Norton.

Cherry-Paul, S., & Johansen, D. (2019). *Breathing new life into book clubs: A practical guide for teachers.* Heinemann.

Cioè-Peña, M. (2021). *(M)othering labeled children.* Multilingual Matters.

Cisneros, S. (1991). *The house on Mango Street.* Vintage Books.

Clark, M. R. (2005). Negotiating the freshman year: Challenges and strategies among first-year college students. *Journal of College Student Development, 46*(3), 296–316.

Coates, T. (2015). *Between the world and me.* One World.

Coleridge, S. T. (2017). *The complete works of Samuel Taylor Coleridge: Poetry, plays, literary essays, lectures, autobiography and letters.* Nabu Press.

Columbus, G. M., Smith, K., & Hinchman, K. (2004). Exploring the African American oral tradition: Instructional implications for literacy learning. *Urbana, 81*(6), 481–490.

Comer, J. (1988). Educating poor minority children. *Scientific American, 259*(5), 42–48.

Connell, W., & Pugliese, S. (Eds.). (2019). *The Routledge history of Italian Americans.* Routledge.

Connor, D. J. (2008). *Urban narratives: Portraits-in-progress—life at the intersections of learning disability, race, and social class.* Peter Lang.

Connor, D. J. (2017). Who is responsible for the racialized practices evident within (special) education and what can be done to change them? *Theory Into Practice, 56*(3), 226–233.

Connor, D. J. (2018). *Contemplating dis/ability in schools and society: A life in education.* Lexington Books.

Connor, D. J. (2022). Revamping a graduate course to (in)fuse disability studies: The politics of representation in "The study of learning disabilities in children and adolescents." *Journal of Teaching Disability Studies.* https://jtds.commons.gc.cuny.edu/revamping-a-graduate-course-to-infuse-disability-studies-the-politics-of-representation-in-the-study-of-learning-disabilities-in-children-and-adolescents-program/

Connor, D. J., Cavendish, W., Gonzalez, T., & Jean-Pierre, P. (2019). Is a bridge even possible over troubled waters? The field of special education negates the overrepresentation of minority students: A DisCrit analysis. *Race Ethnicity and Education, 22*(6), 723–745.

Conrad, J. (2021). *Heart of darkness.* Reader's Library Classics.

Corbin Frazier, L., & Eick, C. (2015). Approaches to critical reflection: Written and video journaling. *Reflective Practice, 16*(5), 575–594.

Cottle, M. (2021, September 6). America's schoolboard meetings are getting weird—and scary. *The New York Times* [Opinion]. https://www.nytimes.com/2021/09/06/opinion/coronavirus-masks-school-board-meetings.html

Cowhey, M. (2022). *Families with power: Centering students by engaging with families and community.* Teachers College Press.

Creamer, J. (2020, September 15). Inequalities persist despite decline in poverty for all major race and Hispanic origin groups. U.S. Census Bureau. https://www.census.gov/library/stories/2020/09/poverty-rates-for-blacks-and-hispanics-reached-historic-lows-in-2019.html

Crenshaw, K., Gotanda, N., Peller, G., & Thomas, K. (Eds.). (1996). *Critical race theory: The key writings that have formed the movement.* New Press.

Cropanzano, R., Li, A., & Benson, L. (2011). Peer justice and teamwork process. *Group & Organizational Management, 36*(5), 567–596.

Crosby, S. D., Howell, P. B., & Thomas, S. (2018). Social justice education through trauma-informed teaching, *Middle School Journal, 49*(4), 15–23.

Crosby, S. D., Howell, P. B., & Thomas, S. (2020). Teaching through collective trauma in the era of COVID-19: Trauma informed practices for middlelevel learners. *Middle Grades Review, 6*(2). https://scholarworks.uvm.edu/mgreview/vol6/iss2/5

Cruz, A. (2020). *Dominicana.* Flatiron.

Cuauhtin, R. T., Zavala, M., Sleeter, C., & Au, W. (Eds.). (2019). *Rethinking ethnic studies.* Rethinking Schools.

Cullen, C. (2023). *Color: Poems of Black America in the 1920s.* Harper & Brothers. Independently Published.

Danforth, E. (2012). *The miseducation of Cameron Post.* Balzer and Bray.

Danforth, S., & Smith, T. J. (2004). *Engaging troubling students: A constructivist approach.* Corwin.

Danielson, C. (2013). *Framework for teaching: Evaluation instrument.* Danielson Group.

Danticat, E. (2013). *The farming of bones.* Soho Press.

Danticat, E. (2015). *Breath, eyes, memory.* Soho Press.

Delpit, L. (1996). *Other people's children: Cultural conflict in the classroom.* New Press.

Denby, D. (1995). *The trouble with* "Heart of darkness." https://www.newyorker.com/magazine/1995/11/06/the-trouble-with-heart-of-darkness

DeWitt, P. M. (2012). *Dignity for all: Safeguarding LGBT students.* Corwin.

DiAngelo, R. (2018). *White fragility: Why it's so hard for White people to talk about racism.* Beacon Press.

Diaz, J. (2008). *The brief, wondrous life of Oscar Wao.* Riverhead Books.

Dickens, C. (1986). *A Christmas carol.* Bantam Classics.

Dickinson, E. (2019). Hope is the thing with feathers: *The complete works of Emily Dickinson*. Gibbs Smith.

Dinkins, D. (2013). *A mayor's life: Governing New York's gorgeous mosaic*. Public Affairs.

Du Bois, W. E. B. (1989). *The souls of Black folks*. Create Space.

Durlak, J. A., Domitrovich, C. E., Weissberg, R. P., & Gullotta, T. P. (2016). *Handbook of social and emotional learning: Research & practice*. Guilford Press.

DuVernay, A. (Director & Producer). (2016). *13th* [Film]. Netflix.

Dyches, J. (2017). Shaking off Shakespeare: A White teacher, urban students, and the mediating powers of a canonical counter-curriculum. *Urban Review, 49*(2), 300–325.

Education Trust. (2017). Graduation rates don't tell the full story: Racial gaps in college success are larger than we think. https://edtrust.org/resource/graduation-rates-dont-tell-the-full-story-racial-gaps-in-college-success-are-larger-than-we-think/

Elias, M., Zins, J. E,, Weisberg, R. P., Frey, K. S, M. Greenberg, M. T., Haynes, N. M., Kessler, R., Schwab-Stone, M. E., & Shriver, T. P. (1997). *Promoting social and emotional learning: Guidelines for educators*. Association for Supervision and Curriculum Development.

Ellison, R. (1995). *The invisible man*. Vintage Books.

Emdin, C. (2007). The three C's for urban science education. *Phi Delta Kappan, 89*(10), 772–775.

Emdin, C. (2016). *For White folks who teach in the hood . . . and the rest of ya'll too: Reality pedagogy and urban education*. Beacon Press.

Engzell, P., Frey, A., & Verhagen, M. D. (2021). Learning loss due to school closings during the COVID-19 pandemic. *Proceedings of the National Academy of Sciences in the USA*. https://www.pnas.org/doi/full/10.1073/pnas.2022376118

Erdrich, L. (2008). *The plague of doves*. HarperCollins.

Eugenides, J. (2007). *Middlesex*. Picador.

Faulkner, W. (1991). *As I lay dying*. Vintage Books.

Fausset, R., Bogel-Burroughs, N., & Fazio, M. (2021, March 17). 8 dead in Atlanta spa shootings, with fears of anti-Asian bias. *The New York Times*. https://www.nytimes.com/live/2021/03/17/us/shooting-atlanta-acworth

Ferlazzo, L., & Hammond, L. (2009). *Building parent engagement in schools*. Linworth.

Fernández-Balboa, J. M. (1998). The practice of critical pedagogy: Critical self-reflection as praxis. *Teaching Education, 9*(2), 47–53.

Ferri, B. A., & Connor, D. J. (2005). Tools of exclusion: Race, disability, and (re) segregated education. *Teachers College Record, 107*(3), 453–474.

Ferri, B. A., & Connor, D. J. (2014). Talking (& not talking) about race, social class, & dis/ability: Toward a margin-to-margin approach. *Race Ethnicity and Education, 17*(4), 471–493.

Fierke, J. (2020) Beyond the American dream: Envisioning social justice for 21st century immigrants. *Social Work with Groups, 43*(1–2), 75–79.

Fitzgerald, F. S. (2004). *The great Gatsby*. Scribner.

Foote, N., & Goebel, M. (Eds.). (2017). *Immigration and national identities in Latin America*. University Press of Florida.

Ford, J. M. (2017). *Challenging stereotypes and prejudices.* Cavendish Square.

Forster, E. M. (2005). *Maurice.* Norton.

Fredericks, M. (2004). *The true meaning of cleavage.* Simon Pulse.

Freire, P. (1976). *Education, the practice of freedom* (M. B. Ramos, Trans.). Writers and Readers Collective.

Freire, P. (1985). *The politics of education: Culture, power and liberation.* Macmillan.

Freire, P. (2018). *Pedagogy of the oppressed: 50th anniversary edition.* Bloomsbury.

Gabel, S., & Connor, D. J. (2009). Theorizing disability: Implications and applications for social justice in education. In W. Ayers, T. Quinn, & D. Stovall (Eds.), *Handbook of social justice* (pp. 377–399). Erlbaum.

Gándara, P., & Santibañez, L. (2016). The teachers our English language students need. *ASCD, 73*(5). https://www.ascd.org/el/articles/the-teachers-our-english-language-learners-need

García, C. (1993). *Dreaming in Cuban.* Ballantine.

García Márquez, G. (2014). *Love in the time of cholera.* Knopf.

Garden, A. (1982). *Annie on my mind.* Square Fish.

Gay, G. (1994). *At the essence of learning: Multicultural education.* Kappa Delta Pi.

Gay, G. (2018). *Culturally responsive teaching: Theory, research, and practice.* Teachers College Press.

Gehlbach, H., Robinson, C. D., Finefter-Rosenbluh, I., Benshoof, C., & Schneider, J. (2018). Questionnaires as interventions: Can taking a survey increase teachers' openness to student feedback surveys? *Educational Psychology, 38*(3), 350–367.

Gerber, N. (2020). How are school districts adapting teacher work policies for emergency closures? *National Council on Teacher Quality.* https://www.nctq.org/blog/How-are-school-districts-adapting-teacher-work-policies-for-emergency-closures

Gestwicki, C. (2015). *Home, school, and community relations.* Cengage Learning.

Gillen, A., Wright, A., & Spink, L. (2011). Student perceptions of a positive climate for learning: A case study. *Educational Psychology in Practice, 27*(1), 65–82.

Goleman, D. (1995). *Emotional intelligence: Why it can matter more than IQ.* Random House.

Gonzalez, J. (2011). *Harvest of empire: A history of Latinos in America.* Penguin.

Gonzalez, J. (2015). The big list of class discussion strategies. *Cult of Pedagogy, 15.* https://www.cultofpedagogy.com/speaking-listening-techniques

Goodson, I. F. (2003). *Studying teachers' lives.* Routledge.

Grant, C., & Agosto, V. (2008). Teacher capacity and social justice in education. In M. Cochran-Smith, S. Faiman-Nemser, & D. J. McIntyre (Eds.), *Handbook of research on teacher education* (pp. 175–200). Routledge.

Graves, K. (2009). *And they were wonderful teachers: Florida's purge of gay and lesbian teachers.* University of Illinois Press.

Grech, J. (2021). Critical self-reflection for nurse educators: Now more than ever!. *Teaching and Learning in Nursing, 16*(1), 89–91.

Greenway, R., & Vanourek, G. (2022). The virtual revolution. *Education Next, 22*(2). https://www.educationnext.org/the-virtual-revolution-understanding-online-schools

Greer, A. S. (2018). *Less.* Back Bay Books.

Griffith, J. (2016). *From me to we: Using narrative nonfiction to broaden student perspectives*. Routledge.

Griffith, J. (2021). Troubling Atticus: Letting the mockingbird fly away. *Voices From the Middle, 28*(4), 30–33.

Grinage, J. (2013). Combatting Huck Finn's censorship: A step-by-step guide to discussing the n-word in the classroom. In S. Grineski, J. Landsman, & R. Simmons III (Eds)., *Talking about race: Alleviating the fear* (pp. 137–148). Stylus.

Grissom, J. A., & Andersen, S. (2012). Why superintendents turn over. *American Educational Research Journal, 49*(6), 1146–1180.

Guiffrida, D. A., Kiyama, J. M., Waterman, S. J., & Museus, S. D. (2011). *Moving from cultures of individualism to cultures of collectivism in support of students of color.* Routledge.

Gyasi, Y. (2017). *Homegoing*. Vintage Books.

Hammond, Z. (2014). *Culturally responsive teaching and the brain: Promoting authentic engagement and rigor among culturally and linguistically diverse students.* Corwin.

Hansberry, L. (1959). *A raisin in the sun*. Vintage Books.

Hansen, A., & Smyth, T. S. (2016). Teaching English language arts students about social justice. In R. Papa, D. M. Eadens, & D. W. Eadens (Eds.), *Social justice instruction*. Springer.

Harris, J. (2021). *Christianity and social justice: Religions in conflict.* Reformation Zion Publishing.

Harry, B., & Klingner, J. K. (2006). *Why are so many students in special education? Understanding race and disability in schools.* Teachers College Press.

Harry, B., & Ocasio-Stoutenburg, L. (2020). *Meeting families where they are: Building equity through advocacy with diverse schools and communities.* Teachers College Press.

Harvey, J. (2019). *Raising white kids: Bringing up children in a racially unjust America.* Abingdon Press.

Hastings, C., & Jacob, L. (2016). *Social justice in English language teaching*. TESOL Press.

Hawking, S. (2018). *Brief answers to the big questions*. John Murray.

Hawthorne, N. (2015). *The scarlet letter.* Create Space.

Heitzeg, N. A. (2016). *The school-to-prison pipeline: Education, discipline, and racialized double standards.* Praeger.

Hellman, L. (1934). *The children's hour*. BN Publishing.

Hernandez-Armesto, F. (2014). *Our America: A Hispanic history of the United States.* Norton.

Hess, F. M., & Maranto, R. A. (2000). Tenure's tenuous tenure in public schools. *The Education Digest, 65*(5), 51–55.

Highland Center (n.d.) Strategic convenings. https://highlandercenter.org/programs/strategic-convenings

Higgins, T. (2020, June 15). *Supreme court rules that workers can't be fired for being gay or transgender*. CNBC News. https://www.cnbc.com/2020/06/15/supreme-court-rules-workers-cant-be-fired-for-being-gay-or-transgender.html

Hill, B. C., & Noe, K.L.S. (2003). *Literature circles in middle school: One teacher's journey* (2nd ed.). Christopher Gordon.

Hirsch, E. D. (1988). *Cultural literacy: What every American needs to know*. Vintage Books.

Holbert, R.M.G. (2015). Beginning with bingo—an icebreaker to initiate classroom community. *College Teaching, 63*(4), 181–182.

Homer. (1997). *The odyssey*. Penguin.

hooks, b. (2001). *All about love: New visions*. William Morrow.

hooks, b. (2014). *Teaching to transgress: Education as the practice of freedom*. Routledge.

Hosseini, K. (2003). *The kite runner.* Riverhead Books.

Howard, T. C., & Banks, J. (2020). *Why race and culture matter in schools: Closing the achievement gap in America's classrooms*. Teachers College Press.

Hughes, L. (1995). *The collected poems of Langston Hughes*. Vintage Books.

Hurston, Z. N. (1928, May). *How it feels to be colored me*. American Roots.

Hurston, Z. N. (2006). *Their eyes were watching God*. Amistad.

Hurston, Z. N. (2008). *Mules and men*. Amistad.

Ihimaera, W. (1987). *The whale rider*. Harcourt.

Jablon, J. (2022). *To kill a mockingbird* is a racist book. In G. M. Jacobs & G. V. Crookes (Eds.), *Becoming community-engaged educators* (pp. 17–26). Springer.

Jacobs, D., & Dirlam, J. C. (2016). Politics and economic stratification: Power resources and income inequality in the United States. *American Journal of Sociology, 122*(2), 469–500.

James, A. (2000, June). Oral tradition—A literacy for lifelong learning: Native American approaches to justice and wellness education. In *Proceedings of the 41st Annual Adult Education Research Conference* (p. 549), Vancouver, British Columbia, Canada.

Jansen, J. (2009). On the clash of martyrological memories. *Perspectives in Education, 27*(2), 147–157.

Jen, G. (2008). *Typical American*. Vintage Books.

Jenkins, B. (Director). (2017). *Moonlight* [Film]. Lionsgate.

Jiang, J. (1999). *Red scarf girl: A memoir of the cultural revolution*. HarperCollins.

Jones, H. (2019). *The 1619 project*. One World.

Jones, S. P. (2020). Ending curriculum violence. *Learning for Justice, 64*. https://www.learningforjustice.org/magazine/spring-2020/ending-curriculum-violence

Jones, S. R., & Hill, K. E. (2016). Understanding patterns of commitment: Student motivation for community services involvement. *The Journal of Higher Education, 74*(5), 516–539.

Kahn, E. (2007). Building fires: Raising achievement through class discussion. *English Journal, 96*(4), 16–18.

Kaler-Jones, C. (2020, May 7). When SEL is used as another form of policing. *Medium*. https://medium.com/@justschools/when-sel-is-used-as-another-form-of-policing-fa53cf85dce4

Kauffman, J., Hallahan, D., & Pullen, P. (2017). *The handbook of special education*. Routledge.

Kaufman, M. (1994). *The Laramie project*. Dramatists Play Service.

Kay, M. (2018). *Not light but fire: How to lead meaningful race conversations in the classroom*. Stenhouse.

Kayyali, R. A. (2005). *The Arab Americans*. Greenwood.

Kearney, P. (2021). *Dear Tucker Carlson.* https://patrickjkearney.wordpress.com/2021/07/07/dear-tucker-carlson

Kendi, I. X. (2019). *How to be an antiracist.* Penguin.

Kennedy, R. (2002). *Nigger: The strange career of a troublesome word.* Vintage Books.

Kenney, M. (2013). Of mice and marginalization. *Rethinking Schools, 20*(1). https://rethinkingschools.org/articles/of-mice-and-marginalization

Kibler, A., Valdes, G., & Walqi, A. (Eds.). (2022). *Reconceptualizing the role of critical dialogue in American classrooms.* Routledge.

Kincheloe, J. L. (1999). The struggle to define and reinvent whiteness: A pedagogical analysis. *College Literature, 26*(3), 162–194.

Kingston, M. H. (1976). *The woman warrior: Memoirs of a girlhood among ghosts.* Picador.

Kohl, H. (1995). *I won't learn from you: And other thoughts on creative maladjustment.* New Press.

Koss, M. D., & Paciga, K. A. (2020). Diversity in Newberry-winning titles: A content analysis. *Journal of Language and Literacy Education, 16*(2), 1–36.

Kumashiro, K. K. (2000). Toward a theory of anti-oppressive education. *Review of Educational Research, 70*(1), 25–53.

Kumashiro, K. K. (2003). *Restored selves: Autobiographies of queer Asian/Pacific American activists.* Routledge.

Kumashiro, K. K. (2015). Against common sense: Teaching and learning toward social justice. *Power and Education, 7*(3), 19–33.

Kushner, T. (2013). *Angels in America.* Theater Communications.

Ladson-Billings, G. (1994). *The dreamkeepers: Successful teachers of African American Children.* Jossey-Bass.

Ladson-Billings, G. (2008). It's not the culture of poverty, it's the poverty of culture: The problem of teacher education. *Anthropology and Education Quarterly, 37*(2), 104–109.

Ladson-Billings, G. (2021). *Critical race theory* [Video]. YouTube. https://www.youtube.com/watch?v=ufKusK6dQI8

Lagares, C., & Connor, D. J. (2009). 20 ways to help students prepare for high school examinations. *Intervention in School and Clinic, 45*(1), 68–71.

Lagravanese, R. (Director). (2007). *Freedom writers* [Film]. Jersey Films.

Lalas, J., & Valle, E. (2007). Social justice lenses and authentic student voices: Enhancing leadership for educational justice. *Educational Leadership and Administration: Teaching and Program Development, 19*, 75–102.

Lawrence, C. (2020). Is Lennie a monster? A reconsideration of Steinbeck's *Of Mice and Men* in a 21st century inclusive classroom context. *Palgrave Communications, 6*(1), 1–8.

Lee, C. (1996). *Native speaker.* Riverhead Books.

Lee, H. (1960). *To kill a mockingbird.* Lippincott.

Lee, J. J., & Casey, M. (2007). *Making the Irish American: History & heritage of the Irish in the United States.* NYU Press.

Lensmire, T. J. (2017). *White folks: Race and identity in rural America.* Routledge.

Léon, B. (2021, November 28). *Black and Latino studies get a place in the classroom.* National Public Radio. https://www.ctpublic.org/2021-11-28/black-latino-studies-get-a-place-in-the-classroom

Leonardo, Z. (2009). *Race, Whiteness, and education.* Routledge.

Lianke, Y. (2018). *The day the sun died.* Grove.

Lindner, A. (2018). Defining Whiteness: Perspectives on privilege. *Gnovis Journal, 18*(2), 43–58.

Lindquist, J. (2004). Class, affects, classroom affectations: Working through the paradoxes of strategic empathy. *College English, 67*(2), 187–209.

Lipsitz, G. (2018). *The possessive investment in Whiteness: How White people profit from identity politics.* Temple University Press.

Loewen, J. W. (2018). *Lies my teacher told me: Everything your American history textbook got wrong.* New Press.

London, R., & Ingram, D. (2018). Social isolation in middle school. *School Community Journal, 28*(1), 107–127.

López, F., Scanlan, M., & Gundrum, B. (2013). Preparing teachers of English language learners: Empirical evidence and policy implications. *Education Policy Analysis Archives, 21*(20), 1–35.

Lorde, A. (1982). *Zami: A new spelling of my name.* Crossing Press.

Lorde, A. (2020). *Selected works of Audre Lorde.* Norton.

Losen, D. J., & Orfield, G. (Eds.). (2002). *Racial inequality in special education.* Harvard Education Press.

Loukaitou-Sidens, A., & Soureli, K. (2011). Cultural tourism as an economic development strategy for ethnic neighborhoods. *Economic Development Quarterly, 26*(1), 50–72.

Love, B. L. (2019, March 18). Dear White teachers: You can't love your Black students if you don't know them [Commentary]. *Education Week.*

Lowe, G. M., Prout, P., & Murcia, K. (2013). I see, I think I wonder: An evaluation of journaling as a critical reflective practice tool for aiding teachers in challenging or confronting contexts. *Australian Journal of Teacher Education, 38*(6), 1–16.

Mackler, C. (2003). *The earth, my butt, and other big round things.* Candlewick.

Margolius, M., Doyle Lynch, A., Pufall Jones, E., & Hynes, M. (2020). *The state of young people during COVID 19: Findings from a nationally representative survey of high school youth.* America's Promise Alliance. https://files.eric.ed.gov/fulltext/ED606305.pdf

Markos, V. (2022). The effect of school community service on volunteering and its motives. *Education, Citizenship, & Social Justice.* https://doi.org/10.1177/17461979221103789

Maslow, A. H. (1943). A theory of human motivation. *Psychological Review, 50*(4), 370–396.

Mathabane, M. (1998). *Kaffir boy: The true story of a Black youth's coming of age in apartheid South Africa.* Free Press.

Matias, C. E. (2016a). "Why do you make me hate myself?": Re-teaching Whiteness, abuse, and love in urban teacher education. *Teaching Education, 27*(2), 194–211

Matias, C. E. (2016b). *Feeling White: Whiteness, emotionality, and education.* Sense.

Matias, C. E. (2022). On Whiteness studies: Hope and futurity. *International Journal of Qualitative Studies in Education, 35*(7), 697–702.

Matias, C. E., & Mackey, J. (2016). Breakin' down Whiteness in antiracist teaching: Introducing critical Whiteness pedagogy. *Urban Review, 48*(1), 32–50.

Mayo, C. (2022). LGBTQ youth and education: Policies and practices. *Teachers College Press.*

McBride, J. (1995). *The color of water: A Black man's tribute to his White mother.* Riverhead Books.

McBride, J. (2003). *Miracle at St. Anna.* Riverhead Books.

McBride, J. (2021). *Deacon King Cong.* Riverhead Books.

Mccarthy, C. (2003). Contradictions of power and identity: Whiteness studies and the call of teacher education. *International Journal of Qualitative Studies in Education, 16*(1), 127–133.

McDonald, J. P., Mohr, N., Dichter, A., & McDonald, E. C. (2013). *The power of protocols: An educator's guide to better practice.* Teachers College Press.

McIntosh, P. (1990). *White privilege: Unpacking the invisible knapsack* [Monograph]. Legislative Assembly of the Northwest. https://www.jstor.org/stable/community.30714426?seq=2#metadata_info_tab_contents

Mendenhall, M., & Bartlett, L. (2018) Academic and extracurricular support for refugee students in the US: Lessons learned. *Theory Into Practice, 57*(2), 109–118.

Mikami, A. Y., Griggs, M. S., Reutland, M. M., & Gregory, A. (2012). Teacher practices as predictors of children's classroom social preference. *Journal of School Psychology, 50*(1), 95–111.

Milner, H. R. (2003). Teacher reflection on race in cultural contexts: History, meanings, and methods in teaching. *Theory Into Practice, 42*(3), 173–180.

Milner, H. R., Cunningham, H. B., Delale-O'Connor, L., & Gold-Kestenberg, E. (2018). *"These kids are out of control": Why we must reimagine "classroom management" for equity.* Corwin.

Min, A. (2004). *Wild ginger.* Mariner.

Moeller, M., & Moeller, V. (2016). *Literature circles that engage middle and high school students.* Routledge.

Molnar, A. (Ed.). (2021). *Virtual schools in the U.S. 2021.* National Education Policy Center.

Molnar, A., & Boninger, F. (2021). Executive summary. In A. Molnar (Ed.), *Virtual schools in the U.S. 2021* (pp. 3–9). National Education Policy Center.

Mondale, S. (2002). *School: The history of American public education.* Beacon Press.

Morningside Center (2013). https://www.morningsidecenter.org/teachable-moment/lessons/introduction-circles

Morrison, T. (1977). *Song of Solomon.* Alfred Knopf.

Morrison, T. (1992). *Playing in the dark: Whiteness and the literary imagination.* Harvard University Press.

Morrison, T. (2007). *The bluest eye.* Vintage Books.

Muhammad, G. (2020). *Cultivating genius: An equity framework for culturally and historically responsive teaching.* Scholastic.

National Assessment of Educational Progress. (2019). NAEP report card: 2019 NAEP mathematics assessment. https://www.nationsreportcard.gov/highlights/mathematics/2019

National Center for Education Statistics. (2018). SAT scores. https://nces.ed.gov/fastfacts/display.asp?id=171

National Center for Education Statistics. (2019). Racial/ethnic enrollment in public schools https://nces.ed.gov/programs/coe/indicator_cge.asp

National Center for Education Statistics. (2020). Students with Disabilities. https://nces.ed.gov/programs/coe/indicator_cgg.asp

National Center for Learning Disabilities. (2019). *Forward together: Helping educators unlock the power of students who learn differently*. https://www.ncld.org/wp-content/uploads/2019/05/Forward-Together_NCLD-report.pdf

Naylor, G. (1983). *The women of Brewster Place*. Penguin.

New York State Education Department. (2018). Culturally responsive-sustaining education. http://www.nysed.gov/crs

Newell, G., Bloome, D., & Hirvela, A. (2015). *Teaching and learning argumentative writing in high school English language arts classrooms*. Routledge.

Nicol, J. (2008). Questioning the canon: Issues surrounding the selection of literature for the high school English curriculum. *English Quarterly, 38*(2–3), 22–28.

Nieto, S. (1992). *Affirming diversity: The sociopolitical context of multicultural education*. Longman.

Nieto, S. (2013). *Finding joy in teaching students of diverse backgrounds: Culturally responsive and socially just practices in U.S. classrooms*. Heinemann.

Nieto, S., & Bode, P. (2017). *Affirming diversity: The sociopolitical context of multicultural education*. Pearson.

Nilson, L. B. (2021). *Online teaching at its best*. Jossey-Bass.

Noddings, N. (2005). *Educating citizens for global awareness*. Teachers College Press.

Noddings, N. (2013a). *Caring: A relational approach to ethics and moral education*. University of California Press.

Noddings, N. (2013b). *The challenge to care in schools: An alternative approach to education*. Teachers College Press.

Nomikoudis, M., & Starr, M. (2016). Cultural humility in education and work: A valuable approach for teachers, learners and professionals. In J. Arvanitakis & D. J. Hornsby (Eds.), *Universities, the citizen scholar and the future of higher education* (pp. 54–68). Palgrave Macmillan.

Novak, K., & Rose, D. (2016). *UDL now! A teacher's guide to applying universal design for learning for today's classrooms* (2nd ed.). CAST Professional Publishing.

Oakes, J. (2005). *Keeping track: How schools structure inequality*. Yale University Press.

Orange, T. (2019). *There there*. Vintage.

Orwell, G. (1961). *1984*. Signet Classics.

Orwell, G. (2004). *Animal farm*. Signet Classics.

Osofsky, J. D., Osofsky, H. J., & Mamon, L. Y. (2020). Psychological and social impact of COVID-19. *Psychological Trauma: Theory, Research, Practice, and Policy, 12*(5), 468–469.

Padilla, D. (2016). *Undocumented: A Dominican boy's odyssey from a homeless shelter to the Ivy League*. Penguin.

Paris, D., & Alim, H. S. (2017). *Culturally sustaining pedagogies: Teaching and learning justice in a changing world*. Teachers College Press.

Parker, D. (2019). *Building bridges: Engaging students at risk through the power of relationships*. Solution Tree Press.

Pass, E. (2021). *The hybrid teacher: Using technology to teach in-person and online*. Jossey-Bass.

Philibert, C. T. (2017). *Everyday SEL in high school: Integrating social-emotional learning and mindfulness into your classroom.* Routledge.

Philip, T. (2019). Principled improvisation to support novice teacher learning. *Teachers College Record, 121*(6), 1–32.

Phillips, O. (2015, April 5). *Without janitors, students are in charge of keeping school shipshape.* National Public Radio. https://www.npr.org/sections/ed/2015/04/04/396621542/without-janitors-students-are-in-charge-of-keeping-school-shipshape

Picower, B. (2009). The unexamined Whiteness of teaching: How White teachers maintain and enact dominant racial ideologies. *Race Ethnicity and Education, 12*(2),197–215.

Polleck, J. (2011a). Adolescent literature book clubs: A forum for cultivation and peer relationships with urban adolescent females. *The ALAN Review, 39*(1), 76–95.

Polleck, J. (2011b). Using book clubs to enhance social-emotional and academic learning with urban adolescent females of color. *Reading & Writing Quarterly, 27*(1–2), 101–128.

Polleck, J. (2022). *Facilitating youth-led book clubs as transformative and inclusive spaces.* Teachers College Press.

Polleck, J., & Epstein, T. (2015). Affirmation, analysis, and agency: Book clubs as spaces for critical conversations with young adolescent women of color. *Reading Horizons: Journal of Literacy & Language Arts, 54*(1), 78–107.

Prebel, J. (2016, Summer). Engaging a "pedagogy of discomfort": Emotion as critical inquiry in community-based writing courses. *Composition Forum, 34,* 12.

Pressick-Kilborn, K., & te Riele, K. (2008). Learning from reciprocal peer observation: A collaborative self-study. *Studying Teacher Education, 4*(1), 61–75.

Primamore, E., & Deluise, D. (2010). *Literature and gender.* Pearson.

Proulx, A. (2005). *Brokeback mountain.* Scribner.

Pyun, H. (2018). *City of ash and red.* Arcade.

Quinones, E. (2000). *Bodega dreams.* Vintage Books.

Rand, A. (2005). *The fountainhead.* Plume.

Rappleye, J., & Komatsu, H. (2017). How to make lesson study work in America and worldwide: A Japanese perspective on the onto-cultural basis of (teacher) education. *Research in Comparative and International Education, 12*(4), 298–430.

Remarque, E. (1928). *All quiet on the western front.* Ballantine.

Roanhorse, R. (2018). *Trail of lightning.* Gallery/Saga Press.

Rocha, I. (2019). *Mexican American sonnet.* https://poets.org/poem/mexican-american-sonnet

Rothenberg, P. (2015). *White privilege: Essential readings on the other side of racism.* Worth.

Roy, A. (1998). *The god of small things.* Random House.

Salend, S. (2015). *Creating inclusive classrooms: Effective, differentiated and reflective practices.* Pearson.

Salinger, J. D. (2001). *The catcher in the rye.* Bay Back Books.

Santiago, E. (2006). *When I was Puerto Rican: A memoir.* Da Capo Press.

Sapphire. (2021). *Push.* Vintage Books.

Satrapi, M. (2004). *Persepolis*. Pantheon.

Sauer, J. S., & Rossetti, Z. (2020). *Affirming disability: Strengths-based portraits of culturally diverse families*. Teachers College Press.

Scherer, M. (2016). *On poverty and learning: Readings from Educational Leadership*. Association for Supervision and Curriculum Development.

Schieble, M., Vetter, A., & Martin, K. M. (2020). *Classroom talk for social change: Critical conversations in English language arts*. Teachers College Press.

Selwyn, N. (2020, October 25). How creative use of technology may have helped save schools during the pandemic. *The Conversation*. https://theconversation.com/how-creative-use-of-technology-may-have-helped-save-schooling-during-the-pandemic-146488

Shah, D. (2016). Online education: Should we take it seriously? *Climacteric, 19*(1), 3–6.

Shakespeare, W. (1992). *Hamlet*. Simon & Schuster.

Shakespeare, W. (2003). *Macbeth*. Simon & Schuster.

Shakespeare, W. (2004). *Othello*. Simon & Schuster.

Shakespeare, W. (2006). *Shakespeare's sonnets and poems*. Simon & Schuster.

Shakespeare, W. (2008). *Richard III*. Oxford University Press.

Shakespeare, W. (2014). *Romeo and Juliet*. Cambridge University Press.

Shange, N. (1997). *For colored girls who have considered suicide/when the rainbow is enuf*. Scribner.

Shapiro, A. (2003). *Everybody belongs: Changing negative attitudes towards classmates with disabilities*. Routledge.

Sharma, S., & Lazar, A. (Eds.). (2019). *Rethinking 21st century diversity in teacher preparation, K–12 education, and school policy: Theory, research, and practice*. Springer.

Simien, J. (Director). (2014). *Dear White people*. [Film]. Code Red Films.

Sims Bishop, R. (1990). Mirrors, windows, and sliding glass doors in perspectives: Choosing and using books for the classroom. *Perspectives, 6*(3), ix–xi.

Singleton, G. (2005). *Courageous conversations about race: A field guide for achieving equity in schools*. Corwin.

Sleeter, C. E. (2016). Wrestling with problematics of Whiteness in teacher education. *International Journal of Qualitative Studies in Education, 29*(8), 1065–1068.

Sleeter, C. E. (2017). Critical race theory and the Whiteness of teacher education. *Urban Education, 52*(2), 155–169.

Sleeter, C. E. (2020). *Transformative ethnic studies in schools: Curriculum, pedagogy, and research*. Teachers College Press.

Sleeter, C. E., & Grant, C. A. (1987). An analysis of multicultural education in the United States. *Harvard Educational Review, 7*, 421–444.

Sleeter, C. E., & Grant, C. A. (1988). *Making choices for multicultural education: Five approaches to race, class, and gender*. Merrill.

Smith, J. (Director). (1995). *Dangerous minds*. [Film]. Buena Vista Pictures.

Solgot, H. (2005). Journaling for personal and professional growth: Reflections of a recent student teacher. *Language Arts Journal of Michigan, 21*(1), Article 13. https://doi.org/10.9707/2168-149X.1218

Sophocles. (2005). *Antigone*. Prestwick House.

Souto-Manning, M. (2010). *Freire, teaching, and learning: Culture circles across contexts*. Peter Lang.

Sparks, S. D. (2021, March 31). Data: What we know about student mental health and the pandemic [Special report]. *Education Week*. https://www.edweek.org/leadership/data-what-we-know-about-student-mental-health-and-the-pandemic/2021/03

Spiegelman, A. (1986). *Maus: A survivor's tale: My father bleeds history*. Pantheon.

Spring, J. (2016). *Deculturalization and the struggle for equality* (8th ed.). Routledge.

Stalvey, L. (1970). *The education of a WASP.* University of Wisconsin Press.

Statista. (2021). Total population in the United States by gender from 2010 to 2027. https://www.statista.com/statistics/737923/us-population-by-gender

Steinbeck, J. (1937). *Of mice and men*. Penguin.

Stevenson, B. (2018). *Just mercy (adapted for young adults): A true story of the fight for justice*. Delacorte Press.

Stoddard, J., Marcus, A. S., & Hicks, D. (Eds.). (2017). *Teaching difficult history through film*. Routledge.

Strozewski, Z. (2022, January 21). 'Social emotional learning' becomes latest battleground in school curriculums. *Newsweek*. https://www.newsweek.com/social-emotional-learning-becomes-latest-battleground-school-curriculums-1671698

Tajalli, H., & Garba, H. (2014). Discipline or prejudice? Overrepresentation of minority students in disciplinary alternative education programs. *Urban Review, 46*(4), 620–631.

Tan, A. (2006). *The joy luck club*. Penguin.

Tanner, S. J. (2019). Whiteness is a White problem: Whiteness in English education. *English Education, 51*(2), 182–199.

Taylor, A. K. (2011). Students learn equally well from digital as from paperbound texts. *Teaching of Psychology, 38*(4), 278–281.

Taylor, M. (1976). *Roll of thunder, hear my cry*. Puffin.

Theobald, J., Gardner, F., & Long, N. (2017). Teaching critical reflection in social work field education. *Journal of Social Work Education, 53*(2), 300–311.

Thomas, P. (1967). *Down these mean streets*. Vintage Books.

Thomas, M. S., Crosby, S., & Vanderhaar, J. (2019). Trauma-informed practices in schools across two decades: An interdisciplinary review of research. *Review of Research in Education, 43*(1), 442–452.

Tillman, L. C. (2003). Mentoring, reflection, and reciprocal journaling. *Theory Into Practice, 42*(3), 226–233.

Trainor, J. S. (2002). Critical pedagogy's "other": Constructions of Whiteness in education for social change. *College Composition and Communication, 53*(4), 631–650.

Trotsky, L. (1993). *Fascism: What it is and how to fight it*. Pathfinder.

Twain, M. (1876). *The adventures of Tom Sawyer*. American Publishing Company.

Twain, M. (1884). *The adventures of Huckleberry Finn*. Charles L. Webster & Co.

Valdes-Rodriguez, A. (2003). *The dirty girls social club*. St. Martin's.

Valle, J. W. (2009). *What mothers say about special education: From the 1960s to the present*. Palgrave.

Valle, J. W., & Connor, D. J. (2019). *Rethinking disability: A disability studies guide to inclusive practices* (2nd ed.). Routledge.

Vygotsky, L. S. (1987). *The collected works of L. S. Vygotsky: Problems of general psychology*. Plenum Press.

Walker, A. (2003). *You can't keep a good woman down.* Amistad.

Walker, A. (2019). *The color purple.* Penguin.

Walls, J. (2006). *The glass castle: A memoir.* Scribner.

Wang, H. (2005). Aporias, responsibility, and the im/possibility of teaching multicultural education. *Educational Theory, 55*(1), 45–59.

Weaver, A. D., Philip Scherer, S. H., & Shriver, M. D. (2020). An exploratory investigation of proximity control in a large-group unstructured setting. *Preventing School Failure: Alternative Education for Children & Youth, 64*(3), 261–270.

Weissberg, R. P., & Shriver, T. P. (1996). *School-based prevention programs: A comprehensive strategy.* Mid-Atlantic Lab for Student Success. https://files.eric.ed.gov/fulltext/ED403338.pdf

Weldon Johnson, J. (2000). *Complete poems.* Penguin Classics.

Wheatley, P. (2001). *Phillis Wheatley, complete writings.* Penguin Classics.

White, S. J. (2021). Overcoming barriers: De-tracking to teach for social justice. *Middle Grades Review, 7*(3). https://scholarworks.uvm.edu/mgreview/vol7/iss3

Whitehead, C. (2020). *The underground railroad.*

Whitehead, C. (2020). *The nickel boys.* Knopf Doubleday.

Wiesel, E. (2006). *Night.* Hill & Wang.

Wiggins, G., & McTighe, J. (2005). *Understanding by design* (2nd ed.). Association for Supervision and Curriculum Development.

Wilder, T. (2003). *Our town.* Perennial Classics.

Williams, T. (2004). *A streetcar named desire.* New Directions.

Williamson, T. (2017). Listening to many voices: Enacting social justice literary curriculum. *Teaching and Teacher Education, 61*, 104–114.

Wilson. A. (1986). *Fences.* Plume.

Wilson. A. (1987). *The piano lesson.* Plume.

Woodson, J. (1997). *The house you pass on the way.* Puffin.

Wright, R. (1940). *Native son.* HarperCollins.

Wright, R. (2023). *Black boy.* HarperCollins.

Yacoveone, D. (2022). *Teaching White supremacy: America's democratic ordeal and the forging of our national identity.* Pantheon.

Yang, M. (2022, January 11). GOP state senator walks back comments on Nazi history in schools. *The Guardian.* https://www.theguardian.com/education/2022/jan/11/gop-senator-backtracks-comments-nazism

Yienger, M. E. (2016). Too much tech harms reading retention in young children. *Inquiries: Social Sciences, Arts, & Humanities, 8*(3). http://www.inquiriesjournal.com/articles/1374/too-much-tech-harms-reading-retention-in-young-children

Young, J. (2017). *Rhetoric, embodiment, and the ethos of surveillance.* Lexington Books.

Zembylas, M. (2015). 'Pedagogy of discomfort' and its ethical implications: The tensions of ethical violence in social justice education. *Ethics and Education, 10*(2), 163–174.

Zembylas, M., & McGlynn, C. (2012). Discomforting pedagogies: Emotional tensions, ethical dilemmas and transformative possibilities. *British Educational Research Journal, 38*(1), 41–59.

Zia, H. (2001). *Asian-American dreams: The emergence of an American people.* Farrar, Straus, & Giroux.

Zimman, L. (2019). Pronouns and possibilities: Transgender language activism and reform. In N. Avineri, L. R. Graham, E. J. Johnson, R. Conley Riner, & J. Roser (Eds.), *Language and social justice in practice* (pp. 176–183). Routledge.

Zinn, H. (2005). *A people's history of the United States: 1942–present*. Harper Perennial.

Index

About the Authors

Sarah Bickens graduated with a bachelor's degree in Comparative Literature from Brown University. She earned her initial teaching license through an alternative certification program partnership between City on a Hill Charter School and Northeastern University in Boston. After moving to New York City, she taught 9th–12th-grade English at Manhattan Village Academy, a small, public, Department of Education high school, for 13 years while earning a master's degree in English Education from Hunter College (CUNY). She has since moved to another small, public NYC high school with a performing arts focus, Talent Unlimited High School, where she teaches 12th-grade ELA and AP English Literature and serves as the school's Peer Collaborative Teacher Leader, mentoring novice teachers and supporting teacher professional learning. She recently earned her school-based leadership certificate through the College of Saint Rose. This year marks her 20th year as an educator.

Frances C. Bittman earned a bachelor's degree in English from Georgetown University and a master's degree in English Education from Teachers College, Columbia University. After working at Manhattan Village Academy, a Title I public school, for 11 years, she relocated to Connecticut, where she taught at Darien High School for 3 years and now is in her 6th year at Greenwich High School, where she teaches English 9–12 and Advancement via Individual Determination (a program to help first-generation students prepare for college) and is one of the English learning facilitators for her department.

David J. Connor earned a bachelor's degree in English and American Literature and Film at the University of East Anglia, UK, a master's degree in Learning Disabilities at Hunter College (CUNY), a master's degree in Creative Writing at City College (CUNY), and a doctorate in Curriculum and Teaching (specializing in learning disabilities) at Teachers College, Columbia University. After working 18 years for the New York City Department of Education as a high school teacher, literacy coach, and professional development specialist, he became a professor of Special Education at Hunter College in the Learning Disabilities Program. He also became a faculty member at large in the Urban Education Doctoral Program at the Graduate Center and helped develop, and taught in, the Instructional Leadership Doctoral Program at Hunter College. He has published numerous articles, books, book chapters, and fiction, and is currently professor emeritus.

For more information, see http://hunter-cuny.academia.edu/DavidJConnor